THE UNAUTHORISED
HARRY
POTTER
COMPANION

THE UNAUTHORISED

HARRY POTTER

COMPANION

COLIN DURIEZ

SUTTON PUBLISHING

First published in the United Kingdom in 2007 by
Sutton Publishing, an imprint of NPI Media Group Limited
Cirencester Road · Chalford · Stroud · Gloucestershire · GL6 8PE

British Library Cataloguing in Publication Data
A catalogue record for this book is available from the British Library.

ISBN 978-0-7509-4470-0

Alex Gabriel

Typeset in Sabon.
Typesetting and origination by
NPI Media Group Limited.
Printed and bound in England.

Contents

Preface

Harry Potter is a reading phenomenon. The seven Harry Potter stories, published over a span of ten years, represent a moment of cultural and literary history that might well turn out to be unique. People all over the world have awaited each instalment with baited breath. The characters, setting and plots have been discussed endlessly in excited conversations in classrooms, chatrooms, blogs, pubs, churches, prisons and university campuses. Some people have had to wait longer for the latest instalment, as the books were painstakingly translated into fifty languages. We all know about Harry, Snape, Voldemort, Hogwarts . . . and Muggles. The very word 'Muggle' is now in the major dictionaries, including *The Oxford English Dictionary*.

Some critics have been quick, too quick, to dismiss Harry Potter's popularity as based upon hype and massive marketing, the readership of the books, they claim, further inflated by successful films based on the series. Others have attacked J.K. Rowling's style, accusing her of dumbing-down literature. The fact remains that high-budget marketing and overheated hype cannot create a phenomenon like Harry Potter out of nothing. Why then have the books been so successful? What is it about them that is so interesting to so many people, children and adults, from a rainbow of backgrounds?

The Unauthorised Harry Potter Companion seeks to expound the many qualities in the stories that are the basis of the deep love that so many have towards the books – an attraction that is the real secret of the magic of Harry Potter. It begins with an easily accessible reference section that includes a useful reminder of the plots, a chronology of events and a handy A–Z of characters, magical creatures, things, places and events. I then give some of the context to the books – from the life of J.K. Rowling and the tradition of children's literature of which she is so much a part. This context does much to illuminate the books. I also open up the important themes and features of the phenomenally popular books – such as growing up, love, friendship, betrayal, loss and death, courage, prejudice and the place of education. Some of the themes inevitably lead into the spirituality embodied in the tales, such as the nature of goodness and evil, sacrifice, things not being what they seem, choice, and wholeness and purity. In the process I have tried to present a three-dimensional guide to the seven books that makes sense of some of the rich layers of meaning to be found in the stories. The books can be read on several levels, which is why they can be enjoyed by children and adults alike. Indeed, one of the most satisfying features of the Harry Potter phenomenon has been the way it brings together adults and children in a shared literary experience. Whether or not J.K. Rowling's popularity continues on its present mind-warping scale is immaterial. What is important is that her brilliance as a storyteller and her sheer power of invention have ensured her a place among the greats of children's literature and, I think, a continuing readership in fifty years' time.

I came to admire the books as a result of noticing the excitement of children themselves over the early books in the series, before booksellers realised that they were looking at a pot of gold, and before publishers began looking in vain for a successor to Harry Potter that could command such a popularity and devotion.

In writing this book my thanks are due to my editors at Sutton Publishing, and to those who commented on the initial draft, including Amy Sturgiss, Gina Burkart, Kristie Berglund, Cindy Bunch and Mark Smith. Alex Gabriel has stimulated my thinking about all things Harry Potter with his observations, questions and a myriad theories.

I must also acknowledge Kathy Martin for creating the portrait of J.K. Rowling, and Equinox Publishing, London, for allowing me to draw upon my chapter in Christopher Partridge and Eric Christianson (eds), *The Lure of the Dark Side* (2008).

Colin Duriez
Keswick
August 2007

The brave soul and the pure spirit shall with a merry and a loving heart inherit the kingdom together.

Elizabeth Goudge, *The Little White Horse*

PART ONE

Quick Reference Guide

ONE

The Plot

The seven Harry Potter books tell the story of Harry's years at Hogwarts School of Witchcraft and Wizardry, his close group of friends (Ron Weasley, Hermione Granger, and Rubeus Hagrid in particular) and Harry's long battle against the most powerful wizard of his generation, the Dark Lord Voldemort, and his cohorts. Voldemort's puzzling failure to kill Harry as an infant, using the strongest curse known to the Dark Arts, provides the foundation for the arc of the plot from books one to seven. Even that failure is part of the underlying nature of magic, in which the perversion of magic in the Dark Arts is pitted against a Deeper Magic that is indicated in the freely chosen bonds of love, friendship, moral courage and self-sacrifice. Both the sequence of seven stories and the individual books have a similar pattern, common to fairy tale, which starts with the hero (Harry) in an ordinary setting (such as home, though imperfect, and school life) moving into extraordinary adventures, involving great dangers, before a return to the ordinary – the world of friends, family (albeit dysfunctional), affection, work and study. The Harry Potter stories are tales – and a tale – of 'there and back again'.

The seven stories about Harry Potter are really one story in seven parts. Each book, however, is a complete story in itself, though books six and seven are more closely linked by plot than each of the others is to one another. In fact, book six – *Harry Potter and the Half-Blood Prince* – is, strictly speaking, the first half of a two-book adventure.

The following synopses do not attempt to retell the stories for those who have never read them. They are intended as an overview, to keep in mind while reading the rest of this book.

Harry Potter and the Philosopher's Stone

Harry Potter is an orphan boy living with his Aunt Petunia, Uncle Vernon and cousin Dudley in a quiet suburb in the affluent south-east of England. His bullying guardians force him to live in a cupboard under the stairs and do not tell him the real reason for his parents' deaths – that they were murdered ten years previously by Lord Voldemort, the most powerful wizard of his generation. Harry is at first unaware that there is a magical world of wizards and strange creatures hidden from 'Muggles' (non-magical folk) like his uncle and aunt, though he is puzzled by unusual powers he has, such as the ability to talk to snakes. He has a lightning-shaped scar on his forehead, which, unknown to him, marks Voldemort's failed attempt to slay him as an infant – a failure that resulted in the Dark Wizard's disembodiment. Voldemort did not die, as he had preserved parts of his soul in magical objects called Horcruxes (though we do not learn of these until later stories). It would, however, take him years to become re-embodied and return.

Harry's life changes when he receives an invitation to attend Hogwarts, at which time he discovers that he has these unusual powers because he belongs with the magical community and is, in fact, a wizard. The invitation is given to him in person by the half-giant Hagrid, game-keeper at Hogwarts, on his eleventh birthday. He had been prevented from receiving earlier invitations by the Dursleys, who are frightened of magic and wish to suppress it. The next day Hagrid accompanies Harry to a magical street off Charing Cross, in central London, called Diagon Alley. Harry discovers that he has a vast supply of wizard money in the vaults of the goblin-run Gringotts Bank, and uses some of it to purchase prerequisites for his studies at Hogwarts, including a wand, which is companion to the wand purchased nearly fifty years before by Voldemort when he joined Hogwarts, as an orphan then called Tom Riddle.

A month later Harry catches the Hogwarts Express from Platform 9¾ of London's King's Cross Station, the platform and train magically hidden from Muggles. On the train he meets other first-year students, including Ron Weasley and Hermione Granger, who are soon to become his fast friends. Hogwarts turns out to be a huge castle on high cliffs overlooking a Scottish loch, or lake, behind which are sloping lawns leading to a dangerous forest full of magical creatures like centaurs, giant spiders and mountain trolls. The subjects taught are intended to instil the proper use of magic, shaping the magical powers of the young wizards and witches attending the academy. These include Potions, Charms, Arithmancy, Astronomy and Astrology, Transfiguration, Divination, the Care of Magical Creatures, Flying and Defence Against the Dark Arts. More advanced skills include Apparition, the ability to move instantly from one place to another. Pupils are divided soon after arrival into one of four houses – Hufflepuff, Ravenclaw, Slytherin or Gryffindor – according to their dominant trait by an ancient Sorting Hat. Harry, Ron and Hermione are all placed in Gryffindor.

Harry soon discovers enemies at Hogwarts as well as friends, particularly first-year Draco Malfoy (the son, as it turns out much later on, of one of Voldemort's inner circle of Death Eaters) and bullying potions teacher Severus Snape, an ex-Death Eater now demonstrably loyal to the values of Hogwarts. These values are supremely represented in its headmaster, the powerful white wizard Albus Dumbledore, feared even by Voldemort and his followers. Harry – who is not an intellectual like Hermione – enthusiastically participates in the distinctive wizarding sport of Quidditch, for which he is soon chosen as Seeker. During Harry's first match his broom goes out of control. Hermione, mistaking Snape's muttered counter-spells for a jinx, sets fire to her teacher's robe, which has the effect of distracting the real perpetrator, Professor Quirrell. Quirrell sports a large turban, which hides a hideous fact; that he is sharing his body with Voldemort. In fact the Dark Lord's face takes up the back of Quirrell's head.

One night Harry comes across a trapdoor off the forbidden third-floor corridor, guarded by a fearsome three-headed dog of Hagrid's, characteristically misnamed 'Fluffy'. Unknown to Harry, the trapdoor guards the entrance to underground vaults where the Philosopher's Stone is hidden and guarded by powerful spells. This alchemical stone holds the secret of immortality, sought desperately by Voldemort, through his host, Quirrell. Snape, who suspects Quirrell of seeking the Stone, tries to find a way past Fluffy, but gets bitten in the process. The wound deepens Harry's suspicions of

Snape, though he and his friends are still piecing together the puzzle of what might lay hidden under the trapdoor.

At Christmas Dumbledore passes on to Harry his father's Invisibility Cloak, encouraging him to explore the secrets of Hogwarts Castle. One night he comes across the mysterious Mirror of Erised (desire), which displays a person's deepest wishes. In it he sees his parents, but gradually learns the important lesson that he cannot live in dreams. He returns steadfastly to the task of discovering what is under the trapdoor. The friends work on various clues, such as a break-in at Gringotts (just after the Stone had been moved from there to Hogwarts for safe-keeping) and a mysterious wizard from the past called Nicolas Flamel, who owned the Philosopher's Stone. They find out the properties of the Stone, such as immortality and unlimited wealth. A breakthrough comes when Harry, Ron and Hermione are punished for being caught out of bounds, the punishment being to go at night into the Forbidden Forest with Hagrid, who is investigating the deaths of unicorns. Harry interrupts a hooded figure (later he learns it was Quirrell) drinking the blood of a newly slain unicorn to nourish his sinister guest, Voldemort. The figure tries to assail him. Harry learns from a centaur (Firenze) that Voldemort seeks to return through the power of the Philosopher's Stone.

Harry realises that he must retrieve the stone before Voldemort does. He convinces Ron and Hermione what is at stake, and the trio steal through the dark corridors of Hogwarts one night to the trapdoor, having learned how to get past Fluffy. Once underground they have to go through several trials of wisdom and wizarding skill before approaching the Stone. Only one can reach the final chamber, so Harry proceeds alone, leaving Hermione to tend the injured Ron and contact Dumbledore.

To his surprise Harry finds himself confronting Quirrell, not Snape, who has the Mirror of Erised. Knowing that Harry is seeking the Stone, Quirrell asks Harry what he sees. Harry sees that the Stone has been placed in his pocket, but says he sees himself being presented with the Quidditch cup. Voldemort's voice under the turban says that Harry is lying and asks to speak to him face to face. Thus Voldemort's now snake-like face is revealed to Harry. He knows the Stone is in his pocket. When Quirrell tries to seize the horrified boy, contact with Harry blisters his hands. As Quirrell raises his wand to utter the killing curse, Harry grabs his face and the teacher recoils from the burning pain. In the struggle Harry passes out from the pain in his scar. When he returns to consciousness he is in the hospital wing, watched over by Dumbledore.

When Harry heads down to the year-end banquet, Slytherin house is celebrating, believing the house cup is theirs, until Harry and his friends are awarded points for their house, Gryffindor, for courage. With the end of term Harry has to return to the Dursleys in Little Whinging.

Harry Potter and the Chamber of Secrets

The summer vacation with the Dursleys is, as usual, an unhappy time for Harry. One evening, when Harry is banished to his bedroom while Uncle Vernon has important visitors for dinner, he is surprised to find Dobby there, the house-elf of the Malfoys, the family of his enemy Draco's. Dobby is determined to prevent Harry returning to Hogwarts for the second year as he has discovered he is in grave danger. When Harry disregards the warning, Dobby disrupts the dinner party, for which Harry gets the blame, so that he is imprisoned in his bedroom, the window barred like a prison cell. Ron comes to the rescue, with his twin brothers Fred and George, in an ancient Ford Anglia, which has been magically fixed so that it can fly. During his stay with Ron's family, they visit Diagon Alley for supplies, and Harry meets the narcissistic Gilderoy Lockhart – the newly appointed Defence Against the Dark Arts teacher at Hogwarts – who is having a book launch. Draco's father, Lucius Malfoy, slips a blank diary into Ginny Weasley's books (she is about to start her first year at the school). When Harry makes his way to King's Cross Railway Station with the Weasleys, he and Ron find they cannot get onto Platform 9¾, and miss the Hogwarts Express (Dobby, it later turns out, has prevented them). However, they borrow the Ford and fly back to Hogwarts, crashing into the Whomping Willow as they descend. Much to their surprise, instead of being expelled, they are merely given detention.

The blank diary turns out to contain a portion of Voldemort's soul. It belonged to him as a pupil at Hogwarts fifty years before, when he was Tom Riddle. Through the diary he gradually possesses Ginny, using her against her will to bring terror to the school, perpetrating a fear that a mysterious Chamber of Secrets has been opened. Those in particular fear are half-bloods (children with only one magical parent) and the Muggle-born (those with two Muggle parents). Filch's cat and several pupils, including Hermione, suffer petrification, but not before Hermione has helped Harry and Ron to find out some facts about the Chamber. Hermione also leaves an important clue clutched in her hand about a monster that has been unleashed. Harry has a number of times heard a cold, mysterious voice speaking of killing and destroying, which none of the others can hear. The mystery is solved when it turns out that the monster is a Basilisk, a giant green snake, whose speech Harry can understand as he is a Parselmouth. Among the facts Harry gets to know is that the Chamber had been opened fifty years before, resulting in the death of a pupil whose ghost inhabits an abandoned girl's toilet and who is known as Moaning Myrtle. Another fact is that Hagrid, a pupil at that time, had been expelled, falsely accused of opening the Chamber by Tom Riddle (then the admired head boy). Finding the truth about Hagrid involves Harry and Ron making a night visit to the ancient giant spider, Aragog, in the Forbidden Forest, a venture that almost costs them their lives. They discover that the secret entrance to the Chamber lies somewhere in the girls' toilets inhabited by Moaning Myrtle.

When the two friends hear that Ginny Weasley has been taken into the Chamber of Secrets, they force their fraudulent teacher, Lockhart, to go with them as they slide deep below the school from the secret entrance. Lockhart tries to modify their memories using Ron's broken wand, a spell that backfires and removes his own memory. The misfired spell also causes part of the tunnel to collapse. Harry is forced to go alone through underground tunnels, leaving Ron with Lockhart. He eventually finds Ginny dying below a gigantic statue of Salazar Slytherin, from whom the ideology of the pure-blood arose. There is also the increasingly definite form of the schoolboy Tom Riddle, who is the age of his stored memory in the diary. He intends to kill Harry and let Ginny die (her usefulness to him is over), and holds Harry's wand, which he dropped when he rushed to see if Ginny was all right. Harry can only think of calling on Dumbledore's aid, and a phoenix flies to him, bearing the Sorting Hat. When Tom summons the Basilisk to kill Harry, Fawkes (for it is Dumbledore's pet phoenix) pecks out the bulbous eyes of the monster. Harry finds a gilded sword – an ancient knife once belonging to Godric Gryffindor – in the Sorting Hat and, because of the attacking serpent's blindness, is able to stab through its mouth with it, killing the reptile. One of its razor-like fangs punctures his arm, poisoning him and breaking off. The tears of the phoenix, however, heal the fatal wound and Harry manages to stab the fang through the diary, the deathly fang destroying its power and the malicious memory of Tom Riddle. With the power of the diary dissipated, Ginny awakes.

Later, when Harry is recounting events to Dumbledore and the Weasleys, Lucius Malfoy bursts into the headmaster's office with his house-elf, Dobby, who bears the marks of his abuse. Confronted with evidence of his involvement in Riddle's plan to harm Harry, Lucius is confounded and leaves, kicking Dobby before him. Harry, however, tricks Lucius into freeing Dobby from his obligations to the Malfoys as their house-elf. His release of Dobby from slavery points to the plot of the next book, where Harry rescues others from imprisonment and the threat of death or something worse than death.

Harry Potter and the Prisoner of Azkaban

Sirius Black, Harry Potter's godfather, had been wrongly imprisoned twelve years previously, charged with killing his wizard friend Peter Pettigrew (nicknamed Wormtail) and a number of Muggles shortly before the death of Harry's parents. In fact, Pettigrew was a spy for Lord Voldemort and faked his death, hiding in his Animagus form, which, appropriately, is that of a rat. It ultimately turns out that the rat is one and the same as Ron Weasley's pet, Scabbers. After twelve years in the notorious wizard prison, Azkaban, Sirius escapes, the very first to do so unaided.

Harry learns by accident of Sirius's escape on his thirteenth birthday. He further discovers that Sirius is (apparently) seeking to do away with him on Voldemort's behalf. The truth, not then known to Harry, is that Sirius seeks to help his godson and tracks him protectively in the form of his Animagus, a huge dog.

Harry's unpleasant existence at the Dursleys during the long summer vacation is made more miserable by a visit from Aunt Marge, Vernon's sister and like him a bully. His anger is provoked by her frequent insults about his dead parents, and he accidentally makes her inflate. Unable to take any more abuse, Harry quickly packs and walks out into the night. He is alarmed to see a large black dog (Sirius, as he discovers much later) and is relieved when a wizarding bus suddenly appears – the Knight Bus – and takes him off to the Leaky Cauldron pub in nearby London (after whizzing here and there around Britain). At the public house Harry meets for the first time the Minister of Magic, Cornelius Fudge, who is concerned about his safety now that Sirius is on the loose. Harry gladly lodges at the pub, awaiting the start of the new school year. He meets his friends Hermione and Ron at Diagon Alley close by, where Hermione buys an oddly shaped cat called Crookshanks, which pursues Ron's rat Scabbers.

During the long journey north the Hogwarts Express is stopped and searched by wraith-like Dementors, looking for Sirius. They are attracted by and feed on Harry's early memories of his parents' murders by Voldemort, and he is overcome. A stranger in the apartment (in fact, the new Defence Against the Dark Arts teacher, Professor Lupin) rescues Harry by banishing the intruders. As classes begin Professor Trelawney, the Divination teacher, reads tea-leaf shapes as a Grim, a large black dog portending death (intensifying Harry's fears, as he sees Sirius from time to time in his Animagus form, not knowing the truth behind the appearances). Hagrid has been appointed teacher for the Care of Magical Creatures classes, and introduces the third years to a Hippogriff called Buckbeak (half-horse and half-griffin). The arrogant Draco Malfoy ignores essential etiquette and slights Buckbeak, resulting in a superficial wound, which he plays up as a dangerous attack. As a result Buckbeak is condemned to be beheaded. In Lupin's Defence Against the Darks Arts classes, he teaches Harry and the others to confront their deepest fears, in the form of a shape-shifting Boggart. He also agrees to give Harry private lessons in fighting off the deadly Dementors with a bright Patronus Charm. The Dementors guard the perimeters of Hogwarts grounds against attack by the supposedly evil Sirius but see the vulnerable Harry as prey. They illegally attack him during a Quidditch match, causing him to fall from his hi-spec broomstick, which flies riderless into the Whomping Willow and is destroyed. It is because of such attacks that Lupin agrees to give Harry lessons in summoning a Patronus, which requires very advanced magic.

On two occasions Sirius gets into Hogwarts, his visits terrifying the students by their seeming violence, as he attacks the portrait of the Fat Lady (guarding the Gryffindor common room and dormitories) and the curtains on Ron's four-poster bed. In fact, Sirius is in pursuit of Pettigrew, having discovered he is Ron's pet rat, Scabbers.

Harry acquires the Marauder's Map of Hogwarts, made by a group of four friends in their schooldays years before – Harry's father James, Sirius, Lupin and Pettigrew (Wormtail). This opens up secret passageways to Harry and warns him of the whereabouts of other people. Ron loses Scabbers, and bloodstains suggest that Crookshanks might have killed the rat.

The friendship between Hermione and the two boys becomes strained, and she is constantly tired, because she is employing a time-turning device that allows her to attend an impossible number of classes, normally ruled out by timetable clashes. Differences are forgotten, however, with Buckbeak's impending execution and their friend Hagrid's sorrow. Harry notices Professor Snape feeding a potion to Lupin. After Snape takes one of Lupin's classes while he is ill and gives them an essay to write on the nature of werewolves, Hermione realises Lupin is one, but keeps her knowledge secret.

The day of the execution arrives. During a one-to-one Divination examination, in which Professor Trelawney tests Harry, she suddenly goes into a trance and predicts that Voldemort's servant will set out to return to him before midnight. Harry, Ron and Hermione, under the cover of Harry's Invisibility Cloak, go across the grounds to comfort Hagrid before the execution. At the cabin, Hermione discovers Scabbers hiding in Hagrid's milk jug. Just after they leave, Ron gripping the squirming rat, they hear, as night falls, the sound of the executioner's blade striking. Then a large black dog appears (Sirius), seizes Ron and drags him under and into the Whomping Willow, breaking his leg in the process as he resists. The others are unable to follow because of the flailing branches, but Crookshanks suddenly presses a knot on the trunk, stilling the tree and enabling them to crawl into a hole leading to a tunnel. The passageway takes them to Hogsmeade village, and the Shrieking Shack, where they find Sirius with the injured Ron. Much to their surprise, Professor Lupin arrives and sides with the apparent murderer as a long-lost friend. He has realised that, as Pettigrew has appeared on the Marauder's Map, which never lies, he is alive, which means that Sirius had been framed, and was not a murderer and betrayer of Harry's parents, as he had thought for long years.

Lupin and Sirius explain the truth to Harry, Ron and Hermione, and decide to kill the traitor, Pettigrew. Their explanation is interrupted by the arrival of their old rival, Snape, who relishes the idea of Sirius experiencing the Dementor's Kiss, which leaves a person an empty, soulless body. Harry, Ron and Hermione, however, disarm Snape, who is rendered unconscious by the force of three simultaneous spells. Lupin and Sirius then force Pettigrew to appear as his real self instead of as Scabbers. Pettigrew eventually confesses, but Harry prevents his execution, convinced his father would not have wanted his friends to become killers.

As the strange group make their way to Hogwarts, accompanied by Snape's floating unconscious form, and with Ron limping and in a splint, the full moon appears and Lupin (who has forgotten to take his potion) begins to transform into a werewolf. Sirius shifts shape into his Animagus, the dog, to protect the children from Lupin, and in the confusion Pettigrew, or Wormtail, becomes Scabbers once more and escapes, as predicted by Professor Trelawney. After the dog chases the werewolf into the Forest, they hear his whimpers, and Harry and Hermione set off for the lakeside to help him, leaving Ron with the still prone Snape. They find Sirius back in his human form but terrified as a hundred Dementors approach. All three are overcome – Harry's attempt at a Patronus Charm is too weak to fight them off – and a Dementor begins to suck out his soul. Just then a large Patronus in the form of a stag gallops across the lake from the further shore and drives away the wraiths. Harry sees the figure who had summoned the Patronus, who looks like his dead father. Sirius is then captured by the revived Snape and imprisoned in Hogwarts Castle, awaiting the Dementor's Kiss to finish him off.

Harry, Ron and Hermione find themselves in the school's hospital wing. Minutes before Sirius is subjected to the lethal Kiss, Dumbledore tells Hermione to use her Time-Turner to enable Harry and herself to save two innocent lives. They go back in time three hours, allowing them to rescue Buckbeak and take him into the Forest. Seeing the Dementors flocking to where, in the past, he, Hermione and Sirius are lying beside the lake, Harry looks out for his father but sees no one. Suddenly he realises that it is he who must summon the Patronus, which he does and saves his past self and the others. On Buckbeak's back, Harry and Hermione fly up until they are level with the room high in Hogwarts where Sirius is imprisoned and rescue him through the window just in time. He is able to fly into hiding on Buckbeak, and they return to the hospital wing as if nothing has happened in the meantime. Though saddened by the fact that Lupin is forced to resign because of the events, Harry is cheered up on his return journey to London at the end of the school year by an owl post from Sirius, saying that he is safe and enclosing a guardian's letter of permission for Harry to visit Hogsmeade village. He would no longer need to visit illegally, under his Invisibility Cloak and through secret passageways.

Harry Potter and the Goblet of Fire

Now at home with the Dursleys for the summer as usual, Harry awakes from a vivid nightmare, roused by the pain of his throbbing scar (a scar that links him with Voldemort). What he recalls is not a dream but a cognition of what has happened 200 miles away, near Little Hangleton, in the Riddle ancestral home, now falling into ruin. Frank Bryce, its elderly gardener, investigates a flickering light upstairs in the mansion and comes across Voldemort, his servant Wormtail (who had rejoined his master after escaping from Sirius and Lupin) and the Dark Lord's giant snake, Nagini. In his dream Harry sees the elderly man murdered by Voldemort's killing curse. Unknown to Harry, fifty years earlier Frank had been accused of killing Mr and Mrs Riddle, and their grown-up son, Tom (Muggle father of Lord Voldemort), whereas it was their grandson, Tom Riddle Jr, who had killed them by dark magic. Voldemort is still not fully embodied, but is in a hideous embryonic state, requiring Wormtail's constant care. Because of the dream Harry is concerned that Voldemort is nearby.

The Weasleys invite Harry to accompany them to the Quidditch World Cup, and transport him to The Burrow, their home in the West Country, via the Floo Network. From there they set off early one morning, using a nearby Portkey (which to the unknowing eye looks like a piece of junk, like the old boot they use) to transport them to a camping area near the site of the game. There they pitch small tents whose interiors are magically larger than their exteriors. Mr Weasley works at the Ministry of Magic and, through him, Harry meets Ludo Bagman, of the Department of Magical Games and Sports, and Barty Crouch Sr, of the Department of International Magical Cooperation. Unknown to his colleagues, Crouch Sr engineered the escape of his rogue son, Barty Crouch Jr, from Azkaban.

Because of Mr Weasley's position, Harry and his friends are able to sit in the Top Box at the games, where they meet the house-elf Winky, who is saving a seat for her master, Barty Crouch Sr. The game is won by Ireland, but Seeker Viktor Krum of Bulgaria superbly catches the Snitch. That evening, a group of Death Eaters cause terror by publicly abusing four Muggles. In the chaos, Harry, Ron and Hermione flee into nearby woods, but Harry loses his wand. Someone (later it turns out to be Barty Crouch Jr) employs his wand to fire the Dark Mark, symbol of Voldemort, high into the night sky. Later Barty Crouch Jr imprisons the new teacher for Defence Against the Dark Arts, Mad-Eye Moody, and takes his place, replicating his appearance using Polyjuice Potion.

Back for the new school year at Hogwarts, Harry and his friends learn that the school is hosting an international Triwizard Tournament between three schools, the others being Beauxbatons Academy of Magic and Durmstrang. The apparent Mad-Eye Moody is protective of Harry, turning Draco into a ferret for attacking the boy while his back is turned, but causes disquiet by teaching Harry's year the three Unforgivable Curses. Hermione is discovering that there is more to life than books, and founds the

S.P.E.W., a society dedicated to the welfare of house-elves. Later in the first term, delegates from the other schools arrive, including the celebrity Quidditch Seeker Viktor Krum from Durmstang. He is chosen by the Goblet of Fire to represent his school, Fleur Delacour is chosen for Beauxbatons and Cedric Diggory for Hogwarts. Harry and his friends are too young to enter. To everyone's surprise a fourth champion is chosen by the Goblet of Fire, Harry. (It later turns out that his name was entered by the false Mad-Eye Moody, as part of his plan to get him into Voldemort's clutches.) As the Goblet has chosen him, the rules are that he must participate, despite his youth. Very few believe Harry's protestations that he did not enter his name. Even Ron doubts him, and will not even speak to him for a long time, causing Harry great pain. An unscrupulous reporter for the *Daily Prophet* called Rita Skeeter insists on interviewing Harry, the resulting article about his history being more fiction than fact.

Harry learns that the first of three trials will involve dragons and warns Cedric. Overhearing this, Mad-Eye Moody applauds Harry's chivalry and hints that Harry would do well to use his broomstick to get past the dragon. Sirius's head appears in the Gryffindor Common Room fireplace late one night advising Harry that the headmaster of Durmstrang is a former Death Eater and may be dangerous. Hermione does all she can to help Harry prepare for the trials, and, in the first, Harry succeeds in summoning his broomstick, skilfully using it to get past the dragon and capture the golden egg.

Harry's greatest challenge, he discovers, lies outside the Tournament. The champions and other students must find partners for the forthcoming Yule Ball, and Harry has no idea about how to go about this. He leaves it too late to ask Cho Chang, a student he fancies, who is snapped up by Cedric Diggory. Ron, similarly, is too slow to partner Hermione, who is quickly asked by Krum. At the last minute, Harry asks the Patil sisters to accompany them. Ron's impoverished family can only supply him with ill-fitting and out-of-fashion party robes, and the sight of Hermione with Krum only deepens his misery. Similarly Harry is jealous of Cedric with Cho. After the ball, Cedric returns Harry's earlier favour by hinting that Harry should take a bath with the golden egg, suggesting he use the lavish Prefects' communal bath. Harry also overhears Hagrid telling Madame Maxime (head of Beauxbatons) that he is a half-giant.

During a trip to Hogsmeade village Harry learns from Ludo Bagman that Barty Crouch Sr has stopped attending work, and Hermione tells Rita Skeeter what she thinks of her spurious journalism. Harry, worried about the proximity of the second trial, and no nearer solving the puzzle of the egg, takes up Cedric's advice and goes to the communal baths late one night. The ghost Moaning Myrtle advises him to open the egg underwater (it normally only screeches). As he does so the egg sings that he will have only an hour to retrieve something he values that the merpeople have placed deep in the lake beside Hogwarts. On his way back to his dormitory he notices a figure moving on the Marauder's Map. It is in Snape's office and labelled 'Bartemius Crouch' (in fact it is Barty Crouch Jr, in Mad-Eye Moody's form, but Harry does not know that then). Intrigued, Harry decides to investigate what Crouch is up to, but drops the egg, which emits raucous screeches, alerting Filch, Snape and Mad-Eye Moody. Moody rescues Harry from the others, who hate him and delight to see him in trouble, returns his egg and borrows the Marauder's Map from him.

There remains the problem of how to breathe underwater for an hour, a feat required by the second trial of the Triwizard Tournament. Dobby comes to his rescue with Gillyweed, which has the magical property of providing gills when underwater. The other contestants solve the problem differently. Harry is able to swim efficiently under the lake, and, after some searching and obstacles, he finds Hermione, Ron, Cho and Fleur's sister magically sleeping and bound in an underwater village of the Merpeople. Hermione is rescued by Krum, and Cho by Cedric, but there is no sign of Fleur to rescue her sister so Harry brings her to the surface along with his charge, Ron, ruining his chances, he believes, of doing well in that trial. However, he is awarded high marks for his courage and selflessness, what Ludo Bagman calls his 'moral fibre'.

One evening the four champions go down to the Quidditch pitch to be briefed by Bagman for the final trial. They find the pitch has been turned into a maze, its walls of hedges starting to grow. Bagman explains that the Triwizard Cup will be placed in the centre of the maze, and the first to reach it will win. There will be obstacles of spells and magical creatures. On their way back to the castle Krum takes Harry off into the nearby Forest to ask if there is anything going on between him and Hermione. Harry explains that they are friends but that she is not his girlfriend. Just then Mr Crouch Sr appears out of the Forest, untidy, confused and rambling in his speech, and asking for Dumbledore. He is anxious to tell Dumbledore that the Dark Lord has got stronger. Harry leaves him with Krum and hurries to get the headmaster. When they return they find Krum has been stunned and that Crouch has disappeared, deepening the mystery of his absence from the Ministry.

During a Divination class Harry falls into a doze and dreams, once again, of Voldemort in the Riddle mansion. He wakes screaming with the pain in his scar. He tells Dumbledore about it, who concludes that Voldemort may be growing stronger. Soon the day of the final trial arrives and the four contestants enter one by one into the maze. After encounters with a giant Blast-Ended Skrewt, a Boggart, and enchanted mist that reverses sky and ground, Harry rescues Cedric from an agonising Cruciatus curse. By now just he and Cedric are in the running for the prize. Then Harry has one of his most amazing experiences – coming face to face with a sphinx who posits a riddle he must answer to pass. The answer, 'Spider', is an important clue, for it warns of a giant spider posing a final obstacle for both Cedric and Harry, who are neck and neck to achieve the prize. They help each other to overcome the danger and agree to take hold of the Cup together. Unknown to them, the Cup has been made into a Portkey by the fake Mad-Eye Moody, Barty Crouch Jr, and the two are instantly transported many hundreds of miles to the churchyard in Little Hangleton, where Tom Riddle Sr, Voldemort's father, is buried. The graveyard is overlooked by the old mansion the Riddles once owned.

Wormtail is waiting, carrying the childlike bundle, the embryonic form of Voldemort. On the Dark Lord's orders he utters the killing curse, murdering Cedric. While this is happening Harry is crippled by the pain in his scar. Wormtail ties Harry to the headstone of Riddle's tomb then drags a huge cauldron of water to the grave and heats it. On Voldemort's orders, Wormtail drops the hideous child form of Voldemort into the boiling liquid, adding the dust of a bone from the grave, his own right hand, which he cuts off in front of Harry, and blood from an enemy – which is some of Harry's own blood, taken from his right arm stabbed by Wormtail. This foul mixture allows Voldemort to regenerate into bodily form and rise slowly out of the cauldron. As he presses a tattoo in the shape of the Dark Mark on Wormtail's arm, an action that causes Harry's scar to sear with pain, Voldemort's Death Eaters are summoned, and quickly Apparate around them. It is Voldemort's rebirthing party. His intention is to kill Harry, but just as the killing curse is uttered Harry cries the Disarming Spell and the two similar wands, Harry's and Voldemort's, are locked against each other. The song of the phoenix is heard, giving Harry strength to hold his wand against his enemy's. While they are connected, a *Priori Incantatem* effect is created which causes the traces of Voldemort's previous victims to emerge – Cedric, Frank Bryce, Bertha Jorkins and Harry's parents. They protect Harry while he breaks the connection, grabs Cedric's body and summons the Portkey (the Cup), which whisks him back to Hogwarts, together with Cedric's body.

Thoroughly weakened and limping, Harry is helped back to the castle by Barty Crouch Jr, in the form of Mad-Eye Moody. He informs the boy that he is in fact a Death Eater and intends to kill him. It turns out also that he has murdered his father, Barty Crouch Sr. He reveals his complicity in Harry's unwilling involvement in the Triwizard Tournament, and that he turned the Cup into a Portkey, to send him to Voldemort. Harry is saved by Dumbledore and other teachers stunning the fake Moody. As the Polyjuice Potion wears off the form of Moody is replaced by Crouch, and the real Moody, who has been held captive, is discovered. Snape forces Crouch to drink Veritaserum, under which he reveals how his father rescued him from Azkaban, and kept him hidden with the enforced help of Crouch's house-elf, Winky. Under torture an employee of the Ministry of Magic, Bertha Jorkins, who had found out what had happened, revealed Barty Crouch Jr's location to Voldemort, who had him rescued. As punishment for murder and his other misdeeds Crouch receives the Dementor's Kiss and loses his soul.

Minister of Magic, Cornelius Fudge, refuses to believe Voldemort has re-embodied and is now a dire threat, requiring immediate precautions, such as dismissing the Dementors from Azkaban.

Dumbledore therefore reveals the truth to the school at the end of year banquet. He also informs all who might rally with him against Voldemort, such as Madame Maxime. After this the headmaster is increasingly sidelined by the Ministry – a major theme of the next book. On the Hogwarts Express Hermione reveals that the rogue journalist Rita Skeeter is in fact a secret Animagus, taking the form of a large beetle, and that she has captured her in a glass jar. Rita had been 'bugging' private conversations illegally. Before returning for another summer with the Dursleys Harry gives his prize money for winning the Tournament to the Weasley twins, Fred and George, so that they can fulfil their ambition of starting a joke shop.

Harry Potter and the Order of the Phoenix

The tedium of summer with the Dursleys is viciously interrupted by an attack on Harry and his Muggle cousin Dudley by a gang of Dementors. Harry is forced to break the rules of underage wizardry and use magic to repel them. As a result, a group of wizards belonging to the Order of the Phoenix – a defensive Order set up by Dumbledore – visit 4 Privet Drive and take Harry off to 12 Grimmauld Place, in London. This rambling house, magically hidden from Muggles, belongs to Sirius Black and operates as the Headquarters for the Order. In fact, it is the Blacks' ancestral home. The work of the Order in resisting Voldemort has become urgent with the refusual of Cornelius Fudge and the Ministry of Magic to acknowledge the Dark Lord's return to power.

For his use of underage magic, Harry appears before the supreme wizard court, and he is acquitted of the charge, but only just. Supporters of Voldemort are everywhere. Upon returning to Hogwarts for the start of his fifth year, Harry learns that his new Defence Against the Dark Arts teacher will be Dolores Umbridge, a bullying and sadistic employee of the Ministry, which is attempting to control the school and undermine Dumbledore. The *Daily Prophet* reinforces this strategy by continually criticising Dumbledore; furthermore, it publishes untrue stories about Harry to subvert his witness to Voldemort's return. At the opening banquet the Sorting Hat warns against division in the school, urging Dumbledore's ideal of wholeness and unity. This is the year that

Harry, Ron and Hermione take their important examinations, their Ordinary Wizarding Levels (OWLs).

Professor Umbridge will not teach defensive spells, only theory. The frustration of Harry and friends increases when she is appointed High Inquisitor of Hogwarts, which includes biased inspection of the other teachers' classroom skills. Exasperated, they form, at the risk of expulsion, Dumbledore's Army or the DA, with Harry made leader. (It is like a junior version of the Order of the Phoenix, which is made up of adult wizards and witches loyal to Dumbledore.) In a secret room – the Room of Requirement – Harry teaches the nearly thirty pupils who have enrolled defensive skills against the Dark Arts. Umbridge shows marked animosity to Harry, far worse than Snape's, and he is soon barred from playing Quidditch and has to serve detentions – in which she forces him to write lines that cut into his flesh. Fred and George Weasley can stand no more of the regime and quit Hogwarts in protest, opening their joke shop in Diagon Alley with Harry's start-up money.

Harry has a recurring and disturbing dream of making his way down a corridor deep below the Ministry of Magic, in the Department of Mysteries. Unknown to him he sometimes has access to Voldemort's thoughts and emotions. Eventually, in the dream, he enters a large room stacked with glass phials. These later turn out to contain stored memories of prophecies. In another dream he is in the body of a huge snake, which attacks Mr Weasley, Ron's father. (It is Nagini, Voldemort's serpent.) He tells Dumbledore, who acts on his dream and has the badly wounded Mr Weasley rescued. Dumbledore informs Harry that, for his own protection, he must have Occlumency lessons from Snape, to protect his mind receiving Voldemort's thoughts and emotions. Harry finds this almost impossible, not least because of the mutual dislike between himself and Snape. He continues to suffer from his scar hurting in response to Voldemort's more powerful emotions.

The DA members are very successful in inculcating defences against dark magic. In the end, however, they are caught by Umbridge and several school members loyal to her, such as Draco and his minders, Crabbe and Goyle. To save them Dumbledore pretends to have instigated the 'Army' to resist the Ministry. Consequently Umbridge is installed in his place as head of Hogwarts.

The OWL examinations begin soon after, and during the Astronomy test pupils are horrified to see from the Tower Professor McGonagall hit by four stunning spells as she protests against an attack on Hagrid by Umbridge and her cohorts. In his History of Magic exam in the Great Hall Harry dozes and has a dream of Sirius being attacked in the Department of Mysteries by Voldemort. Unknown to Harry this is a false vision – Voldemort has intruded into his mind, as feared by Dumbledore. He is tricked, therefore, into leading Ron, Hermione, Ginny, Luna Lovegood and Neville into a trap. This is despite Hermione's fears of just that (she remembered Tom Riddle luring Harry into the Chamber of Secrets in their second year) – she in fact persuades him to check if Sirius is at 12 Grimmauld Place, but Kreacher the house-elf leads Harry to believe that he is not. The plan to rescue Sirius is jeopardised when Harry, Hermione, Ron and other DA members are caught by Umbridge. Hermione cleverly pretends that they are hiding a weapon for Dumbledore and she and Harry accompany Umbridge into the Forbidden Forest supposedly to retrieve it, where, as planned, the centaurs drag her away.

Harry and his friends, so they think, need to help Sirius as soon as possible, and fly on Thestrals, strange but powerful winged horses, to the Ministry of Magic. When they reach the Hall of Prophecies they are ambushed by Death Eaters, but not before Harry has seized a glass phial with his name on it. Lucius Malfoy demands that Harry hands over the prophecy, which, it turns out, concerns him and Voldemort. Using the skills they have learned in the sessions with the DA, the six fight off the Death Eaters long enough for help to arrive in the form of members of the Order of the Phoenix, including Sirius. During the battle Harry drops the fragile phial, which shatters. But worse, Bellatrix Lestrange, until recently in Azkaban prison, kills her cousin, Sirius. Dumbledore arrives and the fight is soon over, but not before Harry is faced with Voldemort. Fudge is forced to acknowledge that Harry and Dumbledore have been right about the Dark Lord all along.

Later Dumbledore explains to Harry that the prophecy claimed that Harry has a power Voldemort cannot understand. He is, in fact, protected by love, the love of his mother, who sacrificed herself for him. The protection is sealed by blood. The prophecy also asserted that either Harry or Voldemort would be destroyed in their final confrontation. The prophecy holds the key, says Dumbledore, as to why Harry has to spend at least a part of every year with the Dursleys – as Aunt Petunia is his mother's sister, sharing her blood, her home extends the protection over Harry. Grieving his godfather's loss, Harry returns to the place he must call home for the summer vacation. He knows that all-out war with Voldemort has started.

Harry Potter and the Half-Blood Prince

The impact of Voldemort's reappearance grows through the summer months. Resulting death and destruction are so bad that they cannot be hidden magically from Muggles. Indeed, non-magical folk are among his victims. Voldemort's evil is threatening the Muggle world as well as the wizarding community. Cornelius Fudge, the outgoing Minister for Magic, is forced to reveal the seriousness of Voldemort's return to the Muggle Prime Minister.

While Harry lives out his miserable existence at the Dursleys, very different events are taking place in an industrial town where Professor Severus Snape has his home during the summer vacations. He is visited by Draco's mother Narcissa Malfoy and her sister Bellatrix Lestrange, the Death Eater. Lucius Malfoy is confined in Azkaban, and Narcissa is concerned about Draco's safety. He has been given a dangerous task by Voldemort out of revenge for Lucius's failure to gain the prophecy (the task later turns out to be to kill Dumbledore). Snape makes an Unbreakable Vow to protect Draco and, if necessary, to complete the task. Snape appears to be serving Voldemort despite his membership of the Order of the Phoenix, but he is in fact acting in his role as double agent and still serving the Order. He is working to counteract Bellatrix's overt distrust of him.

In the holidays Dumbledore picks up Harry from 4 Privet Drive, for the first of several occasions when Harry serves as an apprentice, deliberately being initiated into knowledge that he will need to fight Voldemort when his mentor Dumbledore has gone and he is on his own. With the headmaster's assistance, they Disapparate to a small village on their way to The Burrow, the Weasleys' home in the south-west of England. Here Dumbledore persuades a retired colleague, Horace Slughorn, to return to Hogwarts to teach Potions (Snape has been given the long-desired post of teaching Defence Against the Dark Arts). Then Harry joins Ron and Hermione at The Burrow for the remainder of the vacation. They make their usual visit to Diagon Alley for school supplies, where Harry secretly follows Draco to the Dark Arts shop, Borgin and Burkes. He hears Draco bullying Borgin into agreeing to fix something (an object that later turns out to be a Vanishing Cabinet, which will be used by Draco to smuggle Death Eaters into Hogwarts).

Back at Hogwarts Harry acquires an old copy of a required Potions textbook that was once owned by a pupil named 'The Half-Blood Prince'. As he uses annotations and corrections and even new spells written onto the margins of the book, Harry finds himself dramatically improving in Potions, aided by the fact that the class is now taught by Slughorn, rather than Harry's enemy, Snape. Harry also has regular meetings with Dumbledore, who initiates Harry into Voldemort's murky history using stored memories in the headmaster's Pensieve. Dumbledore believes that knowing Voldemort's history is essential for Harry defeating him when the two finally battle, as foretold in the prophecy. Harry learns much about Voldemort's family history, including how his mother, Merope, gained the short-lived love of Tom Riddle Sr by enchantment, and how she was cast off by him, being forced to give birth to Tom Junior in an orphanage. He learns that Tom (i.e. Voldemort) misused fellow orphans with special powers he did not understand until Dumbledore invited him to study at Hogwarts. Later, he learned how to divide his soul and store the portions in Horcruxes. One, Riddle's diary, had been destroyed by Harry in his second year, and another, a ring, had been destroyed recently by Dumbledore at terrible cost, a withered hand. That seemed to leave four to destroy before killing Voldemort himself.

Life goes on as normal in the school (normal, that is, by Hogwarts standards). When Ron starts going out with Lavender Brown, Hermione is jealous, and she and Ron bicker more than ever, isolating Harry, who falls in love with Ginny Weasley. He takes care not to upset Ron by going out with his sister. When Ron and Lavender stop seeing each other, this cheers up Hermione. Harry is preoccupied with his new duties as captain of the Gryffindor

Quidditch team and trying to work out what Draco is plotting – Harry believes he has become a Death Eater. On many occasions Draco does not appear on his Marauder's Map, until Harry realises suddenly that he must be using the Room of Requirement, the room the DA had used the previous year. This explains why Harry cannot get access to it when he tries. Unknown to him, Draco is ready to use a Vanishing Cabinet in there to link with the repaired one at Borgin and Burkes, so that Voldemort's Death Eaters can invade the school.

Dumbledore takes Harry with him on a perilous quest to find and destroy a locket that belonged to Voldemort's mother, Merope. They enter a vast cave beside the sea and pass through traps and trials before reaching a basin on a flat rocky outcrop in the centre of a black lake, which is full of Inferi, corpses that are magically animated. Dumbledore decides he must drink the basin's contents of bitter and poisonous potion that is hiding the locket. He knows he will need a potion from Snape to counteract it. While he slowly empties the basin, Harry fights back the Inferi. They Disapparate back to Hogwarts, Dumbledore very weak, to find a Dark Mark visible over the Astronomy Tower.

When they reach its ramparts Dumbledore realises they have fallen into a trap as he hears someone running up the stairway. He casts a Body-Binding spell on Harry, hidden under his Invisibility Cloak, freezing all his actions. Draco appears, but, as Dumbledore tells the boy he is not a killer and that the Order of the Phoenix can protect his mother and himself from Voldemort's anger, Draco is unable to fulfil the task demanded by the Dark Lord. Snape then appears and quickly takes in what has happened. He points his wand at Dumbledore and utters the *Avada Kedavra* curse, blasting the frail wizard off the ramparts. With Dumbledore gone, the freezing spell on Harry lifts and he pursues Snape down the tower steps and into a battle between Death Eaters and members of the Order of the Phoenix as well as Harry's friends from the DA.

Snape escapes and the shocked Harry looks at the locket gained at such great cost, which he finds by Dumbledore's corpse. It is not the real Horcrux, which had been taken years before by a wizard called only 'R.A.B.', in order to destroy it. After Dumbledore's funeral, attended by magical beasts as well as wizard folk, Harry tells Ron and Hermione that he will not return to Hogwarts after the summer, but rather will search out the remaining Horcruxes and kill Voldemort. His two friends say they will accompany him on the desperate quest, and remind him that first they must all attend the wedding of Bill Weasley and Fleur Delacour. In the light of his resolve Harry stops seeing Ginny for her own safety

Harry Potter and the Deathly Hallows

This book tells the story of a double quest: to solve the mystery of the Deathly Hallows, and to destroy the remaining Horcruxes and Voldemort himself, ending his flight from death. It concludes the story begun as *Harry Potter and the Half-Blood Prince*, with Severus Snape a dominant player in events, and provides the resolution to all seven tales, as Harry the orphan finds a family and ensures the freedom of his friends from tyranny and evil. Much of the action is away from Hogwarts, but the school remains at the moral centre of events, in its resistance to the Dark Lord. Hogwarts is the setting of the climax, and the final battle against Voldemort, and reference is constantly made to it throughout the story. At the end Harry returns to his comfortable bed in Gryffindor Tower.

We learn in the very first chapter that Voldemort has adopted Malfoy Manor as his headquarters. There Snape reveals to him the exact day in the school vacation that Harry intends to flee the Dursley's home before his protection ends on his seventeenth birthday. The Dark Lord and his forces have stepped up their anti-Muggle activities, extending it to wizards who are not pure-bloods and even to those who value Muggles. His cause is helped by the journalist Rita Skeeter, whose biography *The Life and Lies of Albus Dumbledore* gives a distorted picture of the recently killed symbol of resistance. The lies, ironically, are Rita's, but there is enough fact sprinkled in the book to make it seem plausible.

While Harry is packing his trunk for his departure, he comes across a sliver of the broken mirror given to him by Sirius, in which he thinks for an instant that he sees Dumbledore's brilliant blue eye. He also reads an accurate obituary of Dumbledore and an interview with Rita Skeeter about her book, full of distortions. Members of the Order of the Phoenix, as well as Ron and Hermione (already come of age), come to Privet Drive and become Harry lookalikes, using Polyjuice Potion, to confuse the Death Eaters when he escapes. Pursued by Voldemort, Hagrid and Harry reach safety at Ted and Andromeda Tonks's house. As planned they there use a Portkey to get to The Burrow. Harry is anxious to leave as he sees his friends in danger because of him, but is persuaded to stay for Bill and Fleur's wedding. He, Ron and Hermione plan their departure and next moves, unable to divulge their mission on Dumbledore's orders. He is troubled as he sees in a dream Voldemort seeking a distant wandmaker.

On Harry's birthday Scrimgeour, the Minister of Magic, arrives at The Burrow with Dumbledore's will. He has left objects for the three friends that turn out to be important to their quest. Ron is given Dumbledore's Deluminator (which has other properties beside storing lights), Hermione a book of children's tales and Harry a golden snitch, and also the sword of Gryffindor. Scrimgeour hands over all the objects except for the sword.

On the wedding day Harry and Ron serve as stewards in a grand marquee set up in the garden, where a reception and dance follow the simple ceremony. The proceedings are thrown into disarray when Kingsley Shacklebolt's Patronus announces that the Ministry has fallen and Scrimgeour is slain. Their enemies were coming.

Their journeyings now begin. Harry, Ron and Hermione quickly Disapparate to Tottenham Court Road, in London, the first place that comes into Hermione's mind. Two Death Eaters disguised as Muggle workmen attack them. (It turns out they were detected as soon as they used Voldemort's name, which had been jinxed.) The three immobilise their foes and flee to 12 Grimmauld Place.

From an old letter of Harry's mother to Sirius he discovers that she and Bathilda Bagshot were friends in Godric Hollow; this discovery deepens his desire to visit there. They work out that Regulus Black is the 'R.A.B.' who took the locket from the cave hoping to destroy its Horcrux. Later, from Kreacher the house-elf they discover the full story of Regulus's endeavour, the elf's misuse by Voldemort, and something of the complex ways and magic of elves. Realising they wish to complete what Regulus began, Kreacher becomes a strong ally of Harry and the others. Harry orders him to bring Mundungus Fletcher, who stole the locket with other trinkets from Grimmauld Place. They discover from Mundungus that Dolores Umbridge now has the locket.

Harry, Ron and Hermione take it in turns to spy on the Ministry of Magic entrance, and decide their plan of action. They obtain hairs from three ministry employees and use Polyjuice Potion to enter the building as them. They find the Ministry has become Orwellian, with a giant statue in the Atrium portraying wizards subjugating the Muggle population. The three are soon forced to separate. Umbridge takes Hermione off to a session interrogating wizards who are not pure-bloods, Ron finds himself having to fix a jinxed office, and only Harry is left to find Umbridge's office, where there is no sign of the locket. He makes his way to the courts, guarded by Dementors, and unobtrusively joins Hermione. They seize the locket hanging around Umbridge's neck, rescue a number of wizards facing severe punishment, and come across Ron on their way to the Atrium. They Disapparate after almost being captured, but are unable to take refuge again in Grimmauld Place.

Hiding in the same woods in which the Quidditch World Cup had been played, they fail to open and destroy the locket. Harry finds himself more and more in touch with what Voldemort is doing. Through seeing into his mind Harry discovers that a wand Voldemort seeks to possess to defeat him had been stolen long ago by a blond young man. (It later turns out that this was Grindelwald, for a short time in his youth a friend of Dumbledore's.) The three move around the countryside, foraging for food and seeking out places where a Horcrux might be hidden. They overhear a group of fugitives, including two goblins, and learn that the sword of Gryffindor hidden in Gringotts is a fake. Hermione has the idea of summoning Phineas Nigellus Black, through the portrait she has brought with her, who reveals that Dumbledore borrowed the real sword to break open the ring. In this way they find out how to destroy the Horcruxes. The problem remains as to where the genuine sword is. Ron, increasingly disillusioned with doubt and delays, decides to abandon his friends to see how his family is faring. His reasoning is vividly summed up: 'The sword of Gryffindor was hidden they knew not where, and they were three teenagers in a tent whose only achievement was not, yet, to be dead.'

As Christmas approaches Harry again broaches to Hermione the idea of going to Godric's Hollow. To his surprise she agrees. In the dark graveyard of the village, as the sound of familiar carols come from the church, they find many tombs of wizarding families, one tomb of which has the same mysterious mark as in Hermione's children's book and as worn by Xenophilius Lovegood. They find the tombs of Dumbledore's mother and sister, and that of Harry's parents.

Walking through the village in the dark they locate the blasted ruins of the Potters' house. A figure beckons, whom they take to be Bathilda Bagshot, but it is in fact her decaying body possessed by the snake, Nagini, sent to trap them. The figure lures them to Bathilda's house and summons Voldemort. They escape by jumping through the upper window and Disapparating into lonely countryside. In the process Harry's wand is broken into two.

Late on Christmas night Harry and Hermione Disapparate to the Forest of Dean, near the Welsh border, which has happy childhood memories for Hermione. Harry takes first watch and sees a beautiful Patronus, a silvery doe. It leads him to an icy pool at the bottom of which lies the sword of Gryffindor. Harry nearly dies retrieving it, being rescued by Ron, who has been searching for them for a long time. Ron destroys the Horcrux in the locket with the sword. The three then go to find Xenophilius Lovegood. In his odd cylindrical home, which is near The Burrow, Hermione reads out the tale of three brothers from the book Dumbledore left her, and Xenophilius explains about the three Deathly Hallows, the Elder Wand, the Resurrection Stone, and the Cloak, which are reputed to conquer death. He tries to betray them in the hope of getting Luna back, who is held hostage by the Death Eaters.

As they think about the three Hallows over the coming weeks, Harry becomes more and more obsessed by them, and listless. Ron increasingly takes control. They are encouraged by hearing a secret radio broadcast produced by their friends in opposition to Voldemort, but are captured by Snatchers, seeking those on the run. Realising they have Harry Potter, the Snatchers take their captives to Malfoy Manor. Voldemort is still absent, seeking the powerful Elder Wand. While Hermione is tortured for information, Harry and Ron are thrust into a dungeon containing Luna, Mr Ollivander, Dean

Thomas and the goblin, Griphook, weakened by imprisonment. Dobby Apparates, sent to help Harry. While he Disapparates with the others, taking them to safety at Shell Cottage, the home of Bill and Fleur, Harry and Ron go upstairs to rescue Hermione. They fight but are saved only by the returning house-elf. As the three friends Disapparate with Dobby, he is wounded by a knife thrown by Bellatrix.

Dobby dies of his wound. As Harry buries him, he realises that he must destroy the Horcruxes above all else – the conflict of Horcruxes or Hallows is over. He seeks the help of Griphook in breaking into Gringotts Bank in search of a Horcrux hidden in Bellatrix's vault. Matters become urgent when he sees in his mind Voldemort retrieve the Elder Wand from Dumbledore's tomb. Taking Griphook, and with Hermione in the form of Bellatrix, they successfully retrieve the Cup of Helga Hufflepuff from the vault, and escape on the back of a dragon they have freed. From the events at Gringotts Voldemort realises that Harry is pursuing the Horcruxes. From his link into the Dark Lord's mind Harry discovers a Horcrux is hidden at Hogwarts.

Arriving at Hogsmeade, Harry, Ron and Hermione make contact with Dumbledore's brother, Aberforth, proprietor of the Hog's Head pub. They discover it is he who sent Dobby, learning of Harry's danger through his own magic mirror. Aberforth speaks of his family, and of a large portrait of his sister, which hides a recently opened tunnel to Hogwarts. Neville appears in the portrait and then steps into the room. He leads them to the Room of Requirement in Hogwarts, now set up for the needs of Dumbledore's Army, the Order of the Phoenix and others who resist Voldemort. With Harry's arrival Neville summons reinforcements, expecting to overthrow Snape and Death Eaters on the staff, but Harry explains they have a secret task. When he asks for help in finding an object belonging to Rowena Ravenclaw, Luna recognises that there is a lost diadem, depicted on a statue in the Ravenclaw common room. Harry warns McGonagall and other loyal professors that Voldemort is coming. They organise resistance and chase Snape from the school. Meanwhile Ron and Hermione retrieve fangs from the Basilisk's skull in the Chamber of Secrets, which allows the destruction of the Horcrux embodied in Hufflepuff's Cup.

Harry remembers seeing a diadem in the Room of Requirement when he used it to hide his copy of *Advanced Potion-Making* the year before. As Harry, Ron and Hermione attempt to retrieve it, they are set upon by Draco and his friends. Crabbe starts a magical fire that gets out of hand, killing him and destroying the Horcrux.

While they have been doing this, the Battle of Hogwarts is being fought, and Voldemort's forces besiege the castle. Harry, Ron and Hermione are caught up in the fighting. There are many casualties, including Fred, Tonks and Lupin. Harry sees once more into Voldemort's mind: the Dark Lord is in the Shrieking Shack at Hogsmeade with Nagini, summoning Snape. With Hermione and Ron, Harry makes his way there via the Whomping Willow's entrance. Voldemort still considers Snape his faithful servant but orders Nagini to kill him, believing Snape is master of the Elder Wand because he murdered Dumbledore, and that the Wand's allegiance will switch to himself. Harry finds Snape dying, who passes to him his memories, and dies looking into Harry's eyes, so similar to his mother's. Back at Hogwarts, Harry pours the memories into the Pensieve in the headteacher's office. He discovers that Snape was always protecting him, out of undying love for Lily, and was a double agent. Dumbledore, mortally wounded by putting on Marvolo's ring, had asked him to kill him, if that was required, so that Draco did not have to do it. Harry learns that he himself accidentally became a Horcrux when Voldemort killed his parents and failed to kill him. He must die before Voldemort can be destroyed.

Accepting that he must sacrifice himself so that his friends can live, Harry takes up Voldemort's ultimatum that he must go to him in the Forbidden Forest. On the way Harry is able to open the Snitch given to him by Dumbledore, and use the Resurrection Stone to have the spiritual company of his parents, Sirius and Lupin, who accompany him to the clearing in which Voldemort awaits, confident that Harry will come.

Blasted by the Dark Lord's killing curse, Harry finds himself in a world between life and death, which his imagination shapes into a transformed King's Cross, a place of meetings and potential journeys. Dumbledore and a hideously wounded child are there. Dumbledore explains that the Horcrux in him has been destroyed and that he cannot die while Voldemort lives, because the Dark Lord had used Harry's protected blood in returning to life. However, he has the choice of going on or back. Harry chooses the latter, and finds himself prone in the clearing.

Pretending to be dead, Harry is carried in front of Voldemort's triumphant forces towards Hogwarts. Neville confronts them and Voldemort tortures him by summoning the Sorting Hat and causing it to burn as he wears it. Neville, however, finds the sword of Gryffindor within it and slices off Nagini's head, destroying the final Horcrux. Harry faces Voldemort in the ensuing battle. The Dark Lord is confident that he is master of the Elder Wand, but Harry knows that he, in fact, is the true master. He tells Voldemort that Snape did not master the Wand by killing Dumbledore, as his death was with his consent. Draco had, in fact, become master when he disarmed Dumbledore, a mastery that passed to Harry when he in turn disarmed Draco. Furious, Voldemort throws a killing curse at Harry just as he sends a Disarming Spell. Because the Wand is loyal to Harry, the killing curse backfires on Voldemort, killing him. Harry returns the wand to Dumbledore's tomb, leaves the Resurrection Stone in the forest where it fell, and retains the Invisibility Cloak, like the wise brother in the story. He is back home in Hogwarts.

A brief epilogue set nineteen years later reveals that Harry the orphan has gained a family by marrying Ginny, and that he celebrates the courage of Severus Snape. At King's Cross, he and Ginny see two of their children off to Hogwarts, the third eager to go as soon as possible.

TWO

A Timeline

M any of the dates below are interpreted from the stories, and are approximate. Only some are explicitly identified by the author, often because they happen on a key day such as Hallowe'en (All Hallows Eve), St Valentine's Day or Christmas Day.

BC

382   Ollivanders start making magic wands.

AD

10th century Broomsticks are first used for transport. Around this time Hogwarts School of Witchcraft and Wizardry is established by Godric Gryffindor, Helga Hufflepuff, Rowena Ravenclaw and Salazar Slytherin. Schism is caused by Slytherin, who wishes only pure-bloods to study at Hogwarts, and secretly builds the Chamber of Secrets.

1294   First Triwizard Tournament

1473   First Quidditch World Cup match.

1692   Wizards go into hiding.

1881   Albus Dumbledore born.

1925   Morfin Gaunt attacks Muggle Tom Riddle Sr. Morfin's father, Marvolo, attacks Merope, his daughter, for her love for Riddle. Arrest of Morfin and Marvolo.

1926   Tom Riddle Sr abandons Merope before his son Tom is born. She dies, and Tom Riddle Jr is raised in a London orphanage.

Before 1938 Albus Dumbledore begins teaching at Hogwarts (subject, Transfiguration).

1938   Tom Riddle (Voldemort) starts his Wizarding studies at Hogwarts.

1940	Rubeus Hagrid's first year at Hogwarts.
1943	Tom opens the Chamber of Secrets, resulting in the death of a student whose ghost becomes named Moaning Myrtle. He frames Hagrid for opening the Chamber. Tom murders his father and grandparents at Riddle House, and frames his uncle, Morfin Gaunt, for the killings.
1945	Tom finishes his studies at Hogwarts. He unsuccessfully asks the then headteacher, Armando Dippet, to give him a post on the staff. Dumbledore defeats Grindelwald.
c. **1947**	Tom steals ancient treasures of Salazar Slytherin and Helga Hufflepuff, and goes into seclusion.
1956	Professor McGonagall begins teaching at Hogwarts. About this time Tom Riddle requests the post of Defence Against the Dark Arts teacher from Dumbledore. Secretly he has organised Death Eaters and is calling himself Lord Voldemort.
c. **1959**	Lily Evans born 30 January. James Potter born 27 March.
c. **1969**	Marriage of Arthur Weasley and Molly Prewett.
c. **1970**	Voldemort is now actively seeking power and immortality. James Potter and Lily Evans (Harry's parents-to-be), Sirius Black, Remus Lupin, Peter Pettigrew and Severus Snape begin attending Hogwarts.
1979	Sybill Trelawney prophesies the possible downfall of Voldemort (tied up with the birth of Harry Potter) and becomes Divination teacher around this time. Hermione Granger is born on 19 September. Death of Regulus Black, after stealing Slytherin's locket that is a Horcrux of Voldemort's.
1980	Ron Weasley is born on 1 March; Draco Malfoy on 5 June; Neville Longbottom on 30 July; and Harry Potter on 31 July.
1981	Ginny Weasley is born on 11 August. Severus Snape becomes Potions teacher at Hogwarts. Voldemort murders James and Lily Potter on 31 October, his killing curse on Harry rebounding, leaving the infant

with a lightning-shaped scar and Voldemort without a body. Harry is taken to live with the Dursleys, where he is magically protected by his blood kinship with his aunt, his mother's sister. Around 1 November Sirius Black is arrested for the murder of Peter Pettigrew and a number of other deaths.

1991

summer	Voldemort forces Quirrell to host him in his body, moulding his face on the back of Quirrell's head.
31 July	In the early hours of Harry's birthday, Hagrid delivers his invitation to study at Hogwarts. In the morning he takes Harry off to London and Diagon Alley. That same day the half-giant, on Dumbledore's orders, removes the Philosopher's Stone from a vault in Gringotts Bank.
1 September	Harry, Ron and Hermione start their first term at Hogwarts.
31 October	Quirrell lets a troll into the school to create a diversion while he, unsuccessfully, attempts to steal the Philosopher's Stone. Because of the troll, Hermione becomes friends with Harry and Ron.
November	During a Quidditch match, Quirrell hexes Harry's broomstick in an attempt to make him fall to his death, an attempt foiled by Snape and Hermione.
Christmas Day	Dumbledore passes Harry's father's Invisibility Cloak to him.

1992

June	Harry frustrates Voldemort's plans to steal the Philosopher's Stone and gain immortality. In doing so he helps Gryffindor win the house cup.
31 July	On his birthday, Harry meets Dobby the house-elf for the first time. Dobby creates mayhem at the Dursleys.
autumn term	In the new school year Ginny Weasley opens the Chamber of Secrets, her will controlled by Tom Riddle's sinister diary, which had earlier been planted in her school books by Lucius Malfoy.

1993

February	Ginny flushes the diary down the toilet, realising it is dangerous. Angry, Moaning Myrtle creates a flood that carries the diary, to be found by Harry. Tom Riddle (Voldemort) uses it to show Harry a fifty-year old memory that appears to put Hagrid in the blame for opening the Chamber.
spring	Hermione suffers petrification by seeing the Basilisk's reflection. As a precaution, the Minister of Magic sends Hagrid unjustly to Azkaban, and the school board of Governors, at the instigation of Lucius Malfoy, dismisses Dumbledore.
May	Tom Riddle forces Ginny to write her own fate on the wall and abducts her. Harry saves Ginny and destroys the living memory of Tom Riddle stored in the diary, eradicating one of Voldemort's Horcruxes. He tricks Lucius Malfoy into freeing Dobby. Hagrid is released from Azkaban.
summer	Sirius Black escapes from Azkaban prison after recognising Wormtail (Scabbers) in a photo of the Weasley family.
September	Harry encounters Dementors on his journey to Hogwarts for the new term (his third year).
31 October	Sirius tries to break into Gryffindor Tower to catch Wormtail (Scabbers).
December	Fred and George Weasley give Harry the Marauder's Map.
Christmas Day	Sirius anonymously gives Harry the gift of a Firebolt.

1994

January	Harry begins private lessons with Professor Lupin to repel Dementors.
Spring	Pettigrew, as Scabbers, fakes his own death, worried about Sirius's revenge.
6 June	Professor Trelawney gives her second prophecy, that Voldemort's servant (Peter Pettigrew) will return to him. Harry learns of Sirius's innocence, but Pettigrew escapes, as predicted.

August	Voldemort murders the elderly Frank Bryce, and Ireland gains the Quidditch World Cup.
1 September	Mad-Eye Moody is attacked by Barty Crouch Jr and Wormtail, and made captive while Crouch assumes his form. Returning to Hogwarts for the new school year (his fourth), Harry learns the Triwizard Tournament is to be held for the first time in over a century.
30 October	Delegates from the two other schools arrive at Hogwarts for the Tournament.
31 October	Crouch, in the form of Mad-Eye Moody, secretly places Harry's name in the Goblet of Fire, leading him to be chosen as a surprise fourth champion.
24 November	The first trial in the Tournament; Harry successfully gets past his dragon to retrieve a golden egg.
25 December	The Yule Ball. Cedric Diggory gives Harry an important clue for understanding the puzzle of the golden egg, which he in turn had heard from the fake Moody (who wants Harry to go through the next stage of the Tournament).

1995

24 February	The second trial in the Triwizard Tournament. The fake Moody arranges for Harry to hear about Gillyweed, which allows him to swim underwater.
17 May	Barty Crouch Jr learns that his father has escaped captivity and is likely to be heading towards Hogwarts to warn Dumbledore.
24 May	The Tournament champions receive their instructions for the final trial; Barty Crouch Jr stuns Krum and murders his own father.
24 June	With the aid of his servant Pettigrew, Voldemort returns to full power, and Cedric Diggory is murdered, but Harry escapes death. Dumbledore begins to re-form the Order of the Phoenix.
July	The Order of the Phoenix secretly begin guarding Harry at the Dursleys and watching the door to the Department of Mysteries, aware that Voldemort

seeks the prophecy concerning himself and Harry. Hagrid and Madame Maxime set off to try to win the giants over to Dumbledore's cause against Voldemort.

August	The Order sets up its Headquarters in 12 Grimmauld Place and Dumbledore is humiliated by the Ministry, which strips him of honours. Dolores Umbridge sends Dementors to attack Harry in Little Whinging, jeopardising his future as a wizard. He is moved to safety in Grimmauld Place.
12 August	Harry is cleared of misusing magic by the wizarding court.
30 August	The Ministry of Magic begins taking control of Hogwarts with Educational Decree 22, which allows Umbridge to become the new Defence Against the Dark Arts teacher.
1 September	Harry and friends return to Hogwarts for the new school year, his fifth.
October	Dumbledore's Army, the DA, is formed, led by Harry.
November	Umbridge expels Harry from his Quidditch team and locks up his Firebolt. Hagrid brings his dim half-brother, the true giant Grawp, to live secretly in the Forbidden Forest.
December	Harry kisses Cho Chang, and in a dream witnesses Mr Weasley being attacked by Voldemort's snake, Nagini. Harry and the Weasleys spend Christmas at Grimmauld Place.

1996

January	Back at Hogwarts, Harry begins Occlumency lessons with Snape, to break the connection between Voldemort's mind and his. There is a mass breakout of Death Eaters from Azkaban, including Bellatrix Lestrange, Sirius's cousin.
14 February	Harry dates Cho, with disastrous consequences. Hermione orders Rita Skeeter to interview Harry about the return of Voldemort.

March	Umbridge sacks Professor Trelawney from teaching Divination, and Dumbledore takes on the centaur, Firenze, instead.
April	Umbridge finds out about the DA, and Dumbledore is dismissed, Umbridge replacing him as headteacher.
June	Harry takes his fifth year examinations, the OWLs. Hagrid resists being dismissed by Umbridge, and Professor McGonagall is seriously injured as she remonstrates with Umbridge and her cronies.
June	Harry is lured with his friends to the Hall of Prophecy by a false vision of Sirius being attacked, which was planted by Voldemort. Voldemort, however, is foiled in his attempts to gain the prophecy concerning his fate from the Department of Mysteries, thanks to Harry and his friends from the DA. Harry learns of Professor Trelawney's first prediction, that he is the Chosen One who must kill Voldemort. Sirius Black is killed in the battle in the Department of Mysteries. With the exception of Bellatrix Lestrange, the Death Eaters are captured. The Dementors desert Azkaban and Dumbledore is reinstated as headmaster.
July	The Dementors begin breeding. Voldemorts kills members of the Order. Fudge is sacked as Minister of Magic, replaced by the more decisive Rufus Scrimgeour. Dumbledore is severely wounded in destroying a second of Voldemort's Horcruxes, held in Marvolo Gaunt's ring. Draco Malfoy is ordered by Voldemort to destroy Dumbledore. Snape takes an Unbreakable Vow before Draco's mother, Narcissa, and Bellatrix Lestrange to aid and protect Draco, and, if necessary, fulfil his task.
August	Draco begins working on a complex plan to bring Dumbledore down, involving Borgin and Burkes's shop in Knockturn Alley. The Ministry of Magic imposes extra protection around Hogwarts.

September	Harry, Ron, and Hermione start at their sixth and penultimate academic year at Hogwarts. Harry inherits a Potions textbook annotated by former pupil, 'the Half-Blood Prince'. Dumbledore starts showing Harry all he has gleaned about Voldemort's shadowy background, employing memories in his Pensieve.
October	Draco neglects his schoolwork as he works on his plans in the Room of Requirement, guarded by his ugly minders, who, through taking Polyjuice Potion, appear as pretty girls. Draco's inept attempt to poison Dumbledore fails.
December	Under an Imperius curse from Draco, Madam Rosmerta poisons wine intended as a Christmas gift for Dumbledore. Rufus Scrimgeour fails to persuade Harry to use his standing as the Chosen One to bolster the weakened image of the Ministry of Magic.

1997

January	Dumbledore gives Harry the task of retrieving Slughorn's full memory of his conversation long ago with Tom Riddle concerning Horcruxes.
February	Harry and his year begin learning how to Apparate.
April	Harry succeeds in eliciting the memory from Slughorn, which confirms that Voldemort has made a number of Horcruxes.
May	Ginny stands in for Harry as Seeker in an important Quidditch match, and afterwards the two confess their feelings for each other.
June	Dumbledore with Harry retrieves Slytherin's locket from a coastal cave at great cost to the old wizard, not realising that it is a fake – the real Horcrux had been removed by a wizard called simply R.A.B. While the two were away from Hogwarts, Draco seized the opportunity to smuggle Death Eaters into the school, using the now-repaired Vanishing Cabinets. Dumbledore is killed by a killing curse

from Severus Snape. Professor McGonagall becomes acting headteacher. Harry vows to track down the remaining four Horcruxes in which Voldemort has hidden portions of his soul and kill the Dark Lord, and Ron and Hermione insist that they will accompany him.

July	Explosions, crashes and derailments occur frequently in Muggle Britain. Many die or disappear. Fogs are caused by the presence of Dementors.
27 July	Harry narrowly escapes from Privet Drive, pursued by Voldemort and Death Eaters.
31 July	Harry comes of age as a wizard on his seventeenth birthday, allowing him to use magic outside Hogwarts. Scrimgeour reads to him Dumbledore's will, leaving him a Snitch and the sword of Gryffindor.
1 August	Wedding of Bill Weasley and Fleur Delacour at The Burrow. It is attacked, and Harry, Ron and Hermione Disapparate to Tottenham Court Road, London, where they are soon attacked by Death Eaters after revealing themselves by using Voldemort's name. They flee again to 12 Grimmauld Place, wary that its magical shield may be compromised.
2 August	Harry explores Sirius's bedroom for clues, and the three then search R.A.B.'s bedroom. Kreacher the house-elf comes over to their side after his story is revealed. He is sent on a mission to bring back Mundungus Fletcher, who has burgled the locket, one of the remaining Horcruxes.
4 August	Visit of Lupin to Grimmauld Place, and the return of Kreacher with Mundungus, who reveals that Dolores Umbridge seized the locket.
August	Harry, Ron and Hermione take it in turns to spy on the Ministry of Magic over four weeks.
1 September	Beginning of the term and new year at Hogwarts. Harry brings back news from his seven-hour vigil

watching the Ministry entrance that Severus Snape is the new headteacher.

2 September   Harry, Ron and Hermione infiltrate the Ministry building to locate Umbridge and the locket. They flee with it to the woods where the Quidditch World Cup was held in 1994.

3 September   They move on to a quiet market town, in search of food.

September–December

The three travel to isolated places in Britain to remain safe, some of them spots where they think Horcruxes might be hidden. They gradually move northwards to avoid capture, despite the increasing cold of winter's approach. Ron, disillusioned and affected by the locket, deserts Harry and Hermione.

24 December   Harry and Hermione arrive at Godric's Hollow in the evening of Christmas Eve. The two barely escape Voldemort's trap, and Harry's wand is broken.

Christmas Day   Hermione brings Harry to an isolated spot and erects their tent. They read from Rita Skeeter's *Life and Lies of Albus Dumbledore*, which she snatched from Bathilda Bagshot's house.

Christmas night and the early hours of Boxing Day

The two move on to the Forest of Dean, where a Patronus, a silvery doe, leads Harry to the sword of Gryffindor, on the bed of a pond. Ron, who has been seeking them for some time, rescues his friend. The Horcrux in the locket is destroyed.

Boxing Day   Ron fills his friends in on what has been happening in the world, and Harry in turn tells him what has transpired in his long absence. Hermione suggests they find Xenophilius Lovegood, to find the meaning of the triangular rune he wore at the wedding.

27 December   Visit to Xenophilius's house near The Burrow in south Devon in which they learn more about the Deathly Hallows, and also that Luna is held hostage by Death Eaters. She would be released in exchange for Harry. They escape from the trap.

1998

January–March The three friends wander to various isolated places, lacking definite leads. Harry is absorbed and distracted by the Deathly Hallows and Ron gradually takes charge.

End of March–beginning of April

Ron is able to tune into the secret radio broadcast *Potterwatch*. This heartens them. Carried away, Harry uses Voldemort's name, which betrays their location. The Snatchers take their captives to Malfoy Manor, where Draco has just returned from Hogwarts for the Easter holidays. Bellatrix is also present. The prisoners join Luna, Dean Thomas, Mr Ollivander and Griphook the Goblin, who are locked in a dark dungeon. They escape to Shell Cottage, and bury Dobby their rescuer.

April Harry, Ron and Hermione stay at Bill and Fleur's cottage for the rest of the month, and hatch their daring plot to break into Gringotts to retrieve the Hufflepuff Cup with Griphook's reluctant help.

May They break into Gringotts, and then visit Hogsmeade and the Hog's Head pub. In Hogwarts Castle they seek the Ravenclaw diadem, one of the remaining Horcruxes, while the school, helped by the Order of the Phoenix and many others, prepares for defensive battle against Voldemort's besieging forces. There follow the Battle of Hogwarts, Harry's sacrifice and the end of tyranny.

2017

September Harry's second son, Albus Severus Potter, begins at Hogwarts. His elder son, James, already attends, and the youngest child, Lily, is eager to start there in two years' time.

THREE

An A–Z

Abbott, Hannah A Hufflepuff student who is supportive of Harry, and friends with Ernie Macmillan and Justin Finch-Fletchley. In *Harry Potter and the Order of the Phoenix*, she is a committed member of the DA. In *Harry Potter and the Half-Blood Prince*, as Voldemort's reign of terror grows, Hannah is told that her mother has been found dead.

Accidental Magic Reversal Department A branch of the Ministry of Magic that deals with accidental use of magic, for instance, when Dudley's Aunt Marge is inflated by Harry.

accio A summoning spell, usually followed by the name of the object summoned (e.g. 'accio wand'). Latin, accio, 'I summon.'

Acid Pops Magic sweets available from Honeydukes in Hogsmeade.

acromantula A monster spider with eight eyes and possessed of speech.

Advanced Potion-Making A textbook, by Libatius Borage, which was owned by Severus Snape as a student, and annotated by him. The textbook comes into Harry's possession, but he knows the author only as the self-named 'Half-Blood Prince'. Harry discovers that the annotations help him to become top of Horace Slughorn's Potions class, whereas previously his grades were mediocre.

Agrippa (Heinrich Cornelius Agrippa von Nettesheim), 1486–1535 A real historic alchemist featured as a famous wizard on a Chocolate Frog card owned by Ron, which described him as 'celebrated wizard imprisoned by Muggles for his writing, because they thought his books were evil'. He was a German theologian (he wrote commentaries on Paul's Epistles) who became preoccupied with astrology, and believed that anyone taking up magic needs to be thoroughly grounded in theology, physics and mathematics.

Alchemy A science that flourished in the sixteenth century, and included a quest to turn metal to gold. It is the origin of Chemistry and provides many allusions for the stories. Early scientists were often also Alchemists (for example, Sir Isaac Newton). The search for the Philosopher's Stone was central to the science.

Alohomora A spell to unlock doors, frequently used by Hermione.

Amortentia The most powerful love potion in the world. Its appearance is as of mother-of-pearl, and its pleasant odour varies according to what attracts an individual. Rather than creating real love it in fact induces obsession and infatuation.

Animagus A wizard or witch who can turn him or herself into an associated animal at will (for instance, Professor McGonagall can transform into a cat). The ability is rare – only seven were registered with the Ministry of Magic in the twentieth century. A number of unregistered Animagi appear in the stories, such as Peter Pettigrew.

Aparecium A spell to make invisible ink visible.

Apparition The ability to transport oneself instantly to another destination. Most wizarding houses, and Hogwarts, are protected to prevent Apparition for privacy and security. In Harry's sixth year, Apparition lessons are given. If parts of the body become separated in novices this is called 'Splinching.' Ron fails his first test because he leaves half an eyebrow behind when he Disapparates.

Aragog The name of a gargantuan spider, or acromantula, living in the Forbidden Forest, who was nurtured by the giant Hagrid.

Arithmancy Magical study of the science of numbers, particularly prediction based on numbers, a subject favoured by Hermione.

A text used in the Hogwarts class, taught by a female staff member, Professor Vector, was *Numerology and Grammatica*. According to its principles, Harry's birth number yields the master number 11, indicating a stormy and significant life of a talented person.

Astronomy A subject – the science of heavenly bodies – taught at Hogwarts by Professor Sinistra.

Astronomy Tower This is Hogwarts Castle's tallest tower, used for night lessons in Astronomy. In *Harry Potter and the Half-Blood Prince* Professor Sybill Trelawney utters a prophecy of impending calamity concerning a lightning-struck tower, from a card she draws out of her Tarot pack. Soon after a Dark Mark is positioned above it by Death Eaters who have entered Hogwarts, shortly before Dumbledore is killed seemingly without remorse by Professor Snape.

Atrium Large entrance area of the Ministry of Magic reached through a shabby telephone box on a run-down London back street. It contains a security desk, a golden gate to the lifts and a golden fountain, containing large figures of a witch and a wizard, a centaur, a goblin and a house-elf. The Atrium is the scene of a battle between Dumbledore and Voldemort in *Harry Potter and the Order of the Phoenix* after Harry has encountered the Dark Lord following the destruction of the prophecy concerning the two of them.

Auror Someone employed by the Ministry of Magic to pursue Dark Wizards or Witches. During Harry's period at Hogwarts the main task became to find and kill Lord Voldemort. Harry desires a career as an Auror, opposed as he is to the Dark Arts.

Avada Kedavra A killing curse that normally cannot be blocked, one of the three Unforgivable Curses. Harry uniquely survived the killing curse as an infant, shielded by his mother's sacrificial love from Voldemort's act of murder.

Avery A Death Eater, first name unknown, who is part of an ambush in the Department of Mysteries in *Harry Potter and the Order of the*

Phoenix. He with others in Voldemort's force are seeking to kill Harry and obtain from him an old prophecy about Voldemort's destiny.

Azkaban A fortress on a tiny island in the North Sea where criminal wizards and witches are imprisoned. Sirius Black is able to swim, transformed into a large dog, to the British mainland when he escapes. It was guarded by Dementors until their allegiance to Voldemort became unmistakable. It is the Alcatraz of the wizard world.

Bagman, Ludovic 'Ludo' Head of Department of Magical Games and Sports at the Ministry of Magic. Formerly a Quidditch player, he was a Beater for the Wimbourne Wasps and played for England. Bagman is large and blond-haired. His first name, deriving from Latin, is associated with games and sport but also, in conjunction with his family name, might imply a trickster.

Bagshot, Bathilda A noted historian, she was known by generations of Hogwarts students as the author of the standard textbook *A History of Magic*. She was a friend of Harry's parents in Godric's Hollow. At the end of her life she was interviewed by Rita Skeeter for her scurrilous biography of Albus Dumbledore. In *Harry Potter and the Deathly Hallows* her body is possessed after her death by Nagini to deceive Harry.

Bane A formidable centaur in the Forbidden Forest who considers the reading of stars as fatalistic. Though he wishes for little to do with wizarding folk, he attends Dumbledore's funeral.

Barnabas the Barmy A crazy wizard of some unknown significance, but no doubt familiar to readers of the Hogwarts textbook *History of Magic*. On the seventh floor at the school there is a tapestry of him trying to teach ballet to trolls.

Basilisk A giant and startlingly green snake with yellow eyes that are fatal to look at. It may grow up to fifty feet in length and is called the King of Serpents. Even seen in a reflection its eyes turn the beholder rigid, a condition remedied only by a potion painstakingly made from Mandrakes. Like other snakes it speaks and understands Parseltongue and can be controlled by Parselmouths. The Basilisk in *Harry Potter and the Chamber of Secrets* is subject only to Voldemort, the sole surviving heir of Slytherin. Its deadly fang destroys the Horcrux in Tom Riddle's diary, and in *Harry Potter and the Deathly Hallows* a fang is used to destroy another Horcrux in Helga Hufflepuff's Cup.

Battle of Hogwarts Voldemort's siege of the school in *Harry Potter and the Deathly Hallows* in which many die but Voldemort is vanquished by Harry Potter through his sacrifice and courage. Magical creatures as well as wizards fight in the battle. The year before there was a much smaller attack from within the school by Death Eaters, in which Dumbledore was killed.

Beater In Quidditch, the player whose task it is to knock the Bludgers in the direction of the opposing team to deflect players.

Beauxbatons Academy of Magic A school of witchcraft and wizardry in Europe – a more precise location is not disclosed, but the academy may be in France or French-speaking Switzerland. 'Beauxbatons' may mean 'beautiful wands'. In *Harry Potter and the Goblet of Fire* they join Durmstrang Institute at Hogwarts for the Triwizard Tournament. Beautiful Fleur Delacour, a student at Beauxbatons, later stays with the Weasleys and marries Bill Weasley.

Bell, Katie A Chaser for the Gryffindor Quidditch team. In *Harry Potter and the Half-Blood Prince* she tries to bring a bewitched and deadly opal necklace into Hogwarts under the spell of the Imperius curse.

Bertie Bott's Every-Flavour Beans A popular wizarding variety of jelly beans, which sometimes come in eclectic flavors, including liver, tripe, curry, sprout and even vomit.

bezoar A stone from a goat's stomach which is an antidote to most poisons. Harry uses it to save Ron's life.

Binns, Professor The deceased teacher of the History of Magic who has continued his dull routine of teaching ever since leaving his body in the Hogwarts staff room at death, and not appearing to notice the transition. He enters walking through the blackboard at the beginning of classes. Hermione shocks him by asking a question in class about the mysterious Chamber of Secrets. J.K. Rowling modelled him partly on a dreary and unnamed lecturer she had at university.

bitter cup On the island in the Cave of Inferi used by Dumbledore to drink a basin of green potion protecting the magical locket. This is the only way the locket, which Dumbledore believes is a Horcrux, can be obtained. The bitter liquid nearly finishes Dumbledore off and seriously weakens him, and he can drink it only because he has made Harry promise to force him to do it. In *Harry Potter and the Deathly Hallows* Kreacher recounts how Voldemort forced him to drink the potion when he originally placed the Horcrux in the cave, and how Regulus Black drank it to obtain the locket.

Black Forest, Germany It is said that Professor Quirrell came across vampires here.

Black, Phineas Nigellus Great-great-grandfather of Sirius, and (according to Sirius) the least popular headmaster of Hogwarts, who lives an active life in his portrait hanging on the wall of Dumbledore's study. He is an example of a prodigious Slytherin who has eschewed the Dark Arts.

Black, Regulus Arcturus (R.A.B.) Younger brother of Sirius, who was killed by inferi after obtaining the gold locket containing the Horcrux and substituting a fake one.

Black, Sirius In his schooldays at Hogwarts he became fast friends with Harry's parents-to-be, James Potter and Lily Evans, as well as other fellow-pupils Remus Lupin and Peter Pettigrew, and made a bitter enemy of Severus Snape. Like James Potter and Peter Pettigrew he was an Animagus, his animal form being a large dog. Significantly the constellation that bears his name, Sirius, is also known traditionally as the Dog Star. Sirius is the brightest star in the night sky, and other important characters besides Sirius Black have names taken from the night skies, such as Luna Lovegood and Merope Gaunt, but particularly those related to the Black family. His name sounds like 'serious', and his character certainly reflects the psychological scars of his long internment in Azkaban. Though his ancestry is exclusively associated with Slytherin house, he was in Gryffindor at Hogwarts, despite the fact that there was something of Slytherin in his character. For many years it was believed he had murdered a number of people in support of Voldemort and in fact was a double agent for the Dark Lord. Madam Rosmerta, however, found it hard to believe that he had gone over to the Dark Side. He survived the twelve years in Azkaban by holding onto the fact that he was innocent. He was Harry's guardian and godfather. In his will Sirius left all his possessions to Harry, including 12 Grimmauld Place and his house-elf Kreacher. His death in the battle at the Department of Mysteries at the hand of Bellatrix Lestrange left Harry bereft, his only hope of a home free of the Dursleys gone. Sirius passed through the mysterious veil in the Death Chamber – from the other side of which Harry and Luna could hear murmuring voices.

Blast-Ended Skrewt One of Hagrid's many 'pet' creatures – described as a kind of cross between a fire crab and a manticore. They seem to lack head and eyes, and every so often let out a fiery explosion at one end. Male and female are distinguishable by the fact that males have a scorpion-like sting and females sport suckers on their underbellies. Adults possess a grey armour and might reach as much as 10 feet in length.

Blood-Flavoured Lollipops Candy designed for Vampires, and suitable for eaters of black pudding.

Bloody Baron, the An armour-suited ghost at Hogwarts associated with Slytherin house. He likes to groan and clank up on the Astronomy Tower. He is the spirit of a fiery young man who killed Helena Ravenclaw, the Grey Lady, who is Ravenclaw's resident ghost.

Bloxam, Beatrix Author of *Toadstool Tales*, an allusion to Beatrix Potter's stories.

Bludgers In Quidditch, black balls designed to knock players off course.

Bobbin, Melinda A Hogwarts student invited to the Slug Club merely because her family owns an extensive chain of apothecaries.

Bode, Broderick A wizard working in the Ministry of Magic. He is used by Lucius Malfoy, under an Imperius curse, to try to steal the prophecy in the Department of Mysteries relating to the Dark Lord and Harry, and was later murdered while being treated in St Mungo's Hospital.

Body-Bind spell An immobilising charm. Dumbledore uses this on Harry in *Harry Potter and the Half-Blood Prince* to protect him on the Astronomy Tower from Death Eaters.

Boggarts Shape-shifters that assume the form of a person's worst fears (for example, with Ron they appear as a spider, and for Professor Lupin, the werewolf, a full moon). To be rid of them the victim needs to utter 'Riddikulus' while imaging a shape that would make the apparition of their fear into a laughable object.

Bones, Amelia A member of the Order of the Phoenix who was murdered near 10 Downing Street, most probably by Voldemort himself. She was head of Magical Law Enforcement for the Ministry of Magic, wore a monocle, and had a niece at Hogwarts, Susan Bones.

Bogrod A goblin clerk in Gringotts Bank. Harry uses the Imperius curse against him in *Harry Potter and the Deathly Hallows* as part of the raid on Bellatrix's vault.

Borgin and Burkes A shop in Knockturn Alley, a wizarding street devoted to the Dark Arts, whence came the cursed opal necklace that afflicted Katie Bell. Tom Riddle Junior, a.k.a. Lord Voldemort, worked here after leaving Hogwarts, attracted by its dark interests. The shop sold antiques and bric-à-brac that had unusual and powerful magical qualities.

Bowtruckle An intensely shy guardian of trees that mainly inhabits woodland in the west of England and some European forests. It becomes savage, despite its small size, when its tree is in danger. Problems in obtaining wood for wands can be overcome by distracting the Bowtruckle with woodlice, a delicacy.

Bozo A photographer employed by the *Daily Prophet*.

Braithwaite, Betty A reporter on the *Daily Prophet* who in *Harry Potter and the Deathly Hallows* interviews Rita Skeeter about her biography of Albus Dumbledore.

Brockdale bridge This was magically destroyed in July 1996 as a result of the activities of Voldemort's followers. A number of Muggle cars were hurled into the river underneath, alarming and perplexing the government. 'Brockdale' means 'valley of badgers', and therefore could have an association with Helga Hufflepuff, one of the historic founders of Hogwarts hated by Voldemort.

Broomstick Servicing Kit Service kit in a black leather case given by Hermione to Harry for his thirteenth birthday. It contained Tail-Twig Clippers, a jar of Fleetwood's High-Finish Handle Polish, a brass compass and a handbook on broom care.

Brown, Lavender In the same year at Hogwarts as Harry, Lavender is in Gryffindor. For a time in *Harry Potter and the Half-Blood Prince* she is Ron's girlfriend, much to Hermione's chagrin. She is close friends with Parvati Patel.

Bryce, Frank A Muggle who was elderly gardener at Riddle House, in the village of Little Hangleton. He was employed after returning from the war. Voldemort murdered him with the killing curse.

Bubble-Head Charm A spell that allows a person to breathe underwater, employed by Cedric Diggory and Fleur Delacour in the Triwizard Tournament.

bubotuber A bloated plant resembling a black slug. Its swellings hold an ugly solution like pus. The effluence cures acne, but contact with its undiluted form results in boils and sores.

Buckbeak A Hippogriff under the care of Hagrid who is saved from unjust execution by Harry and Hermione and plays a part in the escape of Sirius in *Harry Potter and the Prisoner of Azkaban*. For safety he is temporarily renamed 'Witherwings' in *Harry Potter and the Half-Blood Prince*. He saves Harry from Snape after the murder on the Astronomy Tower, and fights in the Battle of Hogwarts in *Harry Potter and the Deathly Hallows*.

Budleigh Babberton Location of the temporary home of Horace Slughorn in *Harry Potter and the Half-Blood Prince*, 'borrowed' by Slughorn while the owners are on holiday. The village, which has little more than a war memorial and a church, may be in south Devon, perhaps somewhere near Ottery St Catchpole, as its name echoes the coastal town of Budleigh Salterton and nearby East Budleigh, a few miles from Exeter, where J.K. Rowling attended university. There is also a Babbacombe in Torbay, south Devon.

Bulstrode, Millicent A student in Harry's year who belongs to Slytherin house. In her second year Hermione was unlucky enough to have her as a duelling partner.

Burbage, Charity Teacher of Muggle Studies at Hogwarts. She is captured in *Harry Potter and the Deathly Hallows* by Voldemort after writing in defence of 'Mudbloods' in the *Daily Prophet*, and in favour of mixed marriages between wizards and Muggles. She is murdered by Voldemort and fed to Nagini.

Burke, Caractacus Co-founder of the shop Borgin and Burkes, specialising in artefacts to do with the Dark Arts.

Burrow, The The Weasleys' home near Ottery St Catchpole, Harry's second favourite building, and a second home to him. It may be located in Devon, in the Otter valley (where lies Samuel Taylor Coleridge's birthplace, Ottery St Mary). Its high hedges and the trees of its orchard help to keep it hidden from Muggles.

Butterbeer A popular drink with magical folk native to Hogsmeade. It is a sweet and buttery drink, with a head of soft foam like the best Muggle beer. It can be served hot as a winter warmer.

Cadogan, Sir Knight in a portrait in the North Tower at Hogwarts. While the Fat Lady is being repaired, he takes over temporarily as guardian of Gryffindor Tower.

Canary Creams A variety of popular custard-cream biscuits created by Fred and George Weasley that turn their eater into a canary.

Care of Magical Creatures One of the subjects taken at Hogwarts, on how to look after magical creatures. Through most of Harry's time at Hogwarts it was taught by Hagrid.

Carrow, Alecto A Death Eater who is appointed teacher of Muggle Studies at Hogwarts in *Harry Potter and the Deathly Hallows*, replacing Charity Burbage. Sister of Amycus.

Carrow, Amycus A particularly cruel Death Eater who is appointed teacher of Defence Against the Dark Arts (now called simply Dark Arts) in *Harry Potter and the Deathly Hallows*. Brother of Alecto.

cartomancy The practice of fortune telling or divination using a standard pack of cards, which perhaps started when playing cards were first used in Europe in the fourteenth century. Sometimes the Tarot pack is used, as by Professor Trelawney in *Harry Potter and the Half-Blood Prince*, when, only half-sober, she predicts disaster on the Astronomy Tower (using the card of the lightning-struck tower).

Cattermole, Mary Wife of Reg Cattermole who is interrogated by Dolores Umbridge in *Harry Potter and the Deathly Hallows* as a Mudblood on the charge that her magic was stolen. She is the child of greengrocers.

Cattermole, Reg A wizard in the Ministry of Magic's department of Magical Maintenance whose hairs are used by Ron in Polyjuice Potion to masquerade as him in *Harry Potter and the Deathly Hallows*.

Cave of Inferi The location of one of Voldemort's Horcruxes, a locket of Slytherin's. It is located on the coast a great distance from Hogwarts. Here the youthful Tom Riddle frightened two children from his orphanage. Within the vast cave is a black Stygian lake, in the middle of which is a tiny and flat island of rock to which Dumbledore and Harry cross to try to find the Horcrux in *Harry Potter and the Half-Blood Prince*. There Dumbledore drinks the bitter cup. Inferi fill the depth of the lake.

centaurs Magical creatures from classical mythology. They are half human, half horse and fiercely independent. In the Forbidden Forest there is a large herd, including Bane, Ronan and Firenze.

Chamber of Secrets A hidden and vast subterranean vault created by Salazar Slytherin, one of the four founders of Hogwarts, and containing his giant statue. It contains a mystery terror ready to be unleashed by his true heir (Voldemort) to rid the school of those who do not have pure blood, and hence are considered unworthy to study and practise magic. In *Harry Potter and the Chamber of Secrets* the terror, revealed as a Basilisk, is killed by Harry, with help from Fawkes. The Chamber had been hidden for many centuries but was opened on two occasions, the first by Tom Riddle and his friends during his schooldays and the second in *Harry Potter and the Chamber of Secrets* by Ginny Weasley, her will controlled by Voldemort's Horcrux – Tom Riddle's diary. Ron and Hermione go there in *Harry Potter and the Deathly Hallows* to obtain fangs from the Basilisk's skull in order to destroy Horcruxes.

Chang, Cho One time girlfriend of Harry at Hogwarts and a year above him. She is Seeker in the Ravenclaw Quidditch team. In *Harry Potter and the Goblet of Fire* she dates Cedric Diggory and grieves for him long after.

charm A spell that changes the properties or behaviour of a person or object according to the will of the magician, so that a person, for example, might become as rigid as stone or an object might fly somewhere.

Charms A subject taught at Hogwarts by Professor Filius Flitwick. The classroom is located on the third floor.

Chaser A player in Quidditch who uses the Quaffle to attempt to score a goal.

Chocolate Cauldrons Candies containing Firewhisky. They are susceptible to being spiked with love potion.

Chorley, Herbert A Junior Minister in the UK (Muggle) Government who has a severe reaction to the Imperius curse, making him think he is, in fact, a duck. He is stealthily removed to St Mungo's Hospital.

Chosen One The name given by some to Harry in the belief that he might be the one who rids the world of Voldemort, as he is indicated in a mysterious prophecy that was hidden in the Hall of Prophecy. Harry realises, partly because of this prophecy, that he is in fact the Chosen One, and his destiny is to kill Voldemort or be killed by him (for the future is always open, never fully predictable from a human viewpoint).

Clearwater, Penelope A student at Hogwarts belonging to Ravenclaw house. In *Harry Potter and the Prisoner of Azkaban* she is a girlfriend of Percy Weasley.

Cole, Mrs Matron of the orphanage in which Tom Riddle Jr lived, the future Voldemort. She was an intelligent, lean woman with a sharply formed face.

Colloportus A spell to shut and seal doorways.

Coming of Age For people of the wizarding world this is seventeen years of age. After this point wizards and witches are allowed to employ magic outside Hogwarts.

common rooms In the style of traditional universities, Hogwarts has common rooms for students. There are four, one for each house, Gryffindor's and Ravenclaw's in towers, Slytherin's in a dungeon and Hufflepuff's in a basement close to the kitchen. The common rooms are used for relaxation, games such as Wizard Chess and Exploding Snap, and homework.

Confundus Charm A spell that causes confusion and errors of judgement. Hermione uses one on Cormac McLaggen in *Harry Potter and the Half-Blood Prince* to prevent him from being chosen for Harry's Quidditch team. In *Harry Potter and the Prisoner of Azkaban* Snape attributes support of Sirius by Harry, Ron and Hermione to their being under the Charm.

Coote, Ritchie A Beater in Harry's Quidditch team in *Harry Potter and the Half-Blood Prince*.

Crabbe, Vincent A bullying student at Hogwarts who, along with Goyle, acts as a minder for Draco. He and Goyle are troll-like in appearance, with broad body and long arms. In his sixth year he attempts to bring a shrunken head into the school. He dies in *Harry Potter and the Deathly Hallows* after creating magical fire he cannot control to attack Harry and his friends.

Crookshanks Hermione's ginger pet, who is a mixture of cat and Kneazle, a magical creature. He has inherited the independence of the Kneazle, becoming friendly with Sirius's animagus, a large dog. His name reflects his slightly crooked legs. His extraordinary perceptions result in a vicious animosity to Scabbers, Ron's pet rat, who is really Peter Pettigrew's Animagus.

Crouch Jr, Bartemius 'Barty' Straw-haired son of Barty Crouch, Sr, and 'faithful servant' of Voldemort. His father helps him escape

Azkaban, where he had been imprisoned as a Death Eater, and keeps him captive at home, tended by Winky the house-elf. After escaping his father's custody, Crouch Jr captures Mad-Eye Moody in *Harry Potter and the Goblet of Fire* and, by means of Polyjuice Potion, takes his place as teacher of the Defence Against the Dark Arts. When his identity is finally revealed, his soul is sucked from his body by Dementors before he can have a proper trial.

Crouch Sr, Bartemius 'Barty' A senior minister in the wizarding government, Crouch used methods almost as bad as those of the Dark Arts to suppress Voldemort's original rise to power. He consigned wizards to Azkaban without fair trial and legalised Unforgivable Curses on criminals. The discovery that his own son, Barty Crouch Jr, was loyal to Voldemort jeopardised his career, and he was moved sideways to become head of the Department of International Magical Cooperation. Percy Weasley became his fervent assistant. To please his dying wife, he helped his son escape from Azkaban and hid him. Voldemort released his son from the captivity imposed by his father and put Crouch Sr under an Imperius curse. He escaped and travelled to Hogwarts to warn Dumbledore, but his son intercepted and killed him.

Crucio The foul Cruciatus curse belonging to the Dark Arts used on Neville in *Harry Potter and the Order of the Phoenix* by Bellatrix Lestrange, causing him to convulse and scream in extreme pain. It is one of the Unforgivable Curses. It is used by Bellatrix Lestrange to torture Hermione in *Harry Potter and the Deathly Hallows*.

Cuffe, Barnabas Editor of the *Daily Prophet*.

Cup, Helga Hufflepuff's Originally owned by Hepzibah Smith, a descendant of Hufflepuff, the cup is characteristically engraved with a figure of a badger. It is stolen by Voldemort and turned into a Horcrux before being hidden in Bellatrix Lestrange's vault at Gringotts Bank. It is retrieved by Harry, Ron and Hermione and destroyed with a Basilisk fang in *Harry Potter and the Deathly Hallows*.

currency The wizarding community uses a coinage made up of gold Galleons, silver Sickles and bronze Knuts. There are seventeen silver Sickles to a Galleon, and twenty-nine Knuts to a Sickle. Muggle money can be converted into wizarding currency at Gringotts Bank. To give an idea of relative value, the *Daily Prophet* costs five Knuts, the same price as a scoop of beetle eyes. Harry's wand cost him seven Galleons, whereas the rare silver unicorn horn is priced at twenty-one Galleons.

DA *See* Dumbledore's Army

Daily Prophet A popular daily paper for the British wizarding community. Its offices are in Diagon Alley, and it publishes morning and evening editions. Its editor is Barnabas Cuffe.

Dark Arts Magic employed for evil purposes, represented in the desires of Voldemort and his followers, the Death Eaters. Hogwarts as an institution, led by Dumbledore, is opposed to the use of Dark Arts, and teaches only defence against its curses and practices. Harry and his close friends, the wider Dumbledore's Army, and earlier his parents, fervently repudiate the Dark Arts. The Unforgivable Curses characteristic of the Darks Arts are usually punishable by imprisonment in Azkaban. In the extreme circumstance of war, however, it seems that the Imperius curse may be used, as Harry does during the raid on Gringotts Bank in *Harry Potter and the Deathly Hallows*. Similarly Snape employs the killing curse against Dumbledore in *Harry Potter and the Half-Blood Prince*. Here a moral principle of the 'lesser evil' is employed.

Dark Mark A sign of a skull with a serpent issuing from its mouth. It is distinctively put into the sky above a place Death Eaters have entered or the scene of one of their killings. A Dark Mark appears during the Quidditch World Championship in *Harry Potter and the Goblet of Fire* and another is raised above the Astronomy Tower in *Harry Potter and the Half-Blood Prince* to lure Dumbledore to his death. The Mark appears on the forearm of Death Eaters and becomes active at Voldemort's summons. The logo may have been inspired by the Basilisk appearing out of the mouth of the statue of Slytherin (as in *Harry Potter and the Chamber of Secrets*).

Death Eaters Voldemort's close circle of followers, prepared to torture and kill for him. They carry a mark on their arm, which magically indicates their Dark Lord's summons. The group have a cult of the pure-blood, i.e. wizards and witches who have no Muggles in their family or ancestry. The circle includes the betrayer of Harry's parents, Peter Pettigrew, Bellatrix Lestrange, the brothers Rabastan and Rodolphus Lestrange, Lucius Malfoy, possibly Draco Malfoy (in *Harry Potter and the Half-Blood Prince*), Snape (but who left the circle, and now acts as a double agent), Walden Macnair, Evan Rosier, Nott, Jugson, Crabbe Sr, Wilkes, Igor Karkaroff, Antonin Dolohov, Avery, Augustus Rookwood, Barty Crouch Jr and Mulciber. John Granger suggests that they are the dark opposite of those who feed on life in the Lord's Supper of the Eucharist.

Deathly Hallows As told in the story of the three brothers in *The Tales of Beedle the Bard*, the three Deathly Hallows are the Elder Wand, the Resurrection Stone and the Invisibility Cloak. They are represented by a distinctive rune, made up of a straight vertical line, topped with a circle, with both line and circle enclosed in a triangle. If all are possessed and united, the owner becomes master of death. The story owes a debt to Chaucer's *The Pardoner's Tale*.

Decree for the Restriction of Underage Wizardry This law, strictly enforced by the Ministry of Magic, regulates the behaviour of wizards and witches below the age of seventeen – when they come of age and are able to practise magic outside the confines of Hogwarts. Harry first runs foul of this law when he inflates Dudley's Aunt Marge. On a later occasion he is forced to employ the Patronus Charm to protect Dudley and himself from a Dementor attack.

Delacour, Fleur The granddaughter of a Veela, and beautiful student from Beauxbatons who participates in the Triwizard Tournament in *Harry Potter and the Goblet of Fire*. She is a willowy blond who seems to exude a silvery aura, accentuated by her long, silvery hair. After leaving Beauxbatons she works at Gringotts Bank in Diagon Alley to improve her English. In *Harry Potter and the Half-Blood Prince* she is not deterred from her wish to marry Bill Weasley, despite disfiguring injuries he receives from the werewolf Greyback.

After her marriage she and Bill settle in Shell Cottage, where they give refuge to Harry, Ron, Hermione and others.

Delacour, Gabrielle Younger sister of Fleur Delacour, bravely saved by Harry during the Triwizard Tournament.

Deluminator A device invented by Dumbledore that captures and restores lights, and also allows the owner to find others. In *Harry Potter and the Deathly Hallows* Dumbledore leaves it to Ron in his will. With the Deluminator Ron is able to trace his friends when he hears his name spoken by them – the light it emits enters his body and guides him as he Apparates to a spot near them.

Dementors Magical creatures who steal hope and happiness out of people. They are employed by the Ministry of Magic to guard Azkaban prison and, temporarily, after the escape of Sirius, Hogwarts (much to the dismay of Dumbledore). Sirius remembered how they drained Azkaban of any happiness a prisoner might cling to. The tall, hooded and cloaked figures are described in images of decay and corruption. Their hands are like those of a corpse rotting in water, and their breath is like a death rattle. In their presence, characteristically, the air chills, and seems to engulf a person's heart. They can evoke one's worst memories. When Harry encounters Dementors on the Hogwart's Express he hears once again the pleading screams of his terrified mother, who sacrificed herself for him. He hears her pleas for his life again when attacked by Dementors at a Quidditch match in *Harry Potter and the Prisoner of Azkaban*. The best remedy to aid recovery from an encounter with Dementors is to eat chocolate as soon as possible. The worst feature of Dementors is the Dementor's Kiss, where the living soul is sucked out, leaving the person an empty shell, though physically still alive. The Dementor's kiss is attempted on both Harry and Sirius, but is administered successfully on Barty Crouch Jr. The Dementors' name evokes the term 'demon', and indeed their craving to eat souls is reminiscent of the devils in C.S. Lewis's *The Screwtape Letters* (1942). Their numbers increase dramatically in *Harry Potter and the Deathly Hallows*, as they feed off the fear and despair created by Voldemort's return and assertion of power.

Department for the Regulation and Control of Magical Creatures
The section of the Ministry of Magic that is responsible for magical
creatures that are kept hidden from Muggles. The department has to
inform the Muggle Prime Minister if exceptionally dangerous
creatures are brought into the UK (as when dragons are brought
into Scotland for the Triwizard Tournament).

Department of Magical Law Enforcement A section of the Ministry
of Magic that includes the important Auror office, of which
Scrimgeour was Head for many years. Harry's ambition is to work
as an Auror.

Department of Mysteries A section of the Ministry of Magic that
handles top-secret matters, and includes the Hall of Prophecy. It is
located on the ninth floor down. One of the rooms – the Death
Chamber – has descending tiers with a dais on its sunken floor. On
the dais is a curtained archway, through which the stunned Sirius
falls. Harry and Luna could hear murmuring voices from the other
side of the curtains, but Ron and the others could not. Another
important part of the department is the Hall of Prophecy. In *Harry
Potter and the Order of the Phoenix* the department is the scene of
a battle between Harry and his friends, aided by members of the
Order of the Phoenix, and a group of Death Eaters led by Lucius
Malfoy.

Dervish and Banges A shop in Hogsmeade that sells wizarding
equipment.

Devil's Snare A plant with deadly tendrils that tried to ensnare
Harry, Ron, and Hermione when they dropped through the
trapdoor guarded by the fierce three-headed dog, Fluffy, in *Harry
Potter and the Philosopher's Stone*.

Devon An English county where Nicolas Flamel lives. South Devon
is the probable location of the Weasleys' home, The Burrow, and
also Budleigh Babberton, the temporary home of Horace Slughorn.
The City of Exeter, where J.K. Rowling attended university, is in
south Devon.

Diadem of Rowena Ravenclaw A diadem turned into a Horcrux by Voldemort. It was stolen by Rowena Ravenclaw's daughter Helena and hidden in Albania. Tom Riddle retrieved it and in turn hid it in Hogwarts. In *Harry Potter and the Deathly Hallows* Harry and his friends locate it in the Room of Requirement, where the Horcrux is destroyed by a magical fire created by Vincent Crabbe, Draco's friend.

Diagon Alley The primary shopping area for magical folk off Charing Cross Road, central London. After passing through a brick wall in the courtyard at the back of the Leaky Cauldron pub, wizards and witches find themselves in a twisting, cobbled street, with shops at either side. The stores include Eeylops Owl Emporium, Madam Malkin's Robes For All Occasions, as well as Gringotts Bank, which is run by goblins. Branching off Diagon Alley is the sinister shopping area of Knockturn Alley, devoted to the Dark Arts, and containing Borgin and Burkes. The alley's name is, of course, a play upon 'diagonally'.

Diary, Tom Riddle's A diary from the time of Tom Riddle's schooldays into which Tom (Voldemort) has deposited a portion of his soul, giving it an eerie life of its own as a Horcrux. Through the diary Riddle/Voldemort beguiles Ginny Weasley, so that she acts for him against her will. Harry confronts the evil wizard and, with the help of Fawkes, Dumbledore's phoenix, destroys its magical properties and frees Ginny.

Diggle, Daedalus A member of the Order of the Phoenix.

Diggory, Cedric Captain and Seeker in the Hufflepuff Quidditch team. He is tall and good-looking, and popular with the girl students. In *Harry Potter and the Goblet of Fire* he is chosen, along with Harry, to compete in the Triwizard Tournament. He and Harry reach the Cup that marks the end of the third task simultaneously. It turns out to be a Portkey that transports them to a graveyard in Little Hangleton, where Voldemort awaits. Cedric is executed by the killing curse, but Harry succeeds in escaping Voldemort and returning Cedric's body to Hogwarts.

Dippet, Armando Headmaster during Tom Riddle's schooldays.

Divination A subject taught at Hogwarts by Professor Sybill Trelawney, later assisted by the centaur, Firenze. Her unusually furnished classroom is located in the loft of the North Tower, and is accessed via a circular trapdoor. Some insight into the curriculum is given in *Harry Potter and the Prisoner of Azkaban*, where in Harry's third year his class is told they will study tea leaves in the first term, palmistry in the second, and the crystal ball in the third. The subject is disliked by the sceptical Hermione, who walks out of the class in disgust, as predicted by Professor Trelawney in the first lesson.

Dobby A prominent house-elf. In *Harry Potter and the Chamber of Secrets* he tries to prevent Harry returning to Hogwarts for his second year, because he has learnt of a danger he faces. In *Harry Potter and the Deathly Hallows* he is fatally stabbed helping Harry and his friends escape from Malfoy Manor.

Doge, Elphias A close friend and exact contemporary of Albus Dumbledore who writes his obituary in the *Daily Prophet*. He is a member of the Order of the Phoenix and Special Advisor to the Wizengamot. When Rita Skeeter is writing her biography of Dumbledore in *Harry Potter and the Deathly Hallows*, Doge refuses to cooperate with her.

dragons The most well known of the magical creatures. Ten types of dragon are identified, several of which appear in the stories, notably the Norwegian Ridgeback, the Hungarian Horntail, the Common Welsh Green, the Swedish Short-Snout and the Chinese Fireball – the last four part of a task in the Triwizard Tournament. The Common Welsh Green and the Hebridean Black are native to Britain, but, as elsewhere, are carefully hidden from Muggles. For a short time Hagrid has a pet dragon, Norbert, which he raises from the egg. The dragon guarding the deepest vaults under Gringotts is of an unknown breed.

Dudley's gang Dudley is a bully, and surrounds himself with a gang of bullies, who terrorise the children of Little Whinging. The gang is made up of Piers Polkiss, who accompanies him and Harry to the zoo in *Harry Potter and the Philosopher's Stone*, and some other boys called Dennis, Malcolm and Gordon.

Dumbledore, Aberforth Younger brother of Albus and proprietor of the Hog's Head public house in Hogsmeade. Although he has similar bright blue eyes, he is very different from his brother – not academic or in any sense bookish. His preference was to settle things with a fight rather than with reasoning, as when he broke Albus's nose at their sister Ariana's funeral. In *Harry Potter and the Deathly Hallows* Aberforth is significant in the resistance to Voldemort, at one stage sending Dobby the house-elf to help Harry when he is incarcerated in Malfoy Manor.

Dumbledore, Albus Percival Wulfric Brian Headmaster of Hogwarts School of Witchcraft and Wizardry until he is killed at the end of Harry's sixth year by Severus Snape, when Hogwarts is attacked by Death Eaters brought in by Draco. He is in the literary tradition of Thomas Malory's Merlin and Tolkien's Gandalf. In the stories he is the only wizard feared by Voldemort. His living quarters and office are at the top of one of Hogwarts' towers. A gargoyle protects the entrance to the escalating stairs to his office. He was a friend and associate of the long-living alchemist Nicolas Flamel, whose Philosopher's Stone is at the centre of the first Harry Potter story.

As a child Dumbledore is prodigiously talented, and wins many prizes at school. He has a sister, Ariana, and brother, Aberforth. His father Percival is sent to Azkaban for attacking some Muggle youths who traumatised Albus's young sister, thwarting her magical development. The family settles in Godric's Hollow, home of many wizarding families. His mother dies at the hands of the unbalanced Ariana, forcing Albus to abandon plans for a Grand Tour of the world in order to look after his family. He becomes friendly with a foreign wizard, Gellert Grindelwald, and briefly flirts with his ideas about wizards taking over the Muggle world 'for the greater good'. Albus parts with Grindelwald after a savage argument between the two, in which Aberforth is also involved. During the fight Ariana is accidently killed. Albus thereafter abandons any pursuit of power and devotes himself to teaching at Hogwarts, developing ideals of wholeness and diversity, and the protection of Muggles. During the rise of Voldemort Albus creates the original Order of the Phoenix, in which Harry's parents, Sirius, Neville's parents and many others participate.

When Harry first meets Dumbledore, he is of great age, tall and thin. His silver hair and beard are long enough to be tucked into his belt. Bright blue eyes peer through half-moon spectacles. His long nose is crooked, partly as a result of being broken long ago at his sister's funeral by the angry Aberforth. When we are introduced to him in *Harry Potter and the Philosopher's Stone* he is wearing a purple cloak and high-heeled boots with distinctive buckles on them. When younger he has auburn hair and beard. He confesses to reading Muggle magazines if he gets the opportunity and to liking knitting patterns. In *Harry Potter and the Half-Blood Prince* Harry effectively becomes an apprentice of Dumbledore, but the headmaster has already been Harry's mentor throughout the earlier books. He knows that Harry bears a piece of Voldemort's soul as a result of the evil wizard's failure to kill him as a child, and that Harry will have to die in order for Voldemort to be destroyed. Albus prepares Harry for making the choice of self-sacrifice for his friends. Equally bold is Dumbledore's own trust in Severus Snape, and his belief that Snape will protect Harry at the same time as convincing Voldemort that he is his faithful servant and spy in Hogwarts. In all the seriousness of dealing with Voldemort's wickedness, Albus remains light-hearted and often humourous. A.O. Scott comments: 'Dumbledore's benevolent but strict theology, involving the operations of free will in a supernaturally determined world, is classically Miltonian.' 'Dumbledore' is an Early English word for bumblebee.

Dumbledore, Ariana Sister of Albus and Aberforth, whose tragic death comes between the two brothers. She becomes unstable after being traumatised as a young child by Muggle youths who attacked her after noticing her emerging magical abilities. Her family keeps her condition secret so that she is not committed to St Mungo's. One result of her disorder is that she kills her mother. A large portrait of her hangs in the Hog's Head pub, where she is in her right mind once more.

Dumbledore, Kendra Mother of Albus, killed by her unbalanced daughter, Ariana. After her husband, Percival, was imprisoned at Azkaban, she moved her family from Mould-on-the-Wold to Godric's Hollow.

Dumbledore, Percival Father of Albus, who attacks three Muggle youths for traumatising his little daughter, Ariana, and is sent to Azkaban, where he dies.

Dumbledore's Army Group of Hogwarts students centred around Harry's close friends, who receive from him lessons in Defence Against the Dark Arts in *Harry Potter and the Order of the Phoenix*. They are known for short as the DA. Some of them go with Harry to the Department of Mysteries in the belief that Sirius is in danger of his life and valiantly fight the Death Eaters.

Dursley, Dudley Harry Potter's spoilt cousin, with whom he lives in Little Whinging. He looks like a smaller model of his doting father, Harry's Uncle Vernon, with small, piggish eyes in a pink face, head almost neckless in a large body, and smooth blond hair. As a glutton it is fitting that he is nearly turned into a pig by Hagrid in *Harry Potter and the Philosopher's Stone* (as it turns out, the spell only leaves him with a pig's tail, requiring surgical removal). He is somewhat slow-witted, like his friends, and delights in bullying Harry. In *Harry Potter and the Philosopher's Stone* Dudley is destined to go to an expensive private school called Smeltings, while Harry is expected to attend the local, rough secondary school. Harry, of course, is unexpectedly invited to Hogwarts instead. In *Harry Potter and the Order of the Phoenix* Harry rescues his cousin from a Dementor attack, a rare incursion of the magical into the Muggle world. A dramatic development in his character takes place in *Harry Potter and the Deathly Hallows*, when he expresses some concern about Harry's welfare and thanks him for saving his life.

Dursley, Marge Sister of Vernon Dursley and Dudley's aunt, whose bullying includes humiliating Harry whenever possible. Her life centres on the twelve dogs she keeps, including the vicious 'Ripper'.

Dursley, Petunia (née Evans) Harry's aunt, sister of Lily Potter. Like her husband, Vernon, she is opposed to all things magical, yet sometimes betrays her knowledge of the wizarding world. Though she is cruel to Harry, she feels obliged to look after the orphan, and the blood relationship protects him from Voldemort's followers. Petunia is horsey-looking, which made her envious of the attractive Lily. She is also jealous of her sister's magical ability: it is recorded in *Harry Potter and the Deathly Hallows* that she wrote to Hogwarts asking if she might attend.

Dursley, Vernon Harry's bullying uncle, who resents the fact that the orphan lives in his household. He forbids any mention or indication of magic, and initially resists Harry's invitation to study at Hogwarts. He is the director of Grunnings, a firm producing drills.

Dursleys Vernon and Petunia Dursley have one son, Dudley, and are the uncle and aunt of Harry, who lives with them. Petunia is the sister of Harry's mother, Lily. Aunt Marge, Vernon's sister, sometimes visits. They live in Little Whinging, Surrey.

Eeylops The Owl Emporium, a shop devoted to owls in Diagon Alley.

Elder Wand One of the three Deathly Hallows, this is a master wand, believed to be the most powerful of all wands, giving its possessor supremacy in duels. It has a bloody history, as the wand's loyalty transfers when another wizard kills or defeats its owner. In *Harry Potter and the Deathly Hallows* we learn that Gellert Grindelwald possessed it, but that it eventually came into Dumbledore's possession. Most who seek it do not know it was one of the Deathly Hallows. Voldemort seeks it to be able to destroy Harry, having failed to do so when their wands matched in *Harry Potter and the Goblet of Fire*. The twists and turns of its ownership plays an important part in the plot of *Harry Potter and the Deathly Hallows*, where Harry is revealed as its owner, and master of the Deathly Hallows.

enchanted coins Means of communication developed by Hermione employing fake Galleons and used by the DA. Draco borrows the idea to liaise with Madam Rosmerta when she is under an Imperius curse. A spell (a Protean charm) would modify text on the fake coin.

essays During their schooldays Harry and his friends are required to write many essays, on topics including 'The Principles of Re-Materialisation,' giant wars, the use of moonstones and self-fertilising shrubs. The expected length is specified in feet and inches or sides of parchment, and students write using quills.

Everard A previous headteacher at Hogwarts, whose portrait hangs in Dumbledore's study.

Expelliarmus A Disarming spell; literally 'to expel a weapon'. It becomes Harry's signature spell, as a result of his care in avoiding harmful spells.

Famous Witches and Wizards A series of wizard cards that comes packaged with a popular candy, Chocolate Frogs. It includes cards of Agrippa, Ptolemy, Albus Dumbledore and Morgana.

Fantastic Beasts & Where to Find Them Newt Scamander's classic guide to magical creatures, to be found in nearly all wizarding households in Britain.

Fawkes Phoenix belonging to Dumbledore and habitually kept in his study at Hogwarts. He rescues Harry in *Harry Potter and the Chamber of Secrets*, and heals his mortal wound with his tears. His tears also mend the wound inflicted on Harry's leg by the spider in *Harry Potter and the Goblet of Fire*. Fawkes sings a poignant song at the death of his master in *Harry Potter and the Half-Blood Prince*.

Felix Felicis A potion to make a person feel lucky and thus become lucky, described by Hermione as 'liquid luck'. It evokes feelings of infinite possibility and overwhelming confidence. Harry and several members of the DA benefit from it in *Harry Potter and the Half-Blood Prince*. Ginny and others use it when fighting the Death Eaters let into Hogwarts by Draco.

Fidelius Charm A complex spell to conceal a secret inside a person, thereafter called a Secret-Keeper. The information is impossible to discover without the consent of the Secret-Keeper. Sirius initially was a Secret-Keeper for James and Lily Potter, Harry's parents. Dumbledore used the charm to hide 12 Grimmauld Place.

Figg, Mrs Arabella A neighbour of the Durselys who secretly belongs to the wizarding population. She lives in Privett Drive in order to keep on eye on Harry. Mrs Figg is a Squib and so is forced to protect Harry without magic, which makes her less suspicious to Muggles.

Filch, Argus Caretaker at Hogwarts and constantly bitter because he is a Squib. This means that he cannot use magic, for instance, to clean up after the numerous crises of school life. He rues the day the vicious old punishments were abandoned and craves their return, enjoying the brief despotic rule of Dolores Umbridge as replacement Headteacher and High Inquisitor. Filch constantly battles the students, and the anarchic poltergeist, Peeves. He is well suited to his sour, misanthropic cat, Mrs Norris.

Firebolt Latest-model broomstick sent secretly to Harry by Sirius to replace his Nimbus Two Thousand, which had been destroyed.

Firenze A noble centaur from the Forbidden Forest who sets himself against the evil in the Forest. Later he assists in the teaching of Divination at Hogwarts, even though the other centaurs cut him off because of this.

Flamel, Nicolas (1330–1992) An associate of Dumbledore's, and fellow alchemist, who centuries previously made the Stone in *Harry Potter and the Philosopher's Stone* sought by Voldemort in his quest for immortality. He lives with his wife, Perenelle, somewhere in Devon. In an old book discovered in the Hogwarts library Flamel is described as the 'only known maker of the Philosopher's Stone'. The real Flamel, who lived from 1330 to 1418, was so famous that a street is named after him in Paris. The same is true of his wife, Perenelle.

Fletcher, Mundungus ('Dung') Decrepit wizard, member of the Order of the Phoenix, and invariably dealing with stolen goods. In *Harry Potter and the Deathly Hallows* it is discovered that he stole the locket containing a Horcrux from Grimmauld Place. He has bandy legs and long, straggly ginger hair. 'Mundungus' means 'rank-smelling tobacco'.

Flint, Marcus Captain of the Slytherin Quidditch team and in his sixth year when Harry starts Hogwarts. The troll-like Flint is still captain in Harry's third year, even though he should have left after his seventh year; it is possible he had to retake his final exams.

Flitwick, Filius Diminutive teacher of Charms and head of Ravenclaw house at Hogwarts, of Goblin ancestry. He has to resort to standing on a pile of books to see over his desk.

Floo Network A transport network linking the fireplaces of wizarding houses and institutions. Travel is accomplished by sprinkling Floo powder on the fire and calling out one's destination. A fireplace in the Prime Minister's office at 10 Downing Street is included in the network for such times as important information relevant to Muggles needs to be conveyed.

floors at Hogwarts As Hogwarts is a British school, floors are numbered as ground floor, first floor, second floor, and so on. The ground floor therefore is not called the first floor.

Florean Fortesque's Ice Cream Parlour A popular shop in Diagon Alley. Fortesque was dragged off by Voldemort's forces in *Harry Potter and the Half-Blood Prince*.

Flourish and Blotts A bookshop in Diagon Alley that supplies the necessary set textbooks for study at Hogwarts. Professor Gilderoy Lockhart had a four-hour book-signing session there in *Harry Potter and the Chamber of Secrets* for his autobiography, *Magical Me*.

Fluffy A vicious three-headed dog lent by Hagrid to guard the trapdoor leading to the underground chamber in which lies the

Philosopher's Stone. The dog comes from classical mythology, where Cerberus guards the entrance to the underworld, Hades.

Flume, Ambrosius Owner of Honeydukes who sends Horace Slughorn a hamper every birthday.

flying motorbike In *Harry Potter and the Philosopher's Stone* Hagrid brings one-year-old Harry to Little Whinging on a flying motorcycle to be cared for by his surviving family, the Dursleys. Hagrid borrowed the vehicle from Sirius. He uses it again, complete with sidecar, to take Harry away to safety from the Dursleys' house in *Harry Potter and the Deathly Hallows*. Flying vehicles can be charmed to prevent Muggles from seeing them.

Forbidden Forest The setting for many adventures in the stories, the Forest lies to the north-east of Hogwarts Castle, past the Whomping Willow and Hagrid's hut. In *Harry Potter and the Philosopher's Stone*, for instance, when Harry, Hermione, Neville and Draco are in the Forest with Hagrid and Fang at night, they encounter centaurs and then Harry and Draco come across a hooded figure drinking the blood of a dead unicorn – a figure who subsequently turns out to be Professor Quirrell feeding Voldemort, as he slowly resumes physical form. In *Harry Potter and the Deathly Hallows* Harry responds to Voldemort's challenge to go to him there, so that those who resist him will not die. The Forest is a place of many dangers, such as the giant spider Aragog and his many descendants, and later Hagrid's blundering half-brother, the giant Grawp.

Fudge, Cornelius Minister of Magic during Harry's first five years at Hogwarts, after which he is replaced by the more efficient and decisive Rufus Scrimgeour. He is a stout little man who wears a cloak that is pin-striped like a city suit, a bottle-green suit and a lime-green bowler hat. Formerly he was Junior Minister in the Department of Magical Catastrophes, and was first on the scene when a number of people were murdered, apparently by Sirius. He allowed Dementors to guard Hogwarts but conceded they should be removed after they unsuccessfully used the Dementor's Kiss on

Harry. As Minister his job included liaising with the UK Prime Minister. He was a habitual appeaser who refused for a long period to acknowledge Voldemort's return.

Galleon A golden wizarding coin with serial numbers around its edge. Hermione adapts fake Galleons in *Harry Potter and the Order of the Phoenix* so that the numbers change to transmit messages to members of Dumbledore's Army. The method is still used successfully in *Harry Potter and the Deathly Hallows*.

Gaunt, Marvolo The father of Merope, Voldemort's mother, of the surviving line of Slytherin.

Gaunt, Merope Daughter of Marvolo Gaunt, and mother of Tom Riddle (Voldemort). She was one of the last living descendants of Salazar Slytherin. Dumbledore believes that she used a love potion to win the love of Tom Riddle Sr, Voldemort's father. When Riddle Sr discovered Merope was a witch, he abandoned her to bear their child alone. In poverty she took the infant Tom to an orphanage, dying soon after.

Gaunt, Morfin The son of Marvolo Gaunt. He died in Azkaban, wrongly accused of the murder of Tom Riddle Sr and his parents. Voldemort (Tom Riddle Jr) inflicted a false memory of the triple murder on him.

ghosts There are many ghosts at Hogwarts, some associated with particular houses, as Nearly Headless Nick and Gryffindor. When Harry asks Nick what happens after death, the ghost explains that he does not really know: ghosts are those who have clung on to this world and not moved on. Another important ghost is Moaning Myrtle. At one point twenty ghosts congregate at Hogwarts. Peeves, the mischievous spirit, is not a ghost.

Giant Squid A magical creature living in the lake beside Hogwarts. In hot weather it is sometimes visible making its way languidly across the lake, flexing its tentacles drowsily above the water.

Gibbon A Death Eater who sets off the decoy Dark Mark above the Astronomy Tower in *Harry Potter and the Half-Blood Prince*. He is killed accidently by a killing curse during the Battle of Hogwarts.

Gillyweed A small, rubbery water plant native to the Mediterranean that, if swallowed, temporarily creates gills in the neck, allowing the user to breathe underwater. Hands and feet also become weblike for the duration of the Gillyweed's effect, facilitating movement underwater. Gillyweed, supplied by Dobby the house-elf, allows Harry to accomplish the second of the trials in the Triwizard Tournament in *Harry Potter and the Goblet of Fire*.

goblins A clever and grotesque race who can make beautiful artefacts such as tiaras. They are associated with wealth, and indeed run the successful Gringotts Bank. Professor Flitwick has Goblin ancestry, and the Ministry of Magic has a Goblin Liaison Office. The Goblin Wars are notable in wizarding history. In *Harry Potter and the Deathly Hallows* a goblin freed by Harry and his friends called Griphook helps them raid Gringotts Bank for the Cup of Helga Hufflepuff in return for being given the sword of Gryffindor.

Gobstones A game played by magical folk rather like marbles. Stones would gob an evil-smelling liquid into players' faces when they lost a point.

Godric's Hollow An isolated West Country village, perhaps in north Somerset, favoured by the magical community. Ancient wizarding family names adorn many tombstones in the graveyard of the village church. Both the Dumbledore and Potter families lived there. In *Harry Potter and the Deathly Hallows* Harry and Hermione visit the village on Christmas Eve, where the church windows are lit up by a festive service and Christmas decorations are everywhere to be seen. They see the blasted ruins of Harry's house, where he survived Voldemort's killing curse, and are lured into a trap by his serpent, Nagini, hidden in the animated corpse of Bathilda Bagshot, who had lived near the Potters. It is likely that Godric Gryffindor, one of the founders of Hogwarts, was born there and that Godric's Hollow takes its name from him. According to the Sorting Hat's song, he came 'from wild moor.'

Goyle, Gregory Son of a Death Eater. He, like Crabbe, is a bully and protector of Draco. He is shorter than Crabbe with short stubby hair and gorilla-like arms.

Granger, Hermione One of the brightest witches in the school, Hermione is nevertheless chosen for Gryffindor house rather than Ravenclaw. She is easily picked out in a crowd by her bushy brown hair. As both her parents are Muggles (they are dentists, but clearly unable to correct her protruding teeth), Hermione is despised by Slytherins worshipping 'pure-blood'. She is the conscience of the small group of friends around Harry. Her method of learning is bookish – she is a natural inhabitor of the school library. Characteristically, in *Harry Potter and the Philosopher's Stone* she gives a 'lecture' to her friends on broomstick flying, derived entirely from books. The friendship between Harry, Ron and Hermione is effectively formed when they rescue her from a troll and she lies to protect them, despite being a stickler for school rules. She has an instinctive grasp of magic. Her skill is constantly evident in the stories. From the first she can conjure up a bright blue portable fire, magically open locked doors and create potions with ease. Hermione is a swot who colour-codes her revision notes and helps Harry and Ron prepare for end-of-year exams by drawing up a revision timetable for them. In classes she is the first to shoot her hand up and gives textbook answers. Over the course of the years at Hogwarts romance grows between her and Ron, despite their frequent rows and bickering. In *Harry Potter and the Prisoner of Azkaban* she suddenly matures as a person, hitting Draco, stalking out of Divination class in frustration with Professor Trelawney ('the old fraud') and rescuing Harry's Invisibility Cloak. In Shakespeare's *The Winter's Tale* the character Hermione appears as a statue who comes back to life – in *Harry Potter and the Chamber of Secrets* Hermione for a while suffers petrification after encountering the Basilisk. Changing from stone to life again (as in the stone figures in C.S. Lewis's *The Lion, the Witch and the Wardrobe*) is a traditional symbol of resurrection. In *Harry Potter and the Deathly Hallows* she and Ron assist Harry in his task of destroying Voldemort's Horcruxes, and she suffers terribly when tortured by Bellatrix for information. As always her skill and resourcefulness prove to be essential in the downfall of the Dark Lord. She remains loyal to Harry even when Ron forsakes him. The love between Harry and Hermione is like that between brother and sister.

Granger, Mr and Mrs Parents of Hermione. Though Muggles, they visit Knockturn Alley to exchange money at Gringotts Bank and to buy school equipment. They are both dentists. On one occasion, Christmas shopping, Hermione buys them Toothflossing Stringmints from Honeydukes while visiting Hogsmeade. In *Harry Potter and the Deathly Hallows* Hermione modifies their memories to send them to Australia to protect them from Voldemort's increasing tyranny.

Grawp Half-brother of Hagrid who towers over him despite being small compared to other giants. In *Harry Potter and the Order of the Phoenix* Hagrid brings the reluctant Grawp to live in the Forbidden Forest and helps in his socialization – a painful task, often leaving Hagrid bruised. In *Harry Potter and the Deathly Hallows* Grawp fights against Voldemort's forces in the Battle of Hogwarts.

Great Hall The largest assembly hall in Hogwarts, used for meals, for social events and for examinations. The magnificent ceiling magically displays the skies outside. When functioning as a refectory there are four long tables, one for each house, and a table for teaching and other Hogwarts' staff. It has been aptly described as a place of laughter, conversation and the sound of cutlery in use. At Hallowe'en and Christmas it is lavishly and imaginatively decorated. On Valentine's Day in Harry's second year Gilderoy Lockhart causes the Hall to display pink flowers, and confetti hearts to drift down from the ceiling. After the Battle of Hogwarts in *Harry Potter and the Deathly Hallows* the dead and injured are brought here. In the mixture of joy and grief immediately after the final downfall of Voldemort, no one sat in the Hall according to house divisions – 'all were jumbled together, teachers and pupils, ghosts and parents, centaurs and house-elves . . .'. It is a place of wholeness in all the diversity.

Gregorovitch A continental wandmaker known particularly for supplying his wares to students at Durmstrang. In *Harry Potter and the Deathly Hallows* he is sought by Voldemort and reveals under torture that the Elder Wand was stolen from him by Gellert Grindelwald.

Greyback, Fenrir A notorious werewolf and family friend of the Malfoys. He is also a cannibal when not in wolf shape. In *Harry Potter and the Half-Blood Prince* he badly injures Bill Weasley while still in his man form.

Grey Lady, the The resident ghost of the house of Ravenclaw. In *Harry Potter and the Deathly Hallows* Harry discovers that she is the spirit of Helena Ravenclaw, daughter of one of Hogwart's founders, Rowena, killed in rage by the Bloody Baron.

Grim A grim is a huge ghost dog that portends death. When Sirius escapes from Azkaban, he appears first transformed into a dog (Sirius is an Animagus). At that time, when Harry catches glimpses of a huge dog, he thinks it is sinister and soon learns about grims.

Grimmauld Place, 12 Ancestral home of the Black family inherited by Sirius, which becomes Harry's after his death. It appears to be near King's Cross railway station in London. During Sirius's long imprisonment in Azkaban it was disused and started to decay. In *Harry Potter and the Order of the Phoenix* it is used as headquarters by the Order. The building is magically protected, which includes blending into surrounding buildings. It is possible that it was originally a rural mansion before becoming absorbed into London's urban growth. After Dumbledore's death the Order meet at The Burrow. Harry, Ron and Hermione return to Grimmauld Place for some weeks while fugitives in *Harry Potter and the Deathly Hallows* and become attached to its house-elf, Kreacher. The name of the house may reflect J.K. Rowling's dexterous verbal play, combining 'Grim old place', 'mouldy' and even 'Grim', the sinister appearance of Sirius's dog form.

Grindelwald, Gellert A contemporary of Albus Dumbledore and briefly his friend. He was an outstanding student at Durmstrang but was expelled. Like Voldemort he had pretensions for world domination, his belief that might is right hidden under the slogan 'for the greater good'. Dumbledore came under his influence when Grindelwald stayed with his great-aunt Bathilda Bagshot in Godric's Hollow, soon after his expulsion. After Dumbledore firmly rejected his ideology of wizard supremacy, they became enemies, Dumbledore famously defeating him in 1945 (the year of Hitler's downfall). Grindelwald was incarcerated in the prison he had built at Nurmengard until slain there by Voldemort in *Harry Potter and the Deathly Hallows*.

Gringotts Bank Run by Goblins and located in Diagon Alley. Bill Weasley is employed by the bank as a curse-breaker and his fiancée Fleur Delacour worked for it to improve her English. In *Harry Potter and the Deathly Hallows* Harry, Ron and Hermione successfully steal the Hufflepuff Cup from Bellatrix's vault.

Griphook A goblin from Gringotts Bank who in *Harry Potter and the Philosopher's Stone* operates the trolley that takes Hagrid and Harry to the vaults. He is imprisoned in Voldemort's head-quarters at Malfoy Manor in *Harry Potter and the Deathly Hallows* after being snatched while on the run from the oppressive regime. Griphook plays an important part in the theft of the Hufflepuff Cup from Bellatrix Lestrange's vault deep underground the bank.

Grubbly-Plank, Wilhemina Pipe-smoking relief teacher of Care of Magical Creatures classes at Hogwarts.

Gryffindor common room Located in Gryffindor Tower at Hogwarts. Its circular entrance lies behind the protective portrait of the Fat Lady, who requires a password to enter. From the common room spiral staircases lead to a number of small dormitories. Harry's has five four-poster beds. Gryffindor Tower overlooks the lawns leading to the Whomping Willow and the Forbidden Forest. *See* Common Rooms.

Gryffindor house One of the four student houses at Hogwarts. Students are chosen for the house who have the dominant quality of courage. The house colours are gold and scarlet, reflecting the house badge of a lion on a red field. Harry's close friends are in Gryffindor, and his godfather, Sirius, though from a pure-blood family associated with Slytherin, was placed in Gryffindor while at Hogwarts.

Gryffindor Tower One of the many towers of Hogwarts Castle, and location of the Gryffindor common room.

Hagrid, Rubeus Half-giant, Hagrid is Keeper of Keys and Grounds at Hogwarts, also described as its gamekeeper. In Harry's third year he also becomes a professor at Hogwarts, teaching Care of Magical Creatures. Many years before he had been wrongly expelled from the school as a student, blamed for opening the Chamber of Secrets. At that time his wand was broken, a sign of disgrace. He kept it hidden in a pink umbrella and occasionally uses magic (he never qualified as a wizard). Dumbledore trusts him implicitly, to the extent of charging him with bringing the baby Harry to Privet Drive on Sirius's flying motorbike. Because of the reputation of giants, he kept his ancestry secret, even though he was twice the height of a man. He has a deep affinity with magical creatures, and other surprising traits, such as knitting in the London train in *Harry Potter and the Philosopher's Stone*. He is sentimental and comically unrealistic about dangerous creatures such as dragons and giant spiders – he was known to sing lullabies to a baby dragon and give it a teddy bear, and to read stories to the giant spider Aragog, when it was ill. He is often seen in a long Moleskin overcoat with enormous pockets. He becomes a firm friend of Harry, Hermione and Ron before he is made teacher of the Care of Magical Creatures class. The friends in *Harry Potter and the Chamber of Secrets* clear his name over the original expulsion. His care for living creatures is appreciated by the centaurs of the Forbidden Forest. In *Harry Potter and the Deathly Hallows* he hides in a cave above Hogsmeade with Grawp, and plays an active role in the resistance to Voldemort.

Hagrid's cabin The wooden dwelling of Hogwart's teacher of the Care of Magical Creatures, on the fringe of the Forbidden Forest.

Hall of Prophecy A section of the Ministry of Magic building in London that features prominently in *Harry Potter and the Order of the Phoenix*. It contains thousands of prophecies stored in tiny glass orbs, including Professor Trelawney's to Dumbledore concerning Harry and Lord Voldemort, signed 'S.P.T. to A.P.W.B.D.'. When opened or smashed, smoky-white figures, recognisable as those originally uttering the prophecy, begin to speak the stored message. Prophecies can be retrieved only by those whom they concern.

Hand of Glory A shrivelled hand taken from legend by J.K. Rowling. The legend goes that a hand from a hanged man has magical powers, such as opening doors, or, in conjunction with a special candle, immobilising others. For this reason it was used sometimes by burglars. In Rowling's adaptation it provides light only for the bearer. Draco obtains a Hand from Borgin and Burke's store in Knockturn Alley and uses it in *Harry Potter and the Half-Blood Prince* as he smuggles Death Eaters into Hogwarts. An actual Hand of Glory is on display at Whitby Museum, in Yorkshire, England.

Hedwig A magnificent Snowy Owl given to Harry by Hagrid as a birthday present and named by him. Harry comes across her name in *The History of Magic*, a school textbook. She is Harry's close companion until her loss in *Harry Potter and the Deathly Hallows*, and is a constant and comforting connection to the wizarding world when he is at home with the Dursleys. A St Hedwig (1174–1243) was canonised in 1266.

Herbology One of the subjects studied at Hogwarts, taught in the greenhouses beside the castle by Professor Sprout. Students learn about medicinal herbs. Plants they learn to cultivate include Mandrakes. This ancient craft dates back to ancient China. Some modern medicines still employ traditional healing herbs.

herbs J.K. Rowling made use of *Culpeper's Complete Herbal* to find names of herbs that sounded appropriate for Herbology and Potions – e.g. flaxweed, toadflax, fluwort, goatwort, grommel, knot grass and mugwort. Herblore is common in traditional stories, e.g. Aragorn in Tolkien's *The Lord of the Rings* is a healer.

Higgs, Terence Seeker for the Slytherin Quidditch team before Draco.

Hinkypunk A diminutive creature with one leg that takes pleasure in luring unsuspecting travellers into bogs at night with a light.

Hippogriff A magical creature from classical mythology that appears in the stories. The creature is half-bird, half-horse (*hippo* = horse + *griff* = griffin (creature with eagle's head and lion's body)). During a Care of Magical Creatures class Hagrid introduces the hippogriff Buckbeak, who takes to Harry but wounds the arrogant Draco.

History of Magic A subject at Hogwarts taught drearily by Professor Binns.

Hog's Head, the A grimy pub in Hogsmeade. It is much quieter than the other village pub, the Three Broomsticks, though it is frequented by strange characters. (Hagrid obtains the dragon's egg there in *Harry Potter and the Philosopher's Stone*.) Its proprietor is Aberforth Dumbledore. It is the setting of a number of events in the stories, such as the meeting to set up Dumbledore's Army. In *Harry Potter and the Deathly Hallows* a large portrait of the sister of Albus and Aberforth, Ariana, that hangs in the bar becomes important, as it marks the entrance to a new passageway to the Room of Requirement in Hogwarts not known to the Death Eaters who police the school. The pub receives underage students evacuated before the great Battle of Hogwarts.

Hogsmeade is near Hogwarts School of Witchcraft and Wizardry and a loch (lake), in an undisclosed part of rural Scotland. Mountains dominate the skyline. It is the only completely non-Muggle settlement in Britain. (Other villages favoured by wizards have a partial magical community, such as Godric's Hollow.) According to *Sites of Historical Sorcery*, it was the centre of the Goblin Rebellion of 1612. Its Shrieking Shack is wrongly considered Britain's most haunted building. The only Muggle settlement with a name even slightly similar is Hogsthorpe, near Skegness, in Lincolnshire, England.

Hogwarts School of Witchcraft and Wizardry The finest school of wizardry and perhaps the most dangerous educational establishment in Great Britain. Students usually spend seven years of study here, unless they do not sit the highest-level examinations. It is a comprehensive boarding school, taking students of mixed ability and from all ethnic and social backgrounds. All students, however, have displayed an innate magical ability, which is nurtured and developed but not created by the schooling. Some students are unaware until invited to the school of the magical nature of their special gifts. Their magical abilities are magical rather than occult – in no cases do students call on external spiritual powers. They are taught not only to use magic, but also to control it. Even the forbidden Dark Arts, from which the students are merely taught protection, are seen only as the misuse and perversion of natural powers. Hogwarts Castle is a huge and imposing structure, rising on cliffs above a Scottish lake to its south, and having many towers, the tallest of which is the Astronomy Tower. The building rises up many levels, intersected with numerous corridors, and flights of steps to reach them. The castle as a whole has an astonishing 142 stairways. On the ground floor, near the magnificent entrance on the westerly side, is the Great Hall. In the entrance hall is a flagged stone floor leading to a huge marble staircase, giving access to the heart of the castle. Below the ground floor are many basement and dungeon rooms, secret passages and subterranean chambers and vaults. A long, descending drive leads out of the school grounds north-west from the great entrance and onto the twisting road, which passes Hogsmeade and then circles the lake to the railway station on the other side of the lake. Sloping lawns run from the castle, and in the grounds are the Quidditch pitch, the Whomping Willow and, on the fringe of the Forbidden Forest to the north-east, Hagrid's cabin. Beside the castle are greenhouses and vegetable patches used for Herbology. Muggles chancing upon Hogwarts would see only ruins, with a prominent danger sign to keep off. The school crest is made up of a lion, an eagle, a badger and a snake, referring to its four houses and its idea that the four be a whole. The castle becomes exceedingly cold in the dead of winter, despite large fires in the Great Hall and common rooms. The corridors are particularly cold and draught-ridden. At any one time there are perhaps around one thousand students in Hogwarts. It takes over one hundred stagecoaches to carry all but the first years to Hogwarts from the railway station at the beginning of term. In the period of what would have been Harry's seventh year, a decisive Battle against Voldemort is fought here.

Hogwarts: A History A standard school textbook at Hogwarts, often referred to by Hermione.

Home Life and Social Habits of British Muggles A textbook read by Hermione for her course on Muggle Studies.

Honeydukes A popular shop in Hogsmeade that sells candies such as Pepper Imps, Chocoballs, sherbert balls and sugar-spun quills.

Hooch, Madam Teacher of flying at Hogwarts, and, armed with a silver whistle, referees at inter-house Quidditch matches. In *Harry Potter and the Philosopher's Stone* she gives broomstick-flying lessons to Harry and other first years.

Horcrux An object (e.g. a locket or living being) outside a magician's body that stores a hidden part of his or her soul. An ancient textbook found by Hermione – *Magick Moste Evile* – calls it the 'wickedest of magical inventions' and refuses to say more. In *Harry Potter and the Deathly Hallows* Hermione reveals from her wide reading that the only way a person's split soul can be put together is by remorse. The same volume recounts the quest of Harry, Ron and Hermione to destroy remaining Horcruxes created by Voldemort (two had already been destroyed, Tom Riddle's diary by Harry and Marvolo Gaunt's ring by Dumbledore). The motif of such an object occurs in traditional stories from antiquity to Tolkien's Ring.

house-elf A small magical creature who serves like a slave in some well-off wizarding households and institutions such as Hogwarts. A house-elf can be released if its owner gives it a piece of clothing. As most owners are reluctant to risk freeing their house-elves, the creatures usually have to fend for themselves over clothing, wearing an adapted cast-off pillow case or rags for clothing. They have no possessions and are bound, unless released, to serve one family or ancestral house forever. Dobby is probably characteristic when he harms himself in the event of disobeying his master, Lucius Malfoy, or speaking ill of him. House-elves prominent in the stories are Dobby, Winky and Kreacher. Hermione campaigns for the emancipation of house-elves. Dobby reveals that Harry's survival of Voldemort's attack while a helpless infant had given hope to house-elves. House-elves can wield immense magical power, a power restrained by their absolute obedience to their masters. In *Harry Potter and the Deathly Hallows* Kreacher is technically bound to obey Harry as his new master, but comes over to his side willingly only when he realises that Harry is determined to continue what Kreacher's former master, Regulus Black, was attempting to do to thwart Voldemort. He participates in the Battle of Hogwarts, leading the school's house-elves.

houses in Hogwarts At the very beginning of their first year, Hogwarts students are chosen by the ancient Sorting Hat for one of four houses according to their dominant trait. Hermione, for instance, is placed in Gryffindor, where the desired virtue is courage, even though she is academically brilliant and would therefore expect to go into Ravenclaw house, which pre-eminently values intellect and wit. Hufflepuff house is characterised by diligence and loyalty, while Slytherin house champions cunning and ambition. During house Quidditch matches Gryffindor play in scarlet robes, Slytherin in green, Hufflepuffs in canary yellow and Ravenclaw in blue. According to their creator, the houses 'correspond roughly to the four elements', with Gryffindor being fire, Ravenclaw air, Hufflepuff earth and Slytherin water. The ideal in Hogwarts is that the four houses work together, promoting wholeness rather than fragmentation.

Hufflepuff house One of four houses in Hogwarts named after founders, in this case, Helga Hufflepuff. At the period Harry was at Hogwarts the head of house for Hufflepuff was Professor Sprout. The house colour is yellow, and when playing Quidditch the house team wear canary yellow robes. Hufflepuffs value the qualities of patience, fair play and friendship, and the house motif is the badger.

Impedimenta A jinx to impede an attacker, whether beast or person.

Imperius curse One of the three Unforgivable Curses and therefore, unless in exceptional circumstances, part of the Dark Arts. If successful, the spell allows total control of another's will. In *Harry Potter and the Half-Blood Prince* Madam Rosmerta of Hogsmeade is a victim of Draco's Imperius curse – he uses her in his plans to infiltrate Hogwarts and his attempt to kill Dumbledore. In *Harry Potter and the Deathly Hallows*, after the fall of the Ministry of Magic to Voldemort, Harry is forced to use the curse briefly in Gringotts Bank against the clerk Bogrod and the Death Eater Travers, and Professor McGonagall employs it similarly against Amycus Carrow at Hogwarts.

inferi Corpses magically animated to obey the will of a dark wizard or witch. In *Harry Potter and the Half-Blood Prince* Dumbledore takes Harry into a cave in which there is a black lake full of inferi. An inferius is not alive, but is used like a puppet. Harry is nearly overcome by inferi, but rescued by Dumbledore.

Inquisitorial Squad A group of students, all from Slytherin, appointed by Dolores Umbridge to help implement her rule at Hogwarts. The title echoes the notorious Spanish Inquisition. The squad includes Draco, Crabbe and Goyle.

International Statute of Wizarding Secrecy This Statute is fundamental to relations between the wizarding and Muggle worlds. It was ratified in 1692 by the International Confederation of Wizards. It rules that all aspects of the magical world are to be kept hidden from Muggles. In *Harry Potter and the Deathly Hallows* we learn that Dumbledore's father, Percival, was imprisoned in Azkaban for attacking Muggle youths who had traumatised his daughter Ariana. Wizards have a responsibility to uphold the Statute, and violations are punished. With Voldemort's return and his increasing oppression, the Statute is constantly violated. In *Harry Potter and the Order of the Phoenix* Harry is accused of breaking the law when he performs the Patronus Charm in front of Dudley to repel Dementors.

Invisibility Cloak A unique magical Cloak that renders the wearer invisible. Harry is given the Cloak, which previously belonged to his father, James Potter, by Dumbledore at Christmas in his first year for times of need. The Cloak is large enough for Hermione and Ron to hide beneath it as well as Harry and proves essential on many occasions. In *Harry Potter and the Deathly Hallows* Harry discovers that the Cloak is one of the three Deathly Hallows, the only one he wishes to keep.

Jordan, Lee A student at Hogwarts in the same year as his friends, the Weasley twins. He sports dreadlocks and is memorable for his commentaries at school Quidditch matches.

Johnson, Angelina A tall black student at Hogwarts who is a Chaser on the Gryffindor Quidditch team. In Harry's fifth year she is Captain and gets frustrated as his frequent detentions prevent him practising.

Karkaroff, Igor In *Harry Potter and the Goblet of Fire* the Head of the visiting Durmstrang Institute. A former Death Eater, he is knowledgeable about the Dark Arts. About a year after refusing the summons of Voldemort, he is killed by Death Eaters.

Kettleburn, Professor Teacher at Hogwarts of Care of Magical Creatures before Hagrid. He retired at the end of Harry's second year.

killing curse *See Avada Kedavra.*

King's Cross A large railway station in central London, location in the stories for Platform 9¾, where the steam train to Hogwarts departs. It is located beside a cross roads where two highways meet. The spiritual King's Cross that Harry experiences in *Harry Potter and the Deathly Hallows*, after being blasted by Voldemort's killing curse, signifies choice as well as the possibility of further journeys. Both mark a borderland between worlds.

Kneazle A cat-like magical creature with large ears and a leonine tail who will allow itself to be adopted as a pet if it takes to a wizard or witch. It can sense those people who are up to no good or a danger, and is able to lead its owner home if lost. Hermione's pet, Crookshanks, is half-cat and half-Kneazle, with slightly crooked legs, accounting for his slightly odd appearance.

Knockturn Alley A street of shops off Diagon Alley featuring the Dark Arts, including, notably, Borgin and Burkes.

Kreacher An elderly house-elf who served Regulus and Sirius Black. After Sirius's death he becomes the reluctant servant of Harry, before willingly helping him in the resistance against Voldemort.

Krum, Viktor In *Harry Potter and the Goblet of Fire* he is Seeker at the Quidditch World Cup and the chosen champion representing Durmstrang Institute at the Triwizard Tournament. He accompanies Hermione to the Yule Ball and she is his hostage for the second trial. In *Harry Potter and the Deathly Hallows* he is a guest at the wedding of Fleur and Bill Weasley.

lake, black In *Harry Potter and the Half-Blood Prince* Dumbledore takes Harry to a deep cave, located on the coast, in a quest for one of Voldemort's Horcruxes. Inside is a deep black Stygian lake with a tiny flat-rocked island at its centre, on which the Horcrux had been placed in a protective basin. The lake was also filled with guardian inferi. In *Harry Potter and the Deathly Hallows* we learn that Kreacher has been there twice, once while Voldemort set up the protection for his Horcrux, the Slytherin locket, forcing him to drink from the bitter potion, and once when Regulus Black exchanged a fake locket for the real one.

Latin in the Harry Potter stories Though it is not on the Hogwarts curriculum, Latin is used in many names and spells. The use of Latin is part of the classical element in the stories, such as magical creatures like the centaur. Words employed include *draco*, 'a snake or dragon'; *dormiens*, 'sleeping'; *nunquam* 'never'; *titillandus*, 'should be tickled' (as in the Hogwarts motto, *Draco dormiens nunquam titillandus*); *imperium*, 'power, area of supreme authority' (as in the Imperius curse); *Minerva*, the Roman goddess of Wisdom (as in Professor McGonagall's first name); *patronus*, 'a protector, patron or guardian', from the Latin for 'father' (as in the Patronus Charm); *Sirius*, the 'Dog-star'; and *ludo*, 'I play' (as in Ludo Bagman, who is associated with games and sports). J.K. Rowling did some subsidiary Greek and Roman Studies as part of her main degree in French at Exeter University.

Leaky Cauldron, The A shabby wizarding pub and boarding house in the centre of London, on Charing Cross Road, which hides the entrance to Diagon Alley. In *Harry Potter and the Prisoner of Azkaban* Harry stays here briefly while waiting to return to Hogwarts for a new year. In his room, Room 11, there is a talking mirror.

Legilimens Someone with the ability to see into the minds of others. Voldemort is the greatest Legilimens, according to Snape, who shares this ability. Occlumens are able to prevent intrusions into their minds by Legilimens. The term comes from Latin *mens* ('mind') and *legere* ('to read').

Leg-Locker curse *(Locomotor Mortis)* A jinx that causes the legs of the person afflicted to became rigid. In *Harry Potter and the Philosopher's Stone* Draco puts the curse on Neville, but Hermione knows the counter-spell.

Lestrange, Bellatrix ('Bella') *Bellatrix* is Latin for female warrior, as befits a ruthless Death Eater responsible for the death of her cousin, Sirius Black, in the battle within the Department of Mysteries in *Harry Potter and the Order of the Phoenix*. There she showed the marks of her years in captivity in Azkaban; her skin had tightened, making her head skull-like. In *Harry Potter and the Half-Blood Prince* she distrusts Snape even though her master, Voldemort, regards him as a trustworthy servant. In contrast to her sister Narcissa (mother of Draco), she is dark, with hooded eyes and firm jaw. Hermione suffers the Cruciatus curse at her hand in *Harry Potter and the Deathly Hallows* as she is tortured for information. Later in the story Hermione has the satisfaction of taking her appearance, using Polyjuice Potion, to steal the Hufflepuff Cup from her vault in Gringotts Bank, knowing that

Voldemort's anger against her will be savage. In the Battle of Hogwarts Molly Weasley, furious with grief at the loss of her son, and incensed that Bellatrix nearly hits Ginny with a killing curse, fights and kills her.

Levicorpus A spell discovered by Harry in his Potions textbook annotated by the youthful Snape. It causes the victim to hang upside-down in the air by the ankles, and was very popular when Snape was a student at Hogwarts. In fact, in a Pensieve, Harry had seen his father, James, use the spell on Snape. Death Eaters in *Harry Potter and the Goblet of Fire* used the spell for amusement during the Quidditch World Cup gathering of wizards. The counter-jinx is 'Libera corpus'.

Life and Lies of Albus Dumbledore, The In *Harry Potter and the Deathly Hallows* a biography of Dumbledore published shortly after his death by Rita Skeeter, in which she seeks to undermine his moral integrity and reputation, using the mistake he made briefly in his youth of endorsing ideas of Grindelwald. She also claims falsely that he neglected his mentally unbalanced younger sister after she had killed his mother. The lies turn out to be *about* rather than *of* Dumbledore.

lightning-struck tower In *Harry Potter and the Half-Blood Prince* Professor Trelawney draws this card in a Hogwarts corridor from her Tarot pack. She sees it as warning impeding disaster and calamity. This presages the events on the Astronomy Tower soon after, when Dumbledore suffers the killing curse from Snape. Invisible on the Tower, and helpless to act, is Harry, with his lightning-shaped scar from the time as an infant that Voldemort struck him with the killing curse. This is one of several important prophecies by Sybill Trelawney. *See* prophecies and predictions.

Little Hangleton A little village, possibly in Devon, near to Riddle House and the run-down cottage belonging to Marvolo Gaunt. Frank Bryce lived in a little cottage in the grounds of Riddle House. After their murders, the Riddle parents, and Tom Riddle Sr, Voldemort's father, were buried in the village graveyard, the later scene of confrontation between Voldemort and Harry in *Harry Potter and the Goblet of Fire*. As well as its church, the village had a pub, The Hanged Man.

Locket, Salazar Slytherin's This treasure, prominently displaying a letter 'S', originally belonged to Salazar Slytherin, and eventually came into the possession of Merope Gaunt, an heir of Slytherin and mother of Tom Riddle (Voldemort). Merope sold it to Caractacus Burke, desperate for money. It was stolen by Voldemort from its new owner, Hepzibah Smith, who then employed it as a Horcrux and hid it under protective curses in a vast cave, where it was, in turn, stolen by R.A.B. In *Harry Potter and the Deathly Hallows* Harry, Ron and Hermione seek to destroy it, finding that it got into the hands of Dolores Umbridge after being burgled by Mundungus Fletcher from Grimmauld Place.

Longbottom, Alice Mother of Neville Longbottom, who belonged to the original Order of the Phoenix. As a result of her mind being destroyed by torture at the hands of Voldemort's Death Eaters she is now confined to St Mungo's Hospital of Magical Maladies and Injuries.

Longbottom, Augusta Neville Longbottom's formidable grandmother, who in *Harry Potter and the Deathly Hallows* goes on the run from Death Eaters and later fights in the Battle of Hogwarts.

Longbottom, Frank Father of Neville Longbottom. He was part of the original Order of the Phoenix, which led to him being tortured so much by the ruthless Death Eaters that he lost his mind. He is now confined, with his wife Alice, in St Mungo's Hospital of Magical Maladies and Injuries.

Longbottom, Neville A friend of Harry's and committed member of the DA in *Harry Potter and the Order of the Phoenix*. He participates in the battle with Death Eaters in the Department of Mysteries. From a wizarding family, he has been brought up by his intimidating grandmother, as his parents lost their minds when cruelly tortured by Death Eaters. Neville is a talented and pleasant-natured wizard, but lacks confidence and thus appears to be slow. He is clumsy and forgetful but shines in Herbology. In *Harry Potter and the Deathly Hallows* he plays a leading part in the resistance against Voldemort and kills Nagini, the final Horcrux to be destroyed. In later years he becomes herbology teacher at Hogwarts.

love potion Love potions were popular among some girls in Hogwarts. On one occasion Ron accidently eats chocolates spiked with a love potion intended for Harry. Voldemort's mother, Merope Gaunt, used a love potion to gain Tom Riddle Sr as her husband. *See* Amortentia.

Lovegood, Luna A dreamy friend of Harry's at Hogwarts with misty eyes and long, off-blond hair. She likes to wear a necklace of Butterbeer corks and dramatic hats. Like Harry she can see Thestrals and hear murmuring voices behind the veil in the Department of Mysteries, as, like him, she had seen death. She is in the same year as Ginny Weasley, a fervent member of the DA in *Harry Potter and the Order of the Phoenix* and in Ravenclaw. She responds to Hermione's call the night Dumbledore is murdered by Snape and fights the Death Eaters at the Ministry of Magic. Her father Xenophilius is the eccentric editor of the wacky periodical *The Quibbler*. Because of her oddness she has been a lonely figure, making her appreciate Harry and the fellowship of the DA, which she missed the most out of all of them after Dumbledore was restored to Hogwarts. In *Harry Potter and the Deathly Hallows* we learn she has painted on the ceiling of her bedroom a large picture of her friends Harry, Ron, Hermione, Ginny and Neville. She helps Ginny to re-establish Dumbledore's Army when Hogwarts seemingly comes under the control of Death Eaters. Luna has a talent for speaking uncomfortable truths. Her name reflects her character as a lover of goodness, and is one of several in the stories named after heavenly objects, associating her with silver and light, like Albus Dumbledore.

Lovegood, Xenophilius Father of Luna, whose first name, appropriately, given his eccentricity, means 'strange love.' He lives with his daughter in a cylindrical house not far from The Burrow, where he prints *The Quibbler*. When Harry, Ron and Hermione visit him in *Harry Potter and the Deathly Hallows* Xenophilius explains the meaning of the story of the Deathly Hallows. He is forced into curtailing his opposition to Voldemort in the periodical by the hope that the Dark Lord might return Luna to him, who is held hostage in Malfoy Manor.

Lupin, Remus Harry and his friends first meet Lupin in a railway carriage on their way to a new year at Hogwarts in *Harry Potter and the Prisoner of Azkaban*. He repels Dementors, who attack Harry. He is the new Defence Against the Dark Arts teacher. Unknown to them at that time, he is also a werewolf, condemned to transform at the full moon, as a result of being bitten while a child. Only a regular potion from Snape keeps him in human form. In his schooldays he was a close friend of Harry's father, James, and Sirius, going by the appropriate nickname 'Moony'. When he transformed, he would be confined, via a secret tunnel, in the Shrieking Shack, where his wails were thought by the villagers to be the sound of ghosts. He dressed shabbily, and was prematurely ageing, but he was a brilliant and inspiring teacher. It is possible that his characterisation was partly based on a favourite English teacher of J.K. Rowling's, Lucy Shepherd. He privately teaches Harry the Patronus Charm to protect him from further Dementor attacks. For twelve years he had believed Sirius had gone over to the Dark Side and betrayed James and Lily Potter, before being undeceived. With apparent malice, Snape set an essay on werewolves to Harry's class in the hope that Lupin's symptoms would be noticed. In *Harry Potter and the Order of the Phoenix*, after leaving Hogwarts, Lupin is active in the Order of the Phoenix. Tonks is in love with him, but he for a long time avoids love because of his condition. In *Harry Potter and the Deathly Hallows* we learn that he has married Tonks and later that they have a child. Lupin asks Harry if he will be baby Teddy's godfather. Both Lupin and Tonks fail to return from the Battle of Hogwarts, but the epilogue to *Harry Potter and the Deathly Hallows* makes it clear that Harry is a good godfather to Teddy.

McClaggen, Cormac Student at Hogwarts and, in *Harry Potter and the Half-Blood Prince*, persistent wannabe Keeper for Gryffindor's

Quidditch team. Hermione's appraisal of him is that he makes Grawp seem a gentleman.

McGonagall, Minerva Deputy headteacher at Hogwarts, head of Gryffindor house, and teacher of Transfiguration. She is also an Animagus, appearing first as a cat in *Harry Potter and the Philosopher's Stone*. The professor is severe in appearance, her deep-black hair caught in a compressed bun, and her spectacles square. She has a penchant for tartan patterns – items ranging from her dressing gown to a biscuit tin are in tartan. Her surname is Scottish, shared with the nation's celebrated worst poet, William McGonagall. Her first name, Minerva, is that of the Roman goddess of wisdom. Underneath her formidable exterior she has a tender heart. Unlike negative people such as Snape and Umbridge, McGonagall brings good to Harry from the beginning of his time at Hogwarts, for example, unexpectedly spotting him as a natural Seeker for the Gryffindor Quidditch team. She plays a spirited role in the defence of Hogwarts against the besieging forces of Voldemort in *Harry Potter and the Deathly Hallows*.

Macmillan, Ernie Student at Hogwarts in Hufflepuff house. He is inclined to be pompous, and to doubt Harry, but joins the DA.

Macnair, Walden He is the executioner in *Harry Potter and the Prisoner of Azkaban* assigned by the Ministry of Magic to kill Buckbeak. Macnair is later revealed as a Death Eater and he is among those in *Harry Potter and the Half-Blood Prince* who ambush Harry and his friends at the Department of Mysteries.

Madam Puddifoot's Teashop A teashop located in Hogsmeade that is a favourite with young couples from Hogwarts.

magical creatures Such beings are not noticeable by Muggles (non-magical folk), either by a characteristic lack of observation or because the creatures are magically hidden from their view. Sometimes the Ministry of Magic has to resort to altering memories of Muggles who have accidently seen them. Magical creatures vary enormously in scale: they might be giants or dragons, tiny Cornish pixies or fairies. Wizarding folk participate in the concealment of magical creatures using the Disillusionment Charm. (*See Fantastic Beasts & Where to Find Them.*)

Magical Menagerie A shop selling magical creatures in Diagon Alley, where Hermonie buys her ginger cat, Crookshanks, in *Harry Potter and the Prisoner of Azkaban.*

Malfoy, Abraxas Draco's grandfather, who died of dragon pox.

Malfoy, Draco A student in Harry's year at Hogwarts who models himself upon his wicked father, Lucius Malfoy, and represents the worst of Slytherin house, to which he belongs. His face is pointed and pale, with a permafrost sneer. He believes in the superiority of pure-bloods, those without the contamination of Muggle blood in their ancestry. From the first, Harry dislikes him, and soon they are implacable enemies. In fact, Harry hates him more than his bullying cousin, Dudley Dursley. Like Dudley he surrounds himself with protective thugs, his being fellow Slytherins Crabbe and Goyle. Draco's cowardly cruelty is revealed when he stamps on the helpless Harry's face in *Harry Potter and the Half-Blood Prince.* With the pressure of a task Voldemort imposes on Draco, demanding all his energies, a different side of Draco emerges, so that he looks ill and strained, and secretly weeps. At one point Harry even feels some pity for him after he proves unable to kill Dumbledore, even with Voldemort's dire threats hanging over him. In *Harry Potter and the Deathly Hallows* he is often reluctant to carry out orders given by Death Eaters. There are other hints of a slow redemption, and nineteen years after the events of *Harry Potter and the Deathly Hallows* he is at King's Cross seeing his son Scorpius off to Hogwarts. He is a gifted wizard, and succeeds in what was thought impossible: in *Harry Potter and the Half-Blood Prince*, gaining access for Death Eaters into Hogwarts via the Room of Requirement. His name is derived from 'dragon', linked in fantasy and linguistically with 'worm' or 'serpent', echoing his Slytherin loyalties. Like many related to the Black family he is named after a constellation, Draco, represented traditionally as a dragon.

Malfoy, Lucius Draco Malfoy's father, for many years influential school governor in Hogwarts, and a Death Eater. He is married to Narcissa, who is sister of Bellatrix Lestrange and Andromeda Tonks, and cousin of Sirius Black. The family live in a country mansion in Wiltshire. In *Harry Potter and the Chamber of Secrets* he slips Tom Riddle's diary into a book of Ginny Weasley's, ensnaring her into Voldemort's grasp. Voldemort is furious with him for his handling of the diary (a Horcrux), and for his failure to obtain the prophecy at the Department of Mysteries in *Harry Potter and the Order of the Phoenix*, after which he is imprisoned in Azkaban. With Lucius in Azkaban, Voldemort takes his revenge by imposing a dreadful task upon Draco, his son, threatening to kill Lucius and his mother if he fails. In *Harry Potter and the Deathly Hallows* it is clear that Lucius's devotion to his family is stronger than his ties to Voldemort and his Death Eaters.

Malfoy, Narcissa ('Cissy') Draco Malfoy's mother, and sister of Bellatrix Lestrange and Andromeda Tonks, and aunt of Nymphadora Tonks, member of the Order of the Phoenix. From the ancient Black family, she is cousin of Sirius. In *Harry Potter and the Half-Blood Prince* she asks Snape to protect Draco, in danger from the task imposed upon him by Voldemort to kill Dumbledore. Narcissa is light-coloured and blond, with a haughty face, unlike her dark sister Bellatrix, and her name is the feminine form of Narcissus, who, in classical myth, fell in love with his reflection on the water and drowned. On one occasion, when she comes across Harry in Diagon Alley, she threatens him by saying that Dumbledore will not always be around to protect him. In *Harry Potter and the Deathly Hallows* she is sick with worry about Draco, and when Voldemort demands that she check if Harry is really dead, and she discovers that he is alive, she whispers to him for news of her son, and tells the Dark Lord that Harry is dead.

Malkin, Madam Robe-seller in Diagon Alley.

Marauder's Map A gift to Harry from Fred and George Weasley. It was made by Harry's father and friends – Prongs, Moony, Padfoot and Wormtail – and reveals the various secret passageways in

Hogwarts and the location of everyone in the school. In *Harry Potter and the Deathly Hallows*, when Harry spends long months with Hermione and Ron tracking down the Horcruxes, he sometimes looks at the map for signs of Ginny's movements.

Marvolo's Ring A ring owned by Marvolo Gaunt, an heirloom possibly passed down the centuries from Salazar Slytherin. His nephew Tom Riddle (Voldemort) treacherously took it from him and turned it into a Horcrux. We learn in *Harry Potter and the Deathly Hallows* that Dumbledore's hand is terribly withered because he put it on when obtaining it. He knows that it contains the Resurrection Stone, one of the three Deathly Hallows. His hope is that he might say sorry to those he had lost in his family. The fatal maiming means that he will die within a year, even with the best potions that Snape can supply.

Maxime, Olympe The elegant Head of Beauxbatons Academy, with whom Hagrid – like her a half-giant – falls in love. Her eyes are black and her skin olive. She arrives at Hogwarts for the Triwizard Tournament in a giant powder-blue carriage drawn by a dozen Abraxan winged horses. Her spell-work impresses Hagrid when she is with him among the giants deep in Europe in the summer before Harry's sixth year.

Memory Charm Used in memory modification, notably by Gilderoy Lockhart in *Harry Potter and the Chamber of Secrets*, who ends up wiping his own memory by accident. It is employed by the Muggle Liaison Officer of the Ministry of Magic to tweak the memories of Muggles who have seen magical events or creatures. It is revealed in *Harry Potter and the Half-Blood Prince* that even the memory of the US President can be modified. Voldemort modifies the memories of Morfin Gaunt and Hokey the house-elf in order to incriminate them for his wicked deeds.

merpeople Magical creatures who live in the lake beside Hogwarts, taken from folklore and classical myth. In Scotland they would be called Selkies. Their upper body is a little like humans, and they have a fish-like tail. Grey-skinned and purplish-haired, they fish dextrously with spears. Above water their speech is unintelligible to those who do not speak Mermish. Merpeople feature in *Harry Potter and the Goblet of Fire*, where one task in the Triwizard Tournament takes place below the surface of the lake. In *Harry Potter and the Half-Blood Prince* they mourn Dumbledore.

Ministry of Magic Agency of the wizarding government that regulates the activities of magical folk and keeps their buildings and other aspects of their lives hidden from Muggle people. This is not easy, because even when magical folk try to dress as Muggles they can be spotted wearing an odd assortment of Muggle clothes, such as a frock-coat and spats with a bathing costume. Hogwarts Castle appears to Muggles as a dangerous ruin. The Ministry has direct but secret links with the Muggle government of the UK. Harry has dealings with the Minister for Magic, Cornelius Fudge, and his successor Rufus Scrimgeour. The Ministry under Fudge refuses for a long time to acknowledge the return of Voldemort, despite the insistence of Harry and Dumbledore. There is a tension and ideological conflict between the Ministry and Hogwarts, with the school representing Dumbledore and his values. Harry is asked to help the Ministry's public relations, but he refuses, indicating that he is 'Dumbledore's man' through and through. In *Harry Potter and the Deathly Hallows* the Ministry falls to Voldemort's Death Eaters and Scrimgeour is murdered. Those who do not support Voldemort's ideology still continue to work at the Ministry, provided they are pure-bloods. Harry, Ron and Hermione enter the Ministry under disguise to obtain the locket containing a Horcrux from Umbridge and only narrowly escape.

mirror, two-way In *Harry Potter and the Order of the Phoenix* Harry's godfather Sirius gives him a mirror that is one of a pair to enable communication between them, a mirror Harry never uses, but keeps. It shatters, but he keeps a sliver of it in memory of his godfather. Sirius's is filched by Mundungus Fletcher and comes into the hands of Aberforth Dumbledore, who uses it to watch over Harry in *Harry Potter and the Deathly Hallows*. Because of the mirror he realises Harry is in danger at Malfoy Manor and sends Dobby to help him.

Mirror of Erised A magical mirror of desire that first appears in *Harry Potter and the Philosopher's Stone*. Its caption has its letters reversed, and claims to show those who look into it their deepest longing ('Erised' is desire spelt backwards). When Harry looks into the mirror it takes him away from reality and his responsibilities and he becomes obsessed with it. He sees his dead parents smiling and reflected back at him. Ron sees himself as Head Boy at Hogwarts and Quidditch Captain. Dumbledore explains to Harry that the mirror reveals a desperate need, whereas, if the happiest person on earth looked into it, he would see himself, as in a normal mirror. To those in need it reveals neither truth nor knowledge. The mirror features in Harry's confrontation with Quirrell/Voldemort, in the underworld chamber at the end of *Harry Potter and the Philosopher's Stone*.

Moody, Alastor 'Mad-Eye' A member of the Order of the Phoenix who comes out of retirement as a brilliant Auror to teach Defence Against the Dark Arts in Harry's fourth year at Hogwarts in *Harry Potter and the Goblet of Fire*. Barty Crouch Jr, however, kidnaps him and takes on the role, appearing as Moody with the help of Polyjuice Potion. In *Harry Potter and the Deathly Hallows* Moody is lost protecting Harry's escape from Little Whinging. His friends are unable to recover his body, and his magical revolving eye ends up in Umbridge's office door at the Ministry of Magic, allowing her to snoop on her colleagues. His first name, Alastor, signifies an avenging spirit or deity, a befitting name for an Auror, pursuing Death Eaters.

Moony Nickname of Lupin when a schoolboy at Hogwarts, referring to his werewolf form.

Mrs Norris The cat of Hogwarts' caretaker, Argus Filch, intensely disliked by students as she acts as an uncannily successful probe for her master. She is probably named after Jane Austen's unpleasant busybody Mrs Norris in her *Mansfield Park*.

Mudblood An offensive name for a wizard both of whose parents are Muggles.

Muffliato A charm discovered by Harry in his annotated Potions textbook that causes a buzzing to fill the target's ears, preventing conversations being overheard.

Muggle Studies A subject at Hogwarts, necessary as many wizarding folk have had no exposure to Muggle ways. Even though she has Muggle parents, Hermione elects to take this subject, to appreciate how Muggles look from a wizarding perspective. One of the essays she is given to write is 'Explain Why Muggles Need Electricity'. The teacher of Muggle Studies, Charity Burbage, is tortured and killed by Voldemort because of her pro-Muggle views.

Muggles Non-magical people; those, that is, lacking an innate gift of ability in magic. There is a twilight area between Muggles and wizarding folk: Squibs are those from wizarding families who lack magical ability, e.g. Argus Filch and Mrs Figg, a neighbour of the Dursleys. At Hogwarts students can take Muggle Studies. Arthur Weasley is fascinated by Muggle artefacts such as telephones and ticket machines, and is constantly amazed at Muggle ingenuity in getting along without magic. In Muggle society technology and gadgetry replace magic. The worst side of Muggles is displayed in the Dursley family; and more sympathetically in characters such as Mr and Mrs Granger, Frank Bryce or even the harassed British Prime Minister. After Voldemort gained control of the Ministry of Magic in *Harry Potter and the Deathly Hallows*, many rebel wizards protected Muggles and sought to alleviate their suffering.

Nagini The large snake companion of Voldemort upon whose 'milk' (i.e. venom) he feeds as he gradually reconstitutes in physical form. Voldemort controls Nagini by speaking Parseltongue, and uses her as his agent, as when he bids her attack Arthur Weasley. The snake provides a dark counterpart to Dumbledore's phoenix, Fawkes; whereas she destroys, Fawkes heals. Nagini is a Horcrux, the last to be destroyed, killed heroically by Neville, using the sword of Gryffindor. *Nagini* is the female name for 'cobra' in Hindi.

naming, self This is an indication of meglomania or at least an inflated view of oneself. Tom Riddle renames himself Lord

Voldemort (a clever anagram of Tom Marvolo Riddle) while Snape styles himself, with an irony alien to Voldemort, 'the Half-Blood Prince'. Riddle wishes to be separate from and superior to ordinary humanity and particularly despises Muggles and wizards or witches who were not pure-bloods – i.e. from families without Muggle ancestry. Though he was a half-blood himself, he bolstered his image with the fact that he was the sole surviving heir of Slytherin.

NEWTs Nastily Exhausting Wizarding Tests, taken at the end of seven years at Hogwarts, by which time students will have come of age as adult wizards and witches. They are the highest qualification at the school, and top grades are needed in order to work for the Ministry of Magic. Harry, Ron and Hermione delay their examinations by taking out most of their seventh years in *Harry Potter and the Deathly Hallows* to hunt out Horcruxes for destruction.

Nimbus Two Thousand An advanced sporting broomstick owned by Harry until it is destroyed by the Whomping Willow in *Harry Potter and the Prisoner of Azkaban*. Its replacement, a superior and expensive Firebolt, is a gift from Sirius.

Nurmengard A prison for wizards founded by Grindelwald, equivalent to Britain's Azkaban. Its motto is 'For the greater good'. Grindelwald is imprisoned in the prison after his defeat by Dumbledore in 1945. The name suggests an amalgam of Nuremberg, where Nazi war criminals were tried after the war, and Tolkien's Isengard.

Occlumency *See* Legilimens.

Office for the Detection and Confiscation of Counterfeit Defensive Spells and Protective Objects A section of the Ministry of Magic. In *Harry Potter and the Half-Blood Prince* Arthur Weasley is promoted to its head by Rufus Scrimgeour. At this time it had become important, as many false spells and objects were on the market during Voldemort's new reign of terror.

Office of Misinformation A section of the Ministry of Magic responsible for modifying Muggle memories in cases where magical events have been witnessed.

Ogden, Bob Former head of the Magical Law Enforcement squad who allowed Dumbledore to preserve some memories of his visit to the house of Marvolo Gaunt concerning a serious breach in wizarding law. In *Harry Potter and the Half-Blood Prince* Harry is able to experience the memories in Dumbledore's Pensieve.

Ollivanders A shop selling wands in Diagon Alley that was established in 382 BC but closed at the time of Voldemort's increasing power in *Harry Potter and the Half-Blood Prince*. The proprietor, known only as Mr Ollivander, supplies wands to Hogwarts pupils. In *Harry Potter and the Deathly Hallows* Harry discovers that Voldemort has been torturing Ollivander to find out why his wand failed to overcome Harry when they duelled in the graveyard at Little Hangleton just after his restoration to physical form. Harry and his friends rescue Ollivander from his long captivity and he finds haven in Shell Cottage, home of Bill and Fleur Weasley.

Order of the Phoenix A clandestine society, with its characteristic motif of the phoenix, set up by Dumbledore to oppose Voldemort and his Death Eaters. Its original work ended with the Dark Lord's disembodiment after he had failed to kill the infant Harry. With the re-embodiment and return of Voldemort in *Harry Potter and the Goblet of Fire*, Dumbledore realises the necessity of reactivating the society. The Order is paralleled by the student group set up by Harry in *Harry Potter and the Order of the Phoenix*, the DA. Members of the Order at various times included Aberforth Dumbledore, Arabella Figg, Mundungus Fletcher, Hagrid, Lupin, Madame Maxime, Professor McGonagall, Alastor 'Mad-Eye' Moody, Sturgis Podmore, Kingsley Shacklebolt, Nymphadora Tonks, Arthur Weasley, Molly Weasley, Bill Weasley, Charlie Weasley, Sirius Black, James and Lily Potter, Frank and Alice Longbottom, Peter Pettigrew (defected), Severus Snape and Emmeline Vance.

orphanage The home in London of youthful Tom Riddle (Voldemort) from birth until entering Hogwarts aged eleven.

Ottery St Catchpole Nearest village to the Weasleys' home, The Burrow. It is almost certainly in Devon, in the Otter valley (hence 'Ottery'). The village name evokes the Devon town of Ottery St Mary, near and east of Exeter, birthplace of the poet Samuel Taylor Coleridge. Ottery St Mary celebrates Pixie-Day on the Saturday closest to the Summer Solstice and is on the River Otter. The otter is J.K. Rowling's favourite animal.

Owlery, The A Tower at Hogwarts housing the owls used by staff and students for sending and receiving post.

owls Birds that are indispensable to wizarding life, responsible for sending and receiving post. Harry's owl, a gift from Hagrid, is Hedwig. Hogwarts has its own Owlery, and in Diagon Alley there is an Owl Emporium. The Post Office in Hogsmeade has 300 or more owls, the distance of delivery determining the size of owl required.

OWLs Ordinary Wizarding Levels, examinations taken at the end of the fifth year in Hogwarts.

Padfoot The schoolboy nickname for Sirius Black, referring to the animal he becomes as an Animagus – a large dog.

Parselmouth Someone who can converse with snakes, a very rare ability and not exclusive to those practising the Dark Arts. Parselmouths include Salazar Slytherin, Lord Voldemort, and Harry. Harry inherited some of Voldemort's powers when he was scarred as a baby, and speaking Parseltongue was one of them.

Patronus Charm A spell that produces a silvery Patronus, or quickly moving protecting animal, very often to repel Dementors and protect from their attacks. The Patronus can also proclaim messages (as happened with Kingsley Shacklebolt's graceful lynx or Arthur Weasley's weasel) or guide (as Snape's beautiful doe in the Forest of Dean). Harry's Patronus is a stag, while Hermione's is an otter (J.K. Rowling's favourite animal), and Dumbledore's is a phoenix. Goodness often takes a silvery character or the form of light in the stories. The shape of a Patronus can change after a shock or emotional upheaval, as is the case with Tonks, or over time from being in love, as with Severus Snape's. With the Patronus J.K. Rowling has created myth, rather than simply employed it.

Peeves A resident spirit of chaos at Hogwarts, more like a poltergeist than a ghost. He appears as a tiny man wearing gaudy clothes, replete with orange bow tie. He flies and swoops around the school corridors bent on mischief. He looks solid in comparison with the Hogwarts ghosts. Though tied to no one, in times of crisis he sides with those oppressed at Hogwarts, first by Umbridge and then Death Eaters.

Pensieve A shallow basin made of stone that has strange emblems surrounding its brim. It stores and reveals thoughts and memories in great detail. Memories can be stored in other media, such as the glass orbs that filled the shelves of the Hall of Prophecy in the Department of Mysteries, or the sinister magic diary of Tom Riddle. The Pensieve, however, is unique in the fluency of storage and retrieval of memories and thoughts that it allows. Harry learns much of the backstory of Voldemort through being immersed in the memories of Dumbledore and others via Dumbledore's Pensieve. On one occasion he illicitly enters Snape's Pensieve, but does not see the professor's true nature until much later, in *Harry Potter and the Deathly Hallows*, when the dying Snape gives him his memories, which Harry accesses in the Pensieve once owned by Dumbledore.

Petrificus Totalis A spell to immobilise a person totally, also known as the Body-Bind spell or Full Body-Bind curse.

Pettigrew, Peter ('Wormtail') He was a short and fat boy when one of a group of James Potter's friends while studying at Hogwarts. He was an Animagus, who took the form of a rat – called Scabbers when he became Ron's pet many years later. He betrayed James and

Lily Potter to Voldemort and thus was nearly responsible for Harry's death. Before that he had spied for the Dark Lord. For many years, while hiding in his rat form, Pettigrew was believed to be dead, supposedly killed in a duel by Sirius. As Harry saves Pettigrew's life in *Harry Potter and the Prisoner of Azkaban*, Voldemort then has a deputy who is in the boy's debt. This is because, when one wizard saves another, it forges some kind of a bond between them (as Snape has an obligation to James Potter for once saving him). In *Harry Potter and the Goblet of Fire* Voldemort takes Pettigrew's severed hand to help his regeneration, and gives him a replacement silver hand that remains loyal to the Dark Lord. In *Harry Potter and the Half-Blood Prince*, during the summer before Harry's sixth year at Hogwarts, Pettigrew stays at Snape's house in an industrial city. In *Harry Potter and the Deathly Hallows* Pettigrew, in a moment of pity, spares Harry's life, which costs him his own, strangled by his silver hand.

Peverell, Ignotus In *Harry Potter and the Deathly Hallows* Harry and Hermione find his tombstone while searching the churchyard in Godric's Hollow on Christmas Eve. The tombstone bears the triangular rune of the Deathly Hallows. He is an important ancient wizard who is the original of one of the three brothers in the story of the Deathly Hallows in Hermione's book, left to her by Dumbledore. Like many other wizards, Harry is a descendant of his. When choosing a title for *Harry Potter and the Deathly Hallows* one possibility J.K. Rowling considered was 'Harry Potter and the Peverell Quest', but decided that the word 'quest' had worn rather thin.

Philosopher's Stone A stone sought in legend and in Alchemy for its ability to transform a base metal into pure gold. It is also said to produce the Elixir of Life, conferring immortality. In the Harry Potter stories, the stone belongs to the Alchemist Nicolas Flamel, associate and friend of Dumbledore. In *Harry Potter and the Chamber of Secrets* it is hidden first in a vault deep under Gringotts Bank and then in a Secret Chamber below Hogwarts Castle. There it is protected by the three-headed dog, Fluffy, and riddle spells cast by Hogwarts Professors Sprout, Flitwick, McGonagall, Quirrell and

Snape. Voldemort craves to possess it in order to be immortal, having already cheated death when he was disembodied upon failing to kill the infant Harry with the killing curse. Had he obtained it, he would have returned to power three years sooner than he does. Dumbledore reveals, however, that the stone can be found only by someone who wants to find it but not to use it.

phoenix A magical creature taken from classical mythology (the Romans believed that one had appeared in Egypt in the year after Christ's death). It is an elegant and beautiful bird that bursts into flames and resurrects from its ashes. The early Church took the phoenix as an image of Jesus and his resurrection, and in recent literature D.H. Lawrence appropriated the image for himself as artist. Dumbledore explained to Harry that phoenixes 'can carry immensely heavy loads, their tears have healing powers, and they make highly faithful pets'. The headmaster's own pet is a phoenix, Fawkes, who comes to Harry's aid in *Harry Potter and the Chamber of Secrets*. Fawkes sings a haunting lament to Dumbledore in *Harry Potter and the Half-Blood Prince*. In *Fantastic Beasts & Where to Find Them*, Newt Scamander (a pen-name of Rowling's) comments: 'Phoenix song is magical: it is reputed to increase the courage of the pure in heart and to strike fear into the hearts of the impure. Phoenix tears have powerful healing properties.'

Pigwidgeon 'Pig' Ron's owl, replacing his pet rat, Scabbers.

Pince, Madam Formidable librarian at Hogwarts. Her face reminds Harry of a vulture – with sunken cheeks, parchment-like skin, long and hooked nose, and hands like claws.

Polyjuice Potion A mud-like and slow-bubbling concoction employed by wizards to appear like someone else. In *Harry Potter and the Chamber of Secrets* Harry, Ron and Hermione make the juice in order to deceive Draco by appearing as Crabbe, Goyle and a Slytherin girl (though Hermione's potion goes wrong and she partially transforms into a cat). In *Harry Potter and the Goblet of Fire* Barty Crouch Jr uses the potion to assume the shape of Mad-Eye Moody, who is about to start as a teacher at Hogwarts.

In *Harry Potter and the Deathly Hallows* Harry, Ron and Hermione use Polyjuice on many occasions, because of the need to conceal themselves from Death Eaters as they pursue their quest to destroy the Horcruxes. When someone good is impersonated using Polyjuice it seems that the potion takes on an attractive hue. In *Harry Potter and the Deathly Hallows* the potion used by Hermione to look like Malfalda Hopkirk, a Ministry employee, is a 'pleasant heliotrope' and that for a Harry lookalike is bright, clear and golden.

Pomfrey, Poppy Matron of Hogwarts, and responsible for the well-used hospital wing.

Portkey An object, often ordinary (such as the small hairbrush in *Harry Potter and the Deathly Hallows*), charmed to transport anyone who touches it to a particular destination. The charm can set a predetermined time for the Portkey to become active. In *Harry Potter and the Goblet of Fire* Harry and Cedric Diggory, when they touch the Cup that is sought in the final Triwizard trial, are taken almost instantly to the graveyard in Little Hangleton, where Voldemort awaits.

portraits Like any images in the wizarding world, subjects in a painted portrait move at will, and even leave the frame and enter another if they wish (for example, to have a chat with a neighbouring portrait). This is true even if the subjects have died. In the headteacher's study at Hogwarts are portraits of previous headteachers, who take an interest in what is happening in the present. A portrait of the Fat Lady provides security at the hidden circular entrance to the Gryffindor common foom, requiring a current password to go past her.

Potions A subject taught at Hogwarts for many years by Professor Snape, who is fascinated by the subject, even though he longs to teach Defence Against the Dark Arts (an ambition realised in *Harry Potter and the Half-Blood Prince*). In his student days he corrected his copy of the textbook and added his own charms; that copy comes into Harry's possession in *Harry Potter and the Half-Blood Prince* and considerably enhances his grades.

Potter, Harry James The main character in the seven stories, which trace seven years in his life chronologically: from his invitation to study at Hogwarts School of Witchcraft and Wizardry at his eleventh birthday, to his interrupted seventh year. He is an orphan, whose parents died saving him as a baby from Voldemort, the powerful wizard who feared from a prophecy that Harry would grow up to defeat him. No one before had survived a killing curse, and he bore a lightning-shaped scar and a sliver of Voldemort's fractured soul from the attack. He was protected by the love of his mother, Lily, who had stood between Voldemort and his cot pleading for his life. Brought up by his uncaring Uncle Vernon and Aunt Petunia Dursley, and bullied by his cousin Dudley, he has no idea why he has unusual abilities until receiving the invitation to Hogwarts. It is then that he discovers that there is the normal world of Muggles, and a world of wizards, witches and magical creatures carefully hidden from them. At Hogwarts he finds a home and the acceptance of friends, particularly Ron, Hermione and Hagrid, a circle of friends that gradually widens. Soon he is the youngest ever student to play as Seeker in the wizarding game of Quidditch for over one hundred years. He faces constant danger as Voldemort returns to power and threatens the world – he stands as the greatest obstacle in his path. At the height of the Dark Lord's power Harry becomes the symbol of resistance, signifying 'the triumph of good, the power of innocence, the need to keep resisting'. Ultimately Harry is called upon to choose to sacrifice himself for his friends, and indeed for all who are considered unfit to live or to be free by the tyrant.

Potter, James Father of Harry, and husband of Lily. He is viewed differently by various characters, making him a somewhat enigmatic figure. As Harry gradually builds up a picture of his dead father, he is forced to make judgements, balancing conflicting views of James. Professor McGonagall is positive and admiring. Snape's view of him could not be more different, extending into an ill-disguised hatred of his son. James was an Animagus, taking the form of a stag, hence his nickname, 'Prongs.' This is the form that Harry's Patronus takes when he employs the Patronus Charm to repel Dementors. The spirits of James and Lily appear in the graveyard when Harry and Voldemort duel with matching wands, and in more substantial form after Harry employs the Resurrection Stone in *Harry Potter and the Deathly Hallows*. Harry also sees them in his first year at Hogwarts in the Mirror of Erised. James's ideals, and hatred of the Dark Arts, help to guide Harry in his battle against evil, as when he protects Peter Pettigrew from death, despite his treachery against his parents.

Potter, Lily (née Evans) Red-haired mother of Harry, who comes from a Muggle family and marries the wizard, James Potter. She sacrifices her life saving the infant Harry from Voldemort, her love deflecting the power of the killing curse by a Deeper Magic. When attacked by Dementors, Harry relives the pleading screams of his mother buried deep in his memory. Lily is the sister of Petunia Dursley, who reluctantly provides a home for the orphan, Harry, thus activating an ancient protection. She and Petunia grew up in the same town as Severus Snape, who as a child noticed her magical abilities, and told her about the wizarding community and Hogwarts. Snape loved Lily throughout his tormented life, so much so that his Patronus became similar to hers, a doe. Harry is often told that he has Lily's vivid green eyes. Though she had been in Gryffindor house while at Hogwarts, she was a favourite student of Horace Slughorn because of her skill in Potions. The name 'Lily' refers to a person or thing of great purity or whiteness.

Prang, Ernie Elderly driver of the Knight Bus, named after Ernie Rowling, the author's paternal grandfather, and husband of Kathleen Rowling (from whence comes the 'K' in J.K. Rowling).

Prime Minister The head of the UK Government is contacted from time to time by the Minister of Magic when events in the magical community are likely to affect Muggles. In *Harry Potter and the Half-Blood Prince* the return of Voldemort, and his subsequent reign of terror, are causing inexplicable disasters in the Muggle world and so the Prime Minister is briefed by Cornelius Fudge and Rufus Scrimgeour. Chronologically, the Prime Minister in that period of the 1990s would have been John Major, but his portrayal in *Harry Potter and the Half-Blood Prince* is more like Tony Blair.

Prince, Eileen Mother of Severus Snape and witch, married to Tobias Snape. While at Hogwarts she was Captain of the school Gobstones team.

Privet Drive, 4 The house in a well-heeled suburb belonging to Vernon and Petunia Dursley, and their spoilt son, Dudley, and the adopted home of Harry Potter. He must stay there on at least one occasion every school year while he is at Hogwarts and under seventeen to continue enjoying the protection of a home gained through the sacrificial death of his mother Lily, Petunia's sister. The house has four bedrooms. After living for a considerable period in a cupboard under the stairs, Harry is eventually allowed to have Dudley's second bedroom. The fourth bedroom is kept for visitors, such as Aunt Marge Dursley.

Prongs James Potter's nickname while at school at Hogwarts, from the stag that is the form he takes as an Animagus.

prophecies and predictions These abound in the stories, such as the observation by Dumbledore that Harry will be pleased one day that he spared Peter Pettigrew's life. The prophecies include Professor Trelawney's original prophecy about Harry and Voldemort, a prediction that Wormtail will return to his master, her fortune telling about the lightning-struck tower, and possibly her statement about the first to rise from the table of thirteen will be the first to die (which seems to be fulfilled in Sirius's death). Trelawney's original prophecy, to Dumbledore before Harry's birth, is the most significant: 'The one with the power to vanquish the Dark Lord approaches . . . born to those who have thrice defied him, born as the seventh month dies . . . and the Dark Lord will mark him as his equal, but he will have power the Dark Lord knows not . . . and either must die at the hand of the other for neither can live while the other survives . . . the one with the power to vanquish the Dark Lord will be born as the seventh month dies . . .'.

Protego A shield charm.

pumpkin juice A popular drink that, when iced, makes a particularly refreshing drink in hot weather.

pure-bloods A name favoured by Voldemort, his followers and his sympathisers for wizards and witches both of whose parents are wizards. The label is extended to those who have many generations of 'pure' blood. The ideology goes back to one of the founders of Hogwarts, Salazar Slytherin, who wished to restrict a Hogwarts education to racially pure wizards. Ironically Voldemort himself had a Muggle father.

Quality Quidditch Supplies A shop in Diagon Alley.

Quibbler, The A fanciful periodical edited by Luna Lovegood's eccentric father, Xenophilius. Harry is interviewed for the publication in *Harry Potter and the Order of the Phoenix* so that he can reveal the return of Voldemort. In *Harry Potter and the Deathly Hallows*, after the Ministry of Magic comes under Voldemort's control, *The Quibbler* becomes important in resisting his power. Eventually the editor is pressured into following the party line when Luna is held hostage.

Quidditch The national sport in wizarding Britain, and highly popular at Hogwarts, where each house has its team. Harry is a Quidditch enthusiast, chosen as Seeker in his first year, and later becoming Captain of the Gryffindor team. A team consists of seven players, mounted on broomsticks. There are three Chasers, one Keeper, two Beaters, and one Seeker. The game centres around three different kinds of ball – the red Quaffle is used to score a goal, the two black Bludgers are hit by Beaters to deflect opponents, and a Golden Snitch (a tiny ball with silver wings) is sought by the Seeker. Chasers throw the Quaffle between each other in their attempt to score by hurling it through a hoop, of which there are three at each end of the oval pitch. Each score earns ten points, but capturing the Snitch means 150 points, and the end of the match – which means that the Seeker must only seize it if the score will ensure victory. The team Keeper guards the hoops to prevent opposing Chasers from scoring with their Quaffle. The history and development of Quidditch in Britain and around the globe is told in Kennilworthy Wisp's *Quidditch Through the Ages* (*see* Bibliography).

Quirrell, Professor Defence Against the Dark Arts teacher at Hogwarts in Harry's first year, and the 'man with two faces'. He appears unsuited to be a teacher of this subject, with a stutter and a nervous disposition, but in fact turns out to be in league with Voldemort. In his previous travels, which may have included encounters with vampires in the Black Forest in Germany, he had come across the Dark Lord, struggling to return in embodied form after his dissipation upon failing to kill Harry as a baby. Quirrell allows his master to share his body, hiding the appearance of Voldemort's snake-like face on the back of his head with a large turban. He feeds on unicorn blood in the Forbidden Forest to nurture his hideous guest. Voldemort convinces Quirrell to believe only in power, rejecting goodness and any repulsion at evil. He quests the Philosopher's Stone for his master, failing to steal it from a vault under Gringotts Bank. He then pursues it in hidden chambers under Hogwarts after Hagrid lets slip to Quirrell the secret of subduing Fluffy, the fearsome three-headed dog guarding the entrance that leads ultimately down to the stone. Harry confronts Quirrell/Voldemort deep underground and remains protected from his enemy by his mother's love, the efficacy of which still continues as a Deeper Magic not understood by Voldemort. Quirrell's hands burn upon touching Harry and when Harry grabs his face to prevent him uttering the killing curse he is in agony. Quirrell's death as Voldemort abandons his body means he must continue his quest for re-embodiment.

R.A.B. *See* Black, Regulus.

Ragnuk the First According to Griphook in *Harry Potter and the Deathly Hallows*, the original Goblin owner of the sword of Gryffindor.

Ravenclaw, Helena Beautiful daughter of Rowena Ravenclaw, from whom she stole the diadem. In the stories she is the Grey Lady, the resident ghost of Ravenclaw house. Helena was killed in a fit of anger by the volatile Bloody Baron, her lover.

Ravenclaw, Rowena One of the four founders of Hogwarts whose distinctive diadem is made into a Horcrux by Voldemort.

Ravenclaw diadem A treasure once possessed by the founder of Hogwarts, Rowena Ravenclaw, which was stolen by her daughter Helena Ravenclaw and hidden in a hollow tree in Albania. The diadem was retrieved by Tom Riddle (Voldemort), after he had wheedled its location from Helena's ghost, and turned into a Horcrux.

Ravenclaw house One of the four houses at Hogwarts, whose symbol is an eagle, whose colour is blue and whose resident ghost is the Grey Lady. The house is named after one of the four founders of the school, Rowena Ravenclaw. The qualities valued by the house are intelligence, wit and knowledge.

***Reducto* (Reductor curse)** Spell that diminishes or destroys objects, usually obstacles in the path of the wizard or witch.

Remembrall A small glass ball whose interior white smoke magically turns red when its owner has forgotten to do something. The forgetful Neville Longbottom was given one.

Resurrection Stone One of the three Deathly Hallows. In *Harry Potter and the Deathly Hallows* it lies hidden in the golden Snitch left to Harry by Dumbledore in his will. Harry makes use of it in his most difficult trial, to have the company of his parents, Sirius and Lupin as he faces death.

Riddle, Tom Marvolo Voldemort's birth name, which he rejects in favour of the anagram 'I am Lord Voldemort'.

Riddle, Tom, Sr Father of Tom Riddle (Voldemort). He is an aristocratic Muggle living near Little Hangleton who abandons his pregnant wife, Merope, when the Love Potion she cast on him wears off and thereafter never enquires about his son. Voldemort, who despises his Muggle ancestry, murders him, along with his grandparents, and later uses a bone from his father's grave as part of his re-embodiment ritual in *Harry Potter and the Goblet of Fire*.

Robards, Gawain Head of the Auror Office in the Ministry of Magic after Rufus Scrimgeour.

robes Students at Hogwarts wear long black robes during classes, but while playing Quidditch they wear their house colours: green for Slytherin, blue for Ravenclaw, canary yellow for Hufflepuff and scarlet for Gryffindor.

Robins, Demelza A Chaser in Harry's Quidditch team in *Harry Potter and the Half-Blood Prince*.

Ronan One of the herd of centaurs in the Forbidden Forest who generally shares his species' distrust of wizarding folk and other humans but is peaceable. In *Harry Potter and the Order of the Phoenix* he attempts to protect the captured Harry and Hermione on the grounds that they are 'foals'. In *Harry Potter and the Half-Blood Prince* he attends Dumbledore's lakeside funeral with the other centaurs out of deep respect.

Room of Requirement A room in Hogwarts Castle that a person can enter only in time of real need. The entrance is normally invisible from the access corridor. When the room appears, its size and furnishings are determined by the seeker's needs. In *Harry Potter and the Order of the Phoenix* it is used by the DA for training in Defence Against the Dark Arts during Umbridge's inquisitorial rule. Draco employs it in *Harry Potter and the Half-Blood Prince* while setting up a magical means of passage into Hogwarts for Death Eaters. In *Harry Potter and the Deathly Hallows* the room has an important role in the resistance to the hold of the Death Eaters over Hogwarts and in the decisive Battle of Hogwarts. As part of the fulfilment of need, the room provides a new tunnel to the Hog's Head pub in Hogsmeade for secret access to and exit from the school. Others known to use it are Professor Sybill Trelawney, Tom Riddle and the house-elf Dobby.

Rosmerta, Madam The voluptuous and apparently ageless barmaid of the Three Broomsticks in Hogsmeade, who has a pretty face and wears sparkling turquoise high heels. In *Harry*

Potter and the Half-Blood Prince she is put under an Imperius curse by Draco.

Rowle, Thorfinn A blond Death Eater who fought in Hogwarts on the night of Dumbledore's death in *Harry Potter and the Half-Blood Prince*, and who attacked Harry, Ron and Hermione in a café on Tottenham Court Road.

St Mungo's Hospital for Magical Maladies and Injuries The wizarding hospital serving British magical folk, and located in London, but carefully hidden from Muggles. Staff are known as healers and have to be highly qualified in magical arts and knowledge. The hospital was founded by Mungo Bonham, a famous healer of the seventeenth century in the wizarding history of Harry Potter's world. It has specialised departments on various floors, including Artefact Accidents, Creature-Induced Injuries, Magical Bugs and Diseases, Potion and Plant Poisoning, and Spell Damage. The hospital's emblem is a variation of the Red Cross – a magic wand crossed with a bone. St Mungo is a commonly used name for the real St Kentigern, born about AD 518 (also known as Cantigernus (Latin) or Cyndeyrn Garthwys (Welsh)). He was the son of a single mother, abandoned to die by her husband before his birth, and he founded many churches in Britain, including the notable St Kentigern's in Crosthwaite, Keswick. Kentigern has special significance for single parents and children of single parents.

Scabbers Ron's extraordinarily old pet rat, once owned by his brother Percy Weasley. The rat is revealed to be the animal form taken by the Animagus Peter Pettigrew, betrayer of James and Lily Potter, Harry's parents. Upon being discovered, Pettigrew flees and returns to his true master, Voldemort, helping him to be re-embodied and return to power, donating his right hand in the process, literally becoming his right-hand man. Hermione's pet cat, Crookshanks, is suspicious of the rat Scabbers – as part Kneazle the cat can sense unsavoury creatures and people.

Scar, Harry's Harry received his lightning-shaped scar as an infant when Voldemort's killing curse against him failed. Its hurting is a sign of danger, as often as not an indication that Voldemort is working his evil. Harry in fact has access at times to the Dark Lord's mind and emotions, a power of Legilimency conferred when the wound was given. Though the scar remains after Voldemort is gone, he is no longer troubled by it, having lost the fragment of the Dark Lord's soul that lodged within him when the Dark Lord failed to kill him as a baby.

Scotland Northernmost country in Britain. Somewhere in its vast tracts of sparsely populated country Hogwarts School is situated. The Scottish location is revealed, like so much in the stories, by clues. The clearest are the reference in *Harry Potter and the Chamber of Secrets* to the Ford Anglia being spotted over Peebles during its northwards flight, and the note about the location of acromantula in Britain. Newt Scamander's *Fantastic Beasts & Where to Find Them* informs its reader: 'Rumours that a colony of Acromantula has been established in Scotland are unconfirmed.' The book has annotations by Harry and Ron. Harry has crossed out 'unconfirmed' and written 'confirmed by Harry Potter and Ron Weasley' – referring to their adventure in which the car helps their escape from Aragog and his many descendants. Scotland is also the home of J.K. Rowling.

Scrimgeour, Rufus The new Minister for Magic in *Harry Potter and the Half-Blood Prince*, replacing the inept Cornelius Fudge. Formerly he had been Head of Aurors at the Ministry of Magic and has fought Dark Wizards most of his life. In his appearance he gives the appearance of a lion, with his mane of tawny hair. He wears iron-rimmed spectacles and is alert and tough-minded, in contrast to the prevaricating Fudge. From the start there is a palpable tension between himself and Dumbledore, which is inherited by Harry, whom Scrimgeour sees as 'Dumbledore's man, through and through'. The Minister is murdered by Voldemort's Death Eaters when the Ministry of Magic comes under his control. 'Scrymgeour' is an old Scottish name; there is a Scrymgeour Building at the University of Dundee.

Secrecy Sensor A device used by Filch in *Harry Potter and the Order of the Phoenix* to detect dark objects hidden on a person.

Secret-Keeper Someone who, as a result of the use of the Fidelius Charm (from the Latin *fidelis*, meaning 'faithful' or 'loyal'), allows secret information to be hidden in his or her soul. That information cannot then be obtained unless the Secret-Keeper decides to reveal it. Harry's parents originally chose Sirius to be their Secret-Keeper, the charm hiding them from Voldemort. Sirius then persuaded them to use their mutual friend Peter Pettigrew instead as their Secret-Keeper, but Pettigrew betrayed them to the Dark Lord and framed Sirius for their murder. In *Harry Potter and the Order of the Phoenix*, Dumbledore is used as a Secret-Keeper to hide the whereabouts of 12 Grimmauld Place, the location of the head-quarters of the Order of the Phoenix.

secret passageways Hogwarts has many leading out of the castle, all seven known to Fred and George Weasley, though Filch knows only of four. One starts outside the castle buildings, at the Whomping Willow. Another begins at the statue of the one-eyed witch halfway along the third-floor corridor. When they become known after Hogwarts comes under the control of Death Eaters, a new passageway is formed from the Room of Requirement to the Hog's Head pub in Hogsmeade.

Seeker An important team position in the game of Quidditch. The player's sole job is to find a tiny winged ball called the Golden Snitch. The Seeker has to be light, daring and agile, in order to catch the elusive Snitch. Because of his rare talent, Harry, unusually, is chosen as Seeker for the Gryffindor house in his first year at Hogwarts.

Shacklebolt, Kingsley An Auror and member of the restored Order of the Phoenix. In *Harry Potter and the Half-Blood Prince* he is made secretary of the Muggle Prime Minister's Outer Office to protect him from Voldemort. In *Harry Potter and the Deathly Hallows* he plays an important part in the resistance to Voldemort after the Ministry of Magic falls to him.

Shell Cottage In *Harry Potter and the Deathly Hallows*, an isolated coastal cottage near Tinworth, probably in England's West Country.

It is the home of Bill and Fleur Weasley after their wedding, forming a refuge for Harry, Hermione, Ron and others on the run from Voldemort's forces.

Shrieking Shack, the Located at Hogsmeade and wrongly considered to be one of the most haunted places in Britain. In fact, its reputation arose from Lupin's howls as he was voluntarily constrained there as a schoolboy at full moon during his werewolf periods. It lies up a slope past the Three Broomsticks pub a small distance above the remainder of the village. Its windows are boarded up and its garden wild. Even the Hogwarts ghosts avoid it. A secret tunnel links it to a hidden entrance at the foot of the Whomping Willow. In *Harry Potter and the Deathly Hallows* it is briefly used by Voldemort as Hogwarts is besieged by his forces.

Shunpike, Stan Youthful conductor of the Knight Bus in *Harry Potter and the Prisoner of Azkaban*, whom Harry discovers has been unjustly imprisoned by the Ministry of Magic during Voldemort's new reign of terror in *Harry Potter and the Half-Blood Prince*. This is on suspicion of being involved with Death Eaters. Stan lives in Clapham, London, an area famous for the expression 'man in the Clapham Omnibus' – i.e. the 'man in the street' or the ordinary person. He is named after the author's maternal grandfather, Stan Volant, who lived in Tufnell Park, north London. Stan is one of those who try to catch Harry as he escapes from Privet Drive in *Harry Potter and the Deathly Hallows*, but it is probable that he is under the Imperius curse, used widely at that time by Death Eaters. It is because Harry avoids killing Stan that he gives himself away to the pursuing Death Eaters.

Skeeter, Rita In *Harry Potter and the Deathly Hallows*, author of *The Life and Lies of Albus Dumbledore*. She is the worst kind of tabloid journalist, one who invents news stories and twists facts for effect and ratings. She usually writes for the *Daily Prophet*, a paper that frequently attacks Harry with distorted information. She is an unregistered Animagus who uses her animal form, that of a beetle, to 'bug' the conversations of her victims. Her surname, Skeeter, may allude to a slang term for 'mosquito', implying her blood-sucking character. The rhyming of her names might suggest the frenzied speed of media activity.

Slug Club *See* Horace Slughorn.

Slughorn, Horace Former teacher at Hogwarts who in *Harry Potter and the Half-Blood Prince* comes out of retirement at Dumbledore's request to replace Snape in teaching Potions, Snape having taken on Defence Against the Dark Arts classes. He revives the 'Slug Club,' to which talented students or those with good connections are invited. Harry manages with great difficulty to extract from him his memory of the young Tom Riddle (Voldemort), who, as a student, asked Slughorn to explain about Horcruxes. Slughorn bitterly regretted divulging that information to Riddle, especially as it was a subject banned at the school as a gross evil. Slughorn is immensely fat, and bald, the final touch of his large moustache making him look a little like a walrus. He is so short his feet do not touch the ground while he is sitting.

Slytherin, Salazar One of the four ancient founders of Hogwarts, who created the Chamber of Secrets, which features in *Harry Potter and the Chamber of Secrets*. Slytherin house is named after him. In the Chamber is a vast effigy of him, 'ancient and monkey-like, with a long thin beard that fell almost to the bottom of his sweeping robes'. Dumbledore believed that the qualities Slytherin sought in his students were cunning, ambition and purity of blood. An increasing emphasis on blood purity eventually led to a schism between Slytherin and the other founders, who saw purity as an expression of wholeness of character, not blood and status, an ideal embodied in the ethos of the school. This ideal of wholeness encompassed resourcefulness, determination and ambition, and even a certain disregard for school rules, qualities prized in Slytherin house. It is quite likely that Voldemort, the 'heir of Slytherin', pushed the ideology of the pure-blood further than the Hogwarts founder, resorting to terror and murder for a final solution to mixed blood among students. Slytherin is represented by a silver serpent on a green background, and the name is a play on 'slithering', the movement of a snake. His first name may be borrowed from António de Oliveira Salazar, a Portuguese dictator from 1932 to 1968.

Slytherin house One of four houses at Hogwarts. This one was named after Salazar Slytherin, one of the four founders of the school. The house symbol is a silver snake, its colour is green, and its resident ghost is the Bloody Baron. Qualities valued by the house include resourcefulness, cunning and ambition. Its head is Professor Severus Snape, until he apparently defects to Voldemort in *Harry Potter and the Half-Blood Prince*. While it has a reputation for producing wicked wizards, the house of Slytherin itself is not evil, but part of the school's vision for inclusive wholeness. Harry himself has some qualities favoured by Slytherin, and is a Parselmouth (a very rare ability associated with Salazar Slytherin, and explicable by the fact that Harry carries a fragment of Voldemort's soul). Wizards such as Nigellus Black, a former headmaster, and Horace Slughorn have been Slytherins and have repudiated the Dark Arts. The same is true of Severus Snape, even though he makes limited use of the Dark Arts for the sake of his cover.

Smith, Hepzibah An ancient and wealthy witch who has the misfortune to buy Salazar Slytherin's locket from Caractacus Burke. She is murdered by Voldemort for the locket, who caused her house-elf, Hokey, to appear guilty of poisoning her.

Smith, Zacharias A pupil from Hufflepuff house in *Harry Potter and the Order of the Phoenix* who scoffed at Harry for wanting to teach Dumbledore's Army the elements of the Disarming Spell.

Snape, Severus Hogwarts' Potions master, he is head of Slytherin house during Harry's first six years of Hogwarts and, from the first, is hostile to Harry. He sees the boy as the personification of his father, James, whom he hated. This is partly because James had saved his life, and therefore put him under his debt, and partly through envy – he secretly loved Lily Potter. His unpleasant character is reflected in his unsavoury appearance. His long and straight black hair is permanently greasy and his skin is sallow. His frame under his teaching robes is thin. Though his knowledge of Potions is outstanding, he is a bully in the classroom, intimidating those he despises, such as Harry and Neville Longbottom. Even the brilliant Hermione is put down, seemingly because her parents are Muggles. Snape is one of the most complex characters in children's literature. This is because appearances in the stories are often deceptive, as Snape is a double agent, relaying information both to Dumbledore and Voldemort, and brilliantly preserving his cover. He plays a particularly dominant role in the events covered in the last two books, the title of book six explicitly referring to his chosen nickname while a schoolboy – 'the half-blood Prince'. In *Harry Potter and the Deathly Hallows* Snape is appointed headmaster of Hogwarts by Voldemort's regime, a mark of the Dark Lord's trust in him. This allows him secretly to lessen the impact of the sway of Death Eaters on the school. J.K. Rowling commented about him in an interview given after the publication of the last book: 'a very flawed hero. An anti-hero, perhaps. He is not a particularly likeable man in many ways. He remains rather cruel, a bully, riddled with bitterness and insecurity – and yet he loved, and showed loyalty to that love and, ultimately, laid down his life because of it. That's pretty heroic!'

Snape, Tobias Muggle father of Severus Snape, and husband of the witch Eileen Prince. He was hot-tempered and bullying. Severus told Lily Potter (née Evans) about the discord at home when they were childhood friends.

Snatchers In *Harry Potter and the Deathly Hallows*, roaming gangs who earn rewards by snatching wizards who are considered blood-traitors or Mudbloods (those born of Muggle parents).

Snitch, golden A magical ball used in the game of Quidditch, which is golden with silver wings. It is bewitched to make it as difficult as possible for Seekers to catch, and to remember the touch of the Seeker who catches it. Its capture usually determines the game, because of the large number of points given. In *Harry Potter and the Deathly Hallows* Dumbledore leaves Harry in his will the Snitch he caught in his first Quidditch match. The Snitch bequeathed to Harry is enchanted to open as he faces death, remembering his touch. Inside the Snitch is the Resurrection Stone.

Sorting Hat Upon arrival at Hogwarts, new students take it in turn to put on the ancient and grubby hat, which tells them which house has been chosen for them. Harry is told his house would be Gryffindor, but the hat seemed ambivalent, making him fear he should have been put in Slytherin. The hat is old, frayed and contains a patch. A rip near the brim functions as mouth for its voice. The hat features in *Harry Potter and the Chamber of Secrets*, carrying the silver sword of Godric Gryffindor in answer to Harry's cry for help during the attack of the Basilisk. It also appears in *Harry Potter and the Deathly Hallows*, when Voldemort's attempt to torture Neville goes wrong and instead the hat supplies him with the sword of Gryffindor, allowing him to kill Nagini.

spells There is no hard and fast distinction between spells, charms and curses in the world of Harry Potter, but J.K. Rowling revealed her working theory on her official website. 'Spell' is the generic term for a display of magic. A 'charm' merely adds to or changes an object's properties in some way, without substantially altering them. (Transforming a boy into a pig would be a spell, whereas a charm might make his legs dance erratically, as in the *Tarantallegra* charm.) A curse indicates the worst types of dark magic – *see* Unforgivable Curses.

S.P.E.W. A Society for the Protection of Elvish Welfare, set up by Hermione in *Harry Potter and the Goblet of Fire* when she found out the appalling conditions under which house-elves such as Dobby and Winky served, even at Hogwarts.

spies and double agents For many years the ex-Death Eater Snape is trusted by Dumbledore as a double agent, pretending to serve Voldemort. Voldemort meanwhile trusts Snape as his reliable servant. In *Harry Potter and the Half-Blood Prince* Snape kills Dumbledore with the killing curse by prearrangement. Remus

Lupin acts as a spy for Dumbledore, on a dangerous mission spying among the werewolves. Peter Pettigrew spies for Voldemort for a period before murdering Harry's parents.

Spinner's End An area of terraced streets in an unnamed, probably northern, manufacturing town in England that had most likely fallen into decline as its industry dwindled. A mill chimney dominates the neighbourhood. Spinner's End is the home of Severus Snape, in which he lives outside of term time at Hogwarts. In *Harry Potter and the Half-Blood Prince* Narcissa Malfoy visits Snape's home, accompanied by her sister Bellatrix Lestrange, to ask him to help Draco. Lily Evans (the future Lily Potter) and her sister Petunia (see Petunia Dursley) lived in a better-appointed area of the town as children, where Lily and Severus were friends.

Spinnet, Alicia One of the three Chasers in the Gryffindor Quidditch team at Hogwarts in Harry's first year. Alicia is two years above Harry.

Sprout, Pomona Professor who teaches Herbology at Hogwarts in the Greenhouses beside the castle. Her cultivation of Mandrakes provides an essential remedy for petrification after Hermione and others see a reflection of the deadly Basilisk in *Harry Potter and the Chamber of Secrets*. Her first name, Pomona, comes from the Roman goddess of fruit and apple trees.

Squib A child of wizarding parents who has no magical ability. Argus Filch and Arabella Figg, a neighbour of the Dursleys, are squibs. Squibs are rare in the wizarding world.

staff room at Hogwarts A long room with panelled walls that is furnished with ill-matched old chairs. It contains an old wardrobe in which the teachers keep spare robes. When the wardrobe is inhabited by a Boggart, Professor Lupin takes the opportunity to use it for a lesson, bringing his Defence Against the Dark Arts class to the staff room.

Statute of Secrecy *See* International Statute of Wizarding Secrecy.

Stupefy A spell to stun a person, stupefying him or her. It is used frequently by Harry and others in the stories, for example, in the battle with Death Eaters in the Department of Mysteries in *Harry Potter and the Order of the Phoenix*. In the same volume Professor McGonagall is hit by no less than four stunning spells, on the orders of Dolores Umbridge, requiring the professor to be taken to St Mungo's Hospital.

subjects at Hogwarts Those on offer include Arithmancy, Astronomy, the Care of Magical Creatures, Charms, Defence Against the Dark Arts, Divination, Herbology, History of Magic, Muggle Studies, Potions, the Study of Ancient Runes and Transfiguration.

sword of Gryffindor A magical sword made with goblin skill for one of the founders of Hogwarts, Godric Gryffindor, whose name is engraved just below the hilt. It is silver, with a ruby-encrusted handle. In *Harry Potter and the Chamber of Secrets* it is given to Harry in the nick of time from the Sorting Hat, enabling him to kill the huge Basilisk. In the process it is covered with the snake's venom, which has the property of destroying Horcruxes, demonstrated in Harry's removal of the power of Tom Riddle's diary using a detached fang. In *Harry Potter and the Deathly Hallows*, recovery of the sword is vital to Harry's task of hunting down and destroying the remaining Horcruxes. In the same book the Sorting Hat once again produces the sword, this time for Neville, enabling him to destroy Nagini, and thus the single remaining Horcrux.

The Tales of Beedle the Bard A book of fairy stories well known to wizarding children. In *Harry Potter and the Deathly Hallows* a copy of the book is left to Hermione in Dumbledore's will. It includes the story 'The Tale of Three Brothers', which turns out to be the key to understanding the Deathly Hallows. As a story of an attempt to outwit the figure of Death it owes something to Chaucer's *The Pardener's Tale*, from his *The Canterbury Tales*, a reference suggested by J.K. Rowling in an interview. Other stories in Beedle's book include 'The Fountain of Fair Fortune', 'The Wizard and the Hopping Pot' and 'Babbitty Rabbitty and her Cackling Stump'.

Tarantallegra A dancing spell that causes legs to become uncoordinated and to flay crazily.

Thestrals Winged horses that nevertheless are able physically to pull carriages from Hogsmeade station to Hogwarts and to carry people. They are invisible to all except those who have witnessed death, such as Harry (who saw Voldemort slay Cedric Diggory with the killing curse), Neville Longbottom and Luna Lovegood. Thestral wings are vast, and even those who ride them but cannot see them can feel their glossy heads and silken manes.

Thomas, Dean A close friend of Seamus Finnigan, in Harry's year at Hogwarts. As he is from a Muggle family, Dean knows soccer better than Quidditch, calling for a Red Card at one point during a Quidditch match. He shares a room with Harry, Ron, Neville and Seamus in the boy's dormitory area of the Gryffindor Tower. He is courageous and loyal to Harry. Professor Lupin is his favourite teacher, and he is a stalwart member of the DA. In *Harry Potter and the Deathly Hallows* he is on the run from Voldemort's men and ends up imprisoned with Harry in Malfoy Manor.

Three Broomsticks, the A popular pub in Hogsmeade, adorned by the curvaceous barmaid Madam Rosmerta, admired by many generations of Hogwarts school boys. Drinks available include mulled mead, hot butterbeer (good for a snowy day) and redcurrant rum.

Time-Turner An hourglass device hung around the neck, allowing the user to go back in time. Professor McGonagall loans one to Hermione in *Harry Potter and the Prisoner of Azkaban* so that she can take extra subjects that clash on the timetable. The Ministry of Magic's entire stock of Time-Turners is destroyed in *Harry Potter and the Order of the Phoenix* during the battle at the Department of Mysteries.

Tom the inn-keeper The landlord and bartender of the Leaky Cauldron, the pub that provides secret access to Diagon Alley. He is bent with age and toothless.

Tonks, Andromeda Nymphadora Tonks's mother, and sister of Bellatrix Lestrange (whom she resembles) and Narcissa Malfoy. When she married Ted Tonks, who was from a Muggle family, she was cut off from the Black family, fanatical about its pure-blood heritage. She is the favourite cousin of Sirius Black. In *Harry Potter and the Deathly Hallows* she brings up the orphaned Teddy, her grandson. It is possible that Andromeda was in Slytherin house during her schooldays at Hogswart. She is one of several characters related to the Black family named after celestial bodies.

Tonks, Nymphadora ('Tonks', 'Dora') Member of the restored Order of the Phoenix, and a metamorphmagus – that is, she has the ability to change her appearance at will. Though her hair is naturally brown, she tends to vary it, for example, to bubble-gum pink. Tonks, who is probably in her early twenties when Harry first encounters her, is an Auror. Sirius is her first cousin once removed, and the shock of losing him affects her metamorphosing. Like Neville, she is accident-prone. She is in love with and later marries the older Remus Lupin, and they have a child, Teddy, to whom Harry becomes godfather. Remus and Tonks are both casualties of the bloody Battle of Hogwarts.

Tonks, Ted Nymphadora Tonks's stout-bellied and fair-haired father, a Muggle-born wizard – refered to as a Mudblood by those wizards who see themselves as superior 'pure-bloods.' His house provides temporary refuge for Harry in *Harry Potter and the Deathly Hallows*. Later, on the run from Voldemort's henchmen, he is murdered by Snatchers. His grandson Teddy Lupin is named in honour of him.

Trace, the A charm that senses any underage magical activity, alerting the Ministry of Magic to it.

Transfiguration A subject taught at Hogwarts by Professor Minerva McGonagall. Animagi perform a rare form of Transfiguration. McGonagall herself could transform into a cat.

Transfiguration Today A journal read by venerable wizards.

Transport in the wizarding world Occasionally wizarding folk use Muggle transport, but there are various magical modes: employing the Floo Network, using a Portkey, Apparating, and flying a broomstick. In *Harry Potter and the Prisoner of Azkaban* Harry and Hermione bring in Buckbeak the Hippogriff for Sirius's escape, and in *Harry Potter and the Philosopher's Stone* Firenze the centaur very unusually allows Harry to ride to safety on his back. Also in *Harry Potter and the Prisoner of Azkaban*, Hermione and Harry use a Time-Turner to travel back in time. A further type of magical travel involves linking up two Vanishing Cabinets in different places, as Draco does in *Harry Potter and the Half-Blood Prince* to smuggle Death Eaters into Hogwarts.

Trelawney, Sybill (Sibyll in US editions) The teacher of Divination at Hogwarts, who is notorious for predicting the death of a student in each new year. She is a descendant of the great seer Cassandra Trelawney, a fact that helped her land her post at Hogwarts. Hermione sees through the nebulous nature of the subject, and rightly assesses Professor Trelawney as something of a fraud. Nevertheless, Trelawney does make some accurate prophecies, including the pivotal prediction concerning Harry and Voldemort. After being dismissed by Dolores Umbridge, she seeks solace in her cooking sherry, but, even then, her fortune-telling with her Tarot pack seems to portend the catastrophic event on the Astronomy Tower. The comic figure of Trelawney satirises the hocus pocus of reading tea leaves, crystal-ball gazing and fortune-telling from cards, while not denying the possibility of true prophecy. Her first name comes from the Sibyls of the classical world, who made predictions.

Trevor Neville Longbottom's pet toad.

triangular rune In *Harry Potter and the Deathly Hallows* a distinctive rune that Harry, Ron and Hermione keep coming across. It denotes the three Deathly Hallows: the Elder Wand, Invisibility Cloak and Resurrection Stone. The rune is made up of a straight vertical line, topped with a circle, with both line and circle enclosed in a triangle.

Triwizard Tournament An international Triwizard Tournament between Hogwarts, Beauxbatons Academy of Magic and Durmstrang Institute. It is an ancient institution, the first being held in AD 1294. The Triwizard Tournament held in *Harry Potter and the Goblet of Fire*, and dominating the plot of that story, is held for the first time in over a century.

Trolls A variety of giant magical creatures borrowed from northern folklore, the most uncouth being mountain trolls (featured in *Harry Potter and the Philosopher's Stone*, where one enters the girls' toilets, trapping Hermione). More intelligent security trolls are engaged to protect students at Hogwarts from Sirius, thought at that time to be a dangerous murderer intent on killing Harry. Draco's minders, Crabbe and Goyle, are examples of humans having troll-like features.

Tutshill Tornados A famous Quidditch team supported by Cho Chang since she was six years old. They wear distinctive 'sky blue robes with a double T in dark blue on the chest and back'. The author grew up in Tutshill, by the Forest of Dean.

Twycross, Wilkie Apparition Instructor for the Ministry of Magic in Harry's sixth year.

Umbridge, Dolores Jane Senior Undersecretary to the Minister of Magic in *Harry Potter and the Order of the Phoenix*, she becomes Defence Against the Dark Arts teacher in Harry's fifth year, and, with Dumbledore's suspension, becomes acting Headteacher and High Inquisitor at Hogwarts. She subscribes to a pure-blood ideology, like the worst Slytherins, and is sadistic, forcing Harry to write his punishment lines into his own flesh, leaving scars. She is willing to use an Unforgivable Curse, belonging to the realm of the Dark Arts. Before teaching at Hogwarts she had ordered Dementors to attack Harry in Little Whinging. Despite the magnitude of her cruelty, she continues to be employed by the Ministry of Magic under Rufus Scrimgeour in *Harry Potter and the Half-Blood Prince*. When she later becomes Senior Undersecretary to the Minister, her first-floor office has Mad-Eye Moody's eye set in her door, to keep watch over her colleagues. She also has the role of overseeing the Muggle-born Registration Commission. Stephen King described Umbridge as a horror: 'The gently smiling Dolores Umbridge, with her girlish voice, toadlike face, and clutching, stubby fingers, is the greatest make-believe villain to come along since Hannibal Lecter . . .'.

Unbreakable Vow A binding magical vow, requiring the wizard or witch who utters it to complete the promised act or die. In *Harry Potter and the Half-Blood Prince* Snape takes this vow at the request of Narcissa Malfoy – the vow in this case is to protect her son Draco and to help him to fulfil his task (which is to kill Dumbledore). Snape fulfils the vow when he uses the killing curse on the headmaster when Draco proves unwilling to do so.

underage magic Magical folk under the age of seventeen (coming of age) are not allowed to use magic outside school. Acts of underage magic, but not the perpetrator, can be detected instantly by the Ministry of Magic. Thus, in *Harry Potter and the Chamber of Secrets*, Harry is blamed for magic done by Dobby the house-elf in the Dursley's house, as it was assumed he had done it. In *Harry Potter and the Order of the Phoenix* Harry is forced to use the magical Patronus Charm, and apparently to break wizarding law, to ward off Dementors attacking his cousin Dudley and himself in an alleyway near Magnolia Crescent.

Unfogging the Future A set Divination textbook for year three at Hogwarts, by Cassandra Vablatsky. This is a guide to elementary methods of fortune-telling – such as crystal balls, palmistry and bird entrails. The author's name is a play upon Madame Helena Blavatsky, the Theosophist (1831–91).

Unforgivable Curses The most powerful and terrifying of the spells belonging to the Dark Arts. Their use, except in the most extreme circumstances, such as war, is so reprehensible that, if the perpetrator is caught, it means a life sentence in Azkaban. To accomplish any of the curses usually requires a directed hatred, inflexible will and great skill. The three Unforgivable Curses are the

Avada Kedavra (the killing curse), the Cruciatus curse, and the Imperius curse.

unicorn A significantly powerful magical creature that looks like a white horse, with a golden mane and a distinctive golden horn on its head. It symbolises innocence. Its hairs and horn are used in magic – a wand, for instance, might contain a unicorn's hair. In *Harry Potter and the Philosopher's Stone* Voldemort, in Quirrell's body, is sustained by the blood of a slain unicorn. Firenze the centaur tells Harry why it is a despicable evil to kill such a creature. Someone who does so will have a half-life, and a cursed one, from then on. One of J.K. Rowling's favourite stories as a child – *The White Horse* by Elizabeth Goudge – concerns a unicorn.

Vance, Emmeline A member of the restored Order of the Phoenix, murdered by Death Eaters very close to 10 Downing Street, the Muggle Prime Minister's official residence.

Vanishing Cabinets In *Harry Potter and the Order of the Phoenix* Fred and George Weasley use such a magical cabinet to make Montague, from Umbridge's Inquisitorial Squad, disappear for a considerable period, after he attempted to take points from Gryffindor house. In *Harry Potter and the Half-Blood Prince* Malfoy repairs a damaged Vanishing Cabinet stored in the Room of Requirement, and then creates a magical pathway by pairing it with a similar cabinet in Borgin and Burkes. This allows him to smuggle Death Eaters into Hogwarts as part of a plot to get rid of Dumbledore.

Vector, Professor She teaches Arithmancy, one of Hermione's favourite subjects, at Hogwarts. 'Vector', appropriately, is a mathematical term.

Veela Women of great beauty with white-gold hair whom men find irresistibly attractive and entrancing. When angry they sprout beaks and scaly wings and might throw balls of fire. They appear in northern and Celtic mythology as the Vila, Willi or Veela, and are related to nymphs – spirits living in trees, meadows, ponds, and clouds. In *Harry Potter and the Goblet of Fire*, at the Quidditch World Cup, the Bulgarian team has as its mascots about a hundred Veela, who dance in the stadium. Fleur Delacour has Veela ancestry.

Veil, The A veiled arch that stands on a dais in a sunken room – the Death Chamber – in the Department of Mysteries in *Harry Potter and the Order of the Phoenix*. Issuing from the other side of this veil Harry and Luna Lovegood are able to hear mysterious voices from beyond death. Sirius is thrown through the veil after being hit by a stunning curse from his cousin, a Death Eater named Bellatrix Lestrange.

Veritaserum A potion lacking colour or smell that forces whoever drinks it to speak the truth.

Voldemort, Lord (Tom Marvolo Riddle, 'He-Who-Must-Not-Be-Named') Most of what we learn about the Dark Lord, implacably intent on Harry's destruction, is via backstory in the seven books. Harry meets him on several occasions, always under threat for his life. Voldemort's constant quest to escape death dominates the stories. The quest means that he destroys his own humanity, the tendency towards bullying and cruelty as a child turning into a ruthless attempt to take over the wizarding world, with the intention of reducing the Muggle population to slaves.

According to Sirius, Voldemort is the most evil wizard who has ever existed. Elsewhere he is spoken of as the most evil that century. Cornelius Fudge, Minister of Magic, calls him 'one of the most powerful wizards of all time'.

Voldemort was born Tom Marvolo Riddle to a Muggle father, also called Tom Riddle, and Merope Gaunt, from an old wizarding family descended from Slytherin. Abandoned by his father, and with his mother's death, he is brought up in a London orphanage. Dumbledore invites him to mid-twentieth-century Hogwarts and attempts to nurture him, but Tom puts all his brilliance into understanding the Dark Arts. With great skill he learns how to fragment his soul, the parts stored in Horcruxes, to guarantee survival after death. He takes the name Lord Voldemort, an anagram of his Riddle name.

He surrounds himself with Death Eaters, one of whom, Snape, overhears a prophecy that makes Voldemort fear that Harry, then an infant, is destined to be his nemesis. His attempt to kill him is thwarted by Lily Potter's love in sacrificing herself to save Harry, which evokes a Deeper Magic that he fails to understand. Voldemort's killing curse backfires, destroying his body, and leaving Harry with a scar on his forehead and a sliver of his soul within him.

It takes Voldemort many years to reconstitute himself. By the time of Harry's first year at Hogwarts he parasitically shares the body of Professor Quirrell and attempts to find the Philosopher's Stone, to gain immortality. At the end of Harry's fourth year he is able to re-embody himself, and immediately tries and fails to kill the boy. He gradually grows in power, regrouping his followers, and eventually taking over the Ministry of Magic and (as he thinks) Hogwarts school, following the death of his great enemy, Dumbledore. Harry's name becomes a symbol of resistance to the Dark Lord. Voldemort's hold over life is gradually removed as Harry and his friends destroy the Horcuxes storing parts of his soul. When Harry willingly sacrifices himself to be rid of the Horcrux he bears for the sake of his friends, Voldemort is effectively beaten. Once Neville has destroyed the final Horcrux, Nagini the snake, the Dark Lord can be destroyed forever.

wands British wizards normally obtained wands from Ollivander's shop in Diagon Alley. Many continental wizards made use of the wandmaker Gregorovitch, until his demise at the hands of Voldemort in *Harry Potter and the Deathly Hallows*. They are normally used when casting spells, though some are accomplished silently. Green light, and sometimes red or gold, issues from the wand in many cases. Wands have a life of their own; as Ollivander states, it is the 'wand that chooses the wizard'. In *Harry Potter and the Deathly Hallows* the Elder Wand flourished by Voldemort works in Harry's favour, as its proper master. Remarkably, Mr Ollivander remembers all the wands he has sold and tells Harry that the wand belonging to Voldemort is the twin of the one that is suitable for Harry. This matching of the wands proves to be crucial in the duel between Harry and Voldemort in *Harry Potter and the Goblet of*

Fire. Though Voldemort's is made of yew, and Harry's of holly, the wands have a feather from the same phoenix in them – Dumbledore's pet, Fawkes. Wandcraft plays an important part in the plot of *Harry Potter and the Deathly Hallows*, as Voldemort attempts to understand and find the Elder Wand.

Weasley, Arthur Father of Ron and Head of the Misuse of Muggle Artefacts Office at the Ministry of Magic. In *Harry Potter and the Half-Blood Prince* he is promoted by Rufus Scrimgeour. He is, like his children, red-headed, but balding, and wears horn-rimmed spectacles and a long travelling cloak. He has an irrepressible interest in all things to do with Muggles, for example, how aeroplanes stay up in the sky. Muggle ingenuity in getting along without the benefit of magic constantly amazes him. In *Harry Potter and the Order of the Phoenix* Harry saves his life after seeing into Voldemort's mind and thus witnessing a savage attack on him by Nagini the serpent.

Weasley, Bilius Ron's uncle, who died twenty-four hours after seeing a Grim.

Weasley, Bill Brother of Ron who works for Gringotts Bank in Africa as a curse-breaker. In *Harry Potter and the Half-Blood Prince* he is engaged to be married to Fleur Delacour and is horribly disfigured by Greyback in the battle against the Death Eaters at Hogwarts. After his marriage in *Harry Potter and the Deathly Hallows* he and Fleur provide refuge for some of those on the run from Voldemort's forces in their new home, the isolated Shell Cottage.

Weasley, Charlie Second eldest in the Weasley family, he was Seeker and Quidditch Captain for Gryffindor while at Hogwarts. After leaving school the year before Ron, Harry and Hermione started their studies, he worked with dragons in Romania. He helps them smuggle Hagrid's illegal pet dragon Norbert out of the country in *Harry Potter and the Philosopher's Stone*. Later, in *Harry Potter and the Goblet of Fire*, he and his colleagues supply the dragons that are used in the Triwizard Tournament.

Weasley, Fred and George Ron Weasley's older twin brothers, who are two years ahead of him at Hogwarts. They give Harry the Marauder's Map and are constant pranksters. Harry gives them his winnings from his Triwizard Tournament success to start up a business selling jokes and tricks. After leaving Hogwarts in *Harry Potter and the Order of the Phoenix* when it is under Umbridge's tyrannous rule, they set up a joke shop in Diagon Alley, called Weasley's Wizard Wheezes. Fred is an early casualty in the Battle of Hogwarts in *Harry Potter and the Deathly Hallows*, while earlier George is badly wounded helping Harry escape from Privet Drive.

Weasley, Ginevra Molly 'Ginny' Younger sister of Ron, and one year below him at Hogwarts. She worships Harry, but it is not until *Harry Potter and the Half-Blood Prince* that they start going out with each other. Ginny is attractive, with her long red hair and vivid brown eyes, and has a number of boyfriends (not always in succession). She is a highly talented, intelligent and quick-tempered witch, especially appreciated for her skill with the Bat-Bogey Hex, which causes the nasal discharge to turn into an attacking bat. She plays an important part in the plot of *Harry Potter and the Chamber of Secrets*, as Voldemort possesses her through his enchanted schoolboy diary, which is in fact a Horcrux. His aim is to get to Harry through his best friend's sister. Harry rescues her from death and she is restored. In *Harry Potter and the Order of the Phoenix* she is an active member of the DA, and takes part in the battle with the Death Eaters at the Department of Mysteries. In *Harry Potter and the Half-Blood Prince* she is made Chaser in Harry's Quidditch team. She plays a leading role in the resistance of Dumbledore's Army at Hogwarts while Harry is seeking to destroy the Horcruxes with Hermione and Ron. At the end of all the stories she and Harry find happiness together, and through her Harry gains a family at last.

Weasley, Molly Mother of Ron, who has a soft spot for Harry, mothering him, knitting him sweaters for Christmas and inviting him to stay in her crowded household at The Burrow. She is also very fond of Hermione, who is a frequent visitor too. She manages her large family on Arthur Weasley's inadequate wages, the hardships of the Weasleys at Hogwarts frequently mocked by the well-off Draco. When angry she terrifies even her older children, for whom she is often over-protective, and her deepest fear is to find family members dead. This fear is revealed when she attempts to get rid of a Boggart in Grimmauld Place in *Harry Potter and the Order of the Phoenix*. The fear may be based on the fact that her brothers Gideon and Fabian Prewett were killed years before when part of the original Order of the Phoenix. Molly at first disapproves of Bill's engagement to Fleur Delacour in *Harry Potter and the Half-Blood Prince*, but when Fleur sticks by him after his facial disfigurement by Fenrir Greyback her attitude transforms. In *Harry Potter and the Deathly Hallows* Bellatrix Lestrange finds her a formidable opponent, as Molly seeks revenge in the Battle of Hogwarts. She enjoys listening to the Wizarding Wireless Network (the magical equivalent to BBC radio) and uses her wand as a remote control.

Weasley, Percy Ron's self-important and pompous older brother, who is in his final year at Hogwarts when Ron is in his third. He is first a Prefect and then Head Boy, and works for the Ministry of Magic after leaving school, under Mr Barty Crouch Sr. Percy, like all the Weasleys, is in Gryffindor house. He is tall and thin, and wears horn-rimmed glasses to appear grown-up. His girlfriend at school is called Penelope Clearwater. Percy's support for the regime at the Ministry of Magic at the time when Voldemort's return is denied results in his turning his back on his family. In *Harry Potter and the Deathly Hallows* finally Percy realises how wrong he has been and, full of remorse, enthusiastically fights in the Battle of Hogwarts with his brothers and sister.

Weasley, Ron Harry's closest friend at Hogwarts, in the same year and same house, Gryffindor. Like all the Weasleys he has emphatic red hair and freckles. His younger sister, Ginny, his older twin brothers Fred and George and his older brother Percy are also at Hogwarts through much of his studies there. During his time at the school Ron becomes lanky, and has a bickering relationship with Hermione that develops into love. Long before romance blossoms,

Ron loyally defends Hermione, when, for instance, Snape bullies her in a lesson in *Harry Potter and the Prisoner of Azkaban*. His home is The Burrow, near Ottery St Catchpole. Being brought up in a wizarding household, with no experience of non-magical people, he brings an amusing outside perspective on Muggles and their ways. In *Harry Potter and the Philosopher's Stone* he prods Dean Thomas's poster of West Ham soccer team, attempting to make the players move. A girlfriend, Lavender Brown, to his embarrassment, calls him 'Won-Won'. Professor Slughorn, who frequently gets names wrong, at one time in *Harry Potter and the Half-Blood Prince* calls him Rupert (the first name of the actor who plays Ron in the movies). Ron is named after Ronald Ridley, an old family friend of the Rowlings (see the dedication of *Harry Potter and the Goblet of Fire*). In *Harry Potter and the Deathly Hallows* Ron loyally goes off with Harry and Hermione in search of the Horcruxes, but abandons them for a while in disillusionment. Wracked with remorse, he tracks his friends down and makes amends by saving Harry's life. Often lacking confidence, he is full of unexpected abilities, such as his flair for mimicking voices and sounds, which proves indispensable in the fight of the three for survival in their long and hazardous task of defeating Voldemort.

Weasley ghoul A spirit haunting The Burrow that is treated almost like one of the family. In *Harry Potter and the Deathly Hallows* Ron has it transformed so that it looks like him covered in revolting pustules, to lead any Death Eaters searching the house to believe that he is still there, ill in bed and to be avoided, while all the time he is on the quest with Harry and Hermione to destroy the Horcruxes.

Weasleys' Wizard Wheezes Fred and George Weasley's inimitable joke shop in Diagon Alley, started up with money donated by Harry.

weather Hogwarts experiences northern weather, located as it is in Scotland. The changes in weather include warm sunshine, beating rain, frost, snow, wind and thunderstorms. In *Harry Potter and the Prisoner of Azkaban*, the storm during a Quidditch match particularly makes its presence felt.

Weird Sisters, the A popular music group among the wizarding community, whose instruments include guitars, drums, lute, cello and bagpipes.

werewolf In folklore, a person who turns at times into a wolf (possibly from early English wer, man). There are a number of such changelings in the stories, including Remus Lupin and Fenrir Greyback. A bite from a werewolf can turn the victim into one, as happened with Lupin.

Whomping Willow A large and magical tree between Hogwarts Castle and the Forbidden Forest that strikes at anything that comes too close, be it student or broomstick. It was planted while Remus Lupin was a student, and guards the entrance to a secret passageway to the Shrieking Shack at Hogsmeade. The tree is designed to be stilled by pressing a knot on its trunk – Crookshanks, Hermione's cat, is able to stop its attacks in this way. In *Harry Potter and the Chamber of Secrets*, Ron's flying Ford Anglia is battered by the Willow, and in *Harry Potter and the Prisoner of Azkaban* – Harry's third year at Hogwarts – Ron is dragged under the tree to the passageway by Sirius in his dog form and Harry and Hermione follow with difficulty to rescue him. Earlier in that same year the Willow had destroyed Harry's beloved Nimbus Two Thousand sporting broomstick. When in *Harry Potter and the Deathly Hallows* Harry, Ron and Hermione enter the passageway under the Willow, they find it a tight fit, having grown so much since the third year.

Winky A house-elf, originally belonging to the family of Barty Crouch Sr. She then lives at Hogwarts, cared for by Dobby.

wizarding media The main media are the *Daily Prophet*, a newspaper, *The Quibbler*, an eccentric magazine edited by the father of Luna Lovegood, and the Wizarding Wireless Network (WWN) – a radio station. Molly Weasley's favourite singer, Celestine Warbeck, broadcasts on wizarding radio. One of her songs is 'A Cauldron Full of Hot, Strong Love'. The journalist Rita Skeeter often writes for the *Daily Prophet*, which conducts a campaign against Harry, orchestrated by the Ministry of Magic, to discredit his story of Voldemort's return. In *Harry Potter and the Deathly Hallows* both the *Daily Prophet* and *The Quibbler* come under the control of Voldemort's regime.

wizarding population The population of wizards in the world seems to be quite small. In the UK and the Republic of Ireland the number of wizards and witches attending Hogwarts between the ages of eleven and seventeen at any time is likely to be between 600 and 1,000 – a good indication of the small size of the population in the British Isles. On continental Europe, only the wizarding schools of Durmstrang and Beauxbatons are mentioned – again indicating a tiny population for the remainder of Europe.

Wizengamot The Wizarding supreme court of law, the Chief Warlock of which is Albus Dumbledore. In *Harry Potter and the Order of the Phoenix*, Harry is tried, allegedly for violating laws that restrict underage sorcery, after using magic outside Hogwarts to defend himself and his Muggle cousin Dudley Dursley from an attack by Dementors sent by Dolores Umbridge.

Wood, Oliver Intense Captain and Keeper of the Gryffindor Quidditch team until leaving Hogwarts at the end of Harry's third year. In *Harry Potter and the Goblet of Fire* Wood tells Harry that he has been taken on by the reserve team of Puddlemere United, a famous Quidditch team that numbers Albus Dumbledore among its fans.

Wormtail Nickname of Peter Pettigrew, referring to the form he could take as an Animagus – a rat.

Worple, Eldred An ex-student of Horace Slughorn who appears at the Slug Club in *Harry Potter and the Half-Blood Prince* with his friend, the vampire Sanguini. He is author of *Blood Brothers: My Life Amongst the Vampires*. He presses Harry to allow him to write his biography.

Yaxley A tall, blunt-faced Death Eater who in *Harry Potter and the Deathly Hallows* plays a prominent part in the fall of the Ministry of Magic to Voldemort's forces, putting an Imperius curse upon Pius Thicknesse so that he becomes a puppet Minister of Magic. He brings news to Voldermort of when Harry plans to leave Privet Drive.

Zonko's Wizarding joke shop, conveniently located in Hogsmeade. Its wares include Stink Pellets, Dungbombs, Hiccough Sweets, Frog Spawn Soap and Nose-Biting Teacups.

PART TWO

J.K. Rowling and the World of Harry Potter

FOUR

A Life

Joanne Rowling, appropriately for a very humorous writer who likes to store up funny or odd names, was born by Chipping Sodbury, in Yate Cottage Hospital, in 1965, a short broomstick's flight from Bristol, England. Her parents, Peter and Anne Rowling, were originally Londoners who had met on a train journey from King's Cross station to Arbroath in Scotland. (Harry sets off from King's Cross on the Hogwart's Express for his School of Wizardry, which is located somewhere in Scotland.) J.K. Rowling considers that she owes her existence to the fact that her father only just managed to catch that train! When her parents met they were both eighteen. Jo's future father was travelling to join the Royal Navy and her mother-to-be was on her way to enter the WRENs (the woman's division of the Royal Navy). On the journey Anne Volant had been cold and Peter Rowling invited her to share his coat. They married just a year later. Anne Volant was half-French and half-Scottish, and came from the Tufnell Park area of London. Peter Rowling was also a Londoner.

After their very brief flirtation with the Navy, Peter and Anne Rowling moved to near Bristol, where Peter worked at a Rolls-Royce aircraft engine plant and Anne later became a school laboratory technician. Anne was just twenty when Jo was born on 31 July 1965 (Harry Potter shares the birthday). In family photographs Jo appears as a plump, Rubinesque baby. In fact, Jo Rowling comments that she fits the description of Dudley Dursley as an infant in *Harry Potter and the Philosopher's Stone*. There he appears in photographs as 'what looked like a large pink beach ball wearing different-coloured bobble hats'.

She was one of two sisters, the younger, Dianne ('Di'), born nearly two years later on 28 June 1967. Jo vividly remembers the day. She was in the kitchen, occupied with playdough. Her mother was in bed and her father dashing in and out of the bedroom. Later her father took her hand and led her into her mother, who now had beside her a naked baby with a shock of dark hair. While some details of this mental picture may have come later, she believes that the essence was accurate. Rowling's smaller sister provided a captive audience for her early attempts at storytelling. She played to this audience. Both desired rabbits badly, so rabbits featured in the tales. Sometimes Jo had to sit on her sister to keep her listening. But usually Di stayed voluntarily, entranced by a story Jo was telling. There were many times when the stories transfigured into extensive plays in which the two of them featured as main characters. The older sister bossily insisted on directing them, and Dianne acquiesced in return for star roles.

In one story Dianne Rowling heard Jo tell how she tumbled down a rabbit hole, where a kind rabbit family gave her strawberries to eat. In the first story Jo remembered recording, around the age of five or six, the rabbit concerned was given the plain and gender-neutral name 'Rabbit'. His (or her) adventures were colourful enough, however. Rabbit was afflicted by measles, and friends began visiting, the most memorable being Miss Bee, a giant-sized insect. Creating Rabbit and Miss Bee made Jo want to become a writer, though she disclosed her wish to few, in case people discouraged her. Perhaps in memory of those early days, there is a story 'Babbitty Rabbitty and her Cackling Stump' in *The Tales of Beedle the Bard*, the children's book left to Hermione by Dumbledore in *Harry Potter and the Deathly Hallows*.

Dianne's hair was dark, almost black, with dark brown eyes like her mother's, and clear skin – in contrast to Jo's red hair, pale complexion, freckles and blue eyes. In the older sister's view, Dianne was prettier, while she was regarded as the 'bright one'. The contrast between the two, and more significantly others' attitude to it, contributed significantly, Rowling believes, to the constant bickering between them during their childhood. She remembers: 'We spent about three quarters of our childhood fighting like a pair of wildcats imprisoned together in a very small cage.' One vestige of their battles is a scar above Dianne's eyebrow. Jo had thrown a battery at her sister, expecting her to duck. This explanation had not convinced her furious mother. Though only one character in the stories, Gilderoy Lockhart, is directly based upon an actual person, Jo said in an interview that Hermione Granger's character is partly a combination of herself and her sister Dianne. She has also spoken of Hermione as a caricature of herself. When they were not fighting Jo and her sister were the best of friends, rather like Ron and Hermione in the Harry Potter stories.

In her early years Jo Rowling lived first in Yate, near Chipping Sodbury and a few miles from Bristol, and then, when she was four, in the village of Winterbourne, even nearer the city. Winterbourne's name is believed to derive from a brook or burn called Bradley Brook, which would dry up during the summer. It shared a parish with Watleys End, and its history may go back several centuries BC, in the form of an ancient barrow or round mound. In Yate they lived in a bungalow, but at Winterbourne the family lived in a semi-detached house. This house, unlike the bungalow, had stairs, which, with Jo's fertile imagination, soon became a steep cliff. She and her sister had a favourite game in which one would dangle from the cliff top (i.e. the top stair) clutching the hand of the other and begging her not to let go. All manner of bribe or blackmail would be used without effect, for inevitably the game would end with a death-fall. The two of them never failed to be amused by the game.

In Winterbourne children in the street formed a gang, which included Jo and Dianne, and a sister and brother surnamed Potter. Sensitive to words even then, Jo liked that surname. She was not too impressed with her own, which led to jokes about rolling pins and other familiar associations. All Jo remembers of the boy is that he rode a 'Chopper' bicycle, like most boys in the 1970s, and on one occasion threw a stone at her sister – in response to which the outraged older girl hit him with a plastic sword. When Jo became famous, the brother claimed to the media that he was the original of Harry and that he and Jo would dress up as wizards, a story denied by Rowling. Her schooldays at Winterbourne were marked by a relaxed classroom in which she enjoyed an abundance of drawing, pottery making and story writing.

TUTSHILL AND THE WYE VALLEY

More significant was her move to Tutshill, a small village near Chepstow, on the edge of the ancient Forest of Dean, a forest that features in *Harry Potter and the Deathly Hallows* as the place where Snape's Patronus of a doe leads Harry to the sword of Gryffindor. It was a place of happy childhood memories for Hermione. Chepstow is just across the Severn estuary from Bristol, across the suspension bridge. The move marked the fulfilment of her parents' dream of living out of the city and in the countryside. Jo was now nine, and she and her sister were free to explore the meadows extending behind her house, leading to ancient Offa's Dyke and the nearby River Wye beyond. Woodlands bordering those fields were mysterious to the children who played in them, such as her neighbour Peter Francis. Her house was beside the Anglican church of St Luke's, overlooking its graveyard. Close by the village, and visible from the fields as they slope down to the river, is a ruined castle perched on cliffs. Chepstow, to which the imposing castle belongs, is just in Wales, the river marking the border. The view over to the castle is a short walk from Church Cottage, where Jo lived. Though there is no evidence that they are direct sources, the castle ruins look as Hogwarts Castle appears to Muggles, non-magical folk, and the woodlands beside the river evoke the fringes of the Forbidden Forest. Though little of her invention is taken literally from people and places she has known, Jo Rowling does admit that Chepstow 'is a town dominated by a castle on a cliff, which might explain a lot'. Some playing fields near the primary school she attended reflected the seasons as boys in school colours arrived to play soccer, hockey, rugby and cricket. Add fantasy, and you could have Quidditch. To complete the picture, a dragon-shaped tree grows beside the cottage – a magical environment for an imaginative child.

Revd Peter Francis today makes no claim on the lore of Jo Rowling's childhood. He has little recollection of her, even though his mother and Jo's were good friends. By sheer coincidence, however, he has a scar over his eye, had a den under his stairs, and took a train to Paddington to attend boarding school. If, however,

Harry Potter ended up as an Anglican priest, he would begin to think that that was more than coincidence!

Jo's happiness in her new surroundings was clouded somewhat by her fervent dislike of her new school. Compared to her previous school she found it tiny and locked back in time, full of vestiges of the past; the desks, for instance, had roll-tops and inkwells for the old dip pens. One of her new teachers, a Mrs Sylvia Morgan, figures large in her early memories of the school, and this, she thinks, may have contributed a little to the characterisation of Severus Snape, the bullying Potions teacher at Hogwarts. Mrs Morgan terrified her from the very beginning. A mannerism of hers was to mutter *twp* (Welsh slang for 'stupid') when something annoyed her. On the first morning Jo was given an arithmetic test. She worked conscientiously at the answers, trying her very best, but succeeded in obtaining merely half a mark out of ten. The problem was that this was her first experience of fractions. As a result Mrs Morgan placed her in a row of desks at the side of the classroom that she eventually worked out was for dull pupils – it was the 'stupid' row. The teacher, she realised, sat the children in the class according to how bright she considered them to be. Like the sheep and the goats in the biblical parable, the cleverest were located on one side of the classroom and the dullest on the other, left and right. At first, Jo was located the furthest to her teacher's right, nearest to the playground, but by the end of that year she had graduated to the second row from the left. There was no joy in the move, however. In the process she was forced to exchange seats with her best friend and to become 'clever' but no longer popular. One consolation was that a boy who had previously occupied her desk had succeeded, after working away through many lessons, in digging out a small hole in the desktop with the sharp pin of his geometry compass. Jo took up where he had left off. By the time she moved on from that classroom the hole was big enough for her to waggle her thumb through it.

As well as the gloom of the school, Jo was saddened by the death of her paternal grandmother Kathleen at the time of the move, from whom later she took her middle name Kathleen, to provide the 'K.' in J.K. when she needed an extra initial as her authorial name. (Her agent, Christopher Little, thought that 'J.K.' would deter boy readers less than 'Joanne'.) Indeed, her first experience of death and loss may have coloured her experience of the new school. She does place a tribute to the village in the Harry Potter world, in the form of a Quidditch team, the Tutshill Tornadoes, who wear 'sky blue robes with a double T in dark blue on the chest and back'.

WYEDEAN SCHOOL

Better times lay ahead for Jo when the time came to move up to the secondary school near the village (corresponding to the age when Harry Potter started at Hogwarts School of Witchcraft and Wizardry). Fears raised by a rumour about Wyedean Comprehensive School proved unfounded – this was the very same rumour Harry's cousin Dudley Dursley mockingly tells him when Harry was still expecting to go to his local secondary school:

> 'They stuff people's heads down the toilet the first day at Stonewall,' he told Harry. 'Want to come upstairs and practise?'
> 'No, thanks,' said Harry. 'The poor toilet's never had anything as horrible as your head down it – it might be sick.' Then he ran, before Dudley could work out what he'd said.

Jo Rowling describes the daunting obstacles facing the raw new pupil at Wyedean: 'I was quiet, freckly, short-sighted and rubbish at sports' – at one stage she broke her arm playing netball, a most unusual event. She was further hampered by the fact that her favourite subject was English. That subject had no rival for her, but she was also attracted to languages. She found friends at the new school, studious and quiet pupils like her, 'swots'. At lunch times she would recount to them long stories, an episode at a time. The stories included them as heroes, involving deeds of great daring that they would never have accomplished in real life, as thinkers not doers. Rowling remembers, however, once being forced into a scrap with the 'toughest girl' in her year. The girl started hitting her, forcing Jo either to retaliate or to 'lie down and play dead'. Jo achieved some fame for a few days as the bully failed to knock her flat. What the others did not realise was that Jo's ability to stand up to her was thanks to her locker, which was right behind her and held her up.

Her English teacher, Lucy Shepherd, was to have a formative power over Jo Rowling. Like Miss Honey, in Roald Dahl's story *Matilda*, she provided hope in an often troubled school, but without the sweetness. She was an inspirational but tough teacher, who inculcated in Jo the need for structure, pacing and other qualities in her writing. The strict and confident woman provided something of a model for the young pupil, and after Jo left school she kept in touch with her. She inspired trust in the budding writer and Jo was able to confide in her, but even so she did not reveal her ambitions to be a writer. When Lucy Shepherd wrote to J.K. Rowling after the publication of *Harry Potter and the Philosopher's Stone* via her publisher, commenting on the story, this meant a great deal to her, especially as her former English teacher *liked* the book.

Jo's short-sightedness at school influenced her decision to give her hero spectacles in the Hogwarts stories. (It is said that wearing glasses is far less of a stigma for children than it used to be, thanks to Harry.) A turning point for her was when she started to wear contact lenses, which lessened her fear of being hit in the face. She remembers becoming more outgoing as she got older. During her teen years she wrote many stories, but showed friends only the amusing ones, which included them all in transparent guises. In her final year at Wyedean she was made Head Girl – a senior pupil honoured annually for exceptional abilities and maturity, chosen at Wyedean by both staff and students. She can recall only two responsibilities as a result of this. One was to take a distinguished woman around the annual school fair. Another was to give an Assembly before the whole school. (Assembly was a daily event that took place before classes began, as part of the state provision for religious and moral education.) Jo decided to play a vinyl record to reduce the time that she would have to speak. The record, however, was scratched, resulting in a line of the song repeating itself until the Deputy Headmistress had the presence of mind to kick the record player.

During her schooling at Wyedean Jo developed a special friendship with a fellow pupil, Sean Harris. Affectionately she dedicated her second book, *Harry Potter and the Chamber of Secrets*, to him. The flying Ford Anglia in that story is based on a car he owned. Among Jo's group of friends he passed his driving test before anyone else. His white and turquoise car came to mean a new freedom for Jo. No longer did she have to ask her father for lifts, a necessary feature of rural life. She was happiest as a teenager heading into the night in Sean Harris's car. It was with Sean that Jo first confided her fervent hope of becoming a writer, and it was he alone who believed that she would succeed in her ambition. His belief was very significant for her at that time.

The event that dominated Jo's memories of her teens was her mother developing a virulent form of multiple sclerosis. She was diagnosed when Jo was fifteen. Unlike many sufferers from the disease, her mother had no periods of remission; she progressively declined in health. Though she was told her mother had an incurable disease, it was only later that she fully realised the implications.

In childhood Jo Rowling was a voracious reader, a habit that continued into adulthood. Her favourites included Tolkien, C.S. Lewis's Narnia stories, Elizabeth Goudge's *The White Horse* (about a plain orphan girl who was red-headed and freckly), Jane Austen, Edith Nesbit and later Roddy Doyle. As a teenager she was introduced to the autobiography of Jessica Mitford, *Hons and Rebels*, who immediately became her heroine, inspired by her moral courage and idealism. Mitford was an investigative journalist and champion of human rights, who had rejected the fascism of her upbringing in pre-war England. She famously quipped, 'You may not be able to change the world, but at least you can embarrass the guilty.' Later Jo was to name her first child after the writer.

After leaving Wyedean in 1983 at the age of eighteen Rowling started the next term in the University of Exeter, about 90 miles to the south-west of her home, near the south Devon coast.

UNIVERSITY, SORROWS AND THE BIRTH OF HARRY

At Exeter Jo took a degree in French, a choice she later decided was a mistake (English Literature was closer to her heart), though it did give her the opportunity to live in Paris for a year as an important element of her course. She had, she felt, been too swayed by her parents, who considered that the study of languages would open up a possible career as a bilingual secretary. In her own estimation (belied by the complexity of structure and plot in her stories) she was a highly disorganised person, because of which, she found after university, she made a poor secretary. Her language degree included a strong component of French literature. She also did some subsidiary study in the classics as part of her Honours degree. This later made its mark in the Harry Potter stories, though she sought help with the phrasing of the Hogwarts motto, 'Draco dormiens nunquam titillandus'.

After graduating she moved to London to seek work. The only redeeming feature of office life, she was to discover, was the chance secretly to put her burgeoning stories onto computer. She found she paid little heed to business meetings, as she was invariably scrawling fragments of stories in progress in the margins of her notepads, or deciding on the best names for characters. This created problems, as she had the task of recording the minutes of meetings. Her most memorable office work was with Amnesty International, an independent charity committed to publicising the abuse of human rights throughout the world, particularly of those in prison. Here she was employed as a research assistant. Hermione's efforts to help the plight of the house-elves may give a slightly self-mocking picture of her own political concerns.

In 1990, three years after leaving Exeter, Jo decided to move up to Manchester with her current boyfriend. With this in mind she spent a weekend in Manchester looking for a suitable flat. While she was travelling back to London on a packed train the concept of the Harry Potter stories 'fell into' her head with many essential plot features taking form on the journey. Though she had been composing stories since she was six years of age, she had never before been so gripped and excited about an idea.

In the flurry of the inspiration inside her head, Jo was horrified to find that she had no pen with her that worked. Though the carriage was crowded she was too reticent to ask any of the travellers if she could borrow one. In countless interviews Rowling has been asked how Harry Potter started life. Looking back she concluded that, all things considered, it was better that she had no pen, even if some details were forgotten. She calmed herself and for the four hours enforced by the train's delay she thought about the unfolding ideas of a boy wizard and a school of wizardry. The elements that bubbled up from what Tolkien calls 'the cauldron of story' were dominated by a vision of a skinny black-haired boy with glasses, a boy who gradually became vivid and tangible. Uninterrupted by the slow process of jotting notes, the ideas teemed in her imagination.

When she finally reached her London home she began writing what became *Harry Potter and the Philosopher's Stone* that very evening. The first pages she drafted were unlike anything in the final version, but they were a significant start on an ambitious writing project that was to span seven books and sixteen years' of writing, and in final form would exceed one million words. As well as the published books there would be many cardboard boxes of notes on characters, places and plot (Rowling's filing method). When she eventually moved into the Manchester flat she took a growing manuscript with her that was taking a variety of quirky directions, and already incorporated seeds of Harry's later years at Hogwarts, not merely the first year as an eleven-year-old. Her preferred method was to compose initially in longhand on a pad and later to type up the text. The Harry Potter story was in fact the third novel she had started, having abandoned her first two in dissatisfaction. The first two, unlike the new one, were written for adults. She did not consciously, however, decide to write for children but wrote about Harry Potter because that was what she deeply wanted to write.

That same year, 1990, an event occurred that was far more significant than the Harry Potter books, as perceived at the time and also in hindsight. This was the death of her mother, Anne, on 30 December. Her MS had led to respiratory failure. Jo was writing a section of what became *Harry Potter and the Philosopher's Stone* when she heard the news. Her loss had a lasting impact on Jo's life, and also her Harry Potter stories, in which, as in the fiction of Tolkien and earlier George MacDonald, death is a major theme, underlined in the final story, *Harry Potter and the Deathly Hallows*. Rowling commented, later in life: 'I think most people believe, deep down, that their mothers are indestructible.' She, her father and her sister Dianne were deeply shocked that Anne Rowling had died at forty-five years of age. They had never imagined she would pass away so soon. They each bore the grief in their own ways. Jo reassessed her life, her succession of secretarial jobs, and the increasing importance of the emerging stories of the boy wizard. Harry Potter had confirmed her desire to be a writer.

So it was that, soon after the birth of Harry, and four years after graduating, when Jo Rowling was twenty-six, she abandoned office work entirely and fled abroad to the new opportunities of Portugal to teach English as a Foreign Language. Her move was just nine months after her mother's death. In some ways it was like being back in childhood Winterbourne, as students played with her name. Instead of the joke being 'rolling pin', however, it was now 'Rolling Stone'. She enjoyed teaching English, and relished the fact that her hours were afternoons and evenings, leaving her mornings free. This meant precious time to write.

The first Harry Potter had already changed as a result of Anne Rowling's death. Jo revealed: 'Harry's feelings about his dead parents had become much deeper, much more real.' Furthermore, during her initial weeks in Aporto, she wrote what turned out to be her favourite chapter in that first book, 'The Mirror of Erised', a chapter where Harry sees his long-dead parents in a magical mirror, which proves important for his own attitude to his loss. This was directly inspired by the death of her mother.

The year after she had begun teaching in Aporto, Jo married a Portuguese man while she was still coming to terms with the loss of her mother. She married Jorge Arantas, a journalist, on 16 October 1992. Though the marriage failed (it was marked by discord and quarrels and Jo was thrown out of her home), it did give her Jessica, her first child, named after the political activist she admired, Jessica Mitford, whose courage and heroism are enshrined in the virtues championed in the house of Gryffindor at Hogwarts. Jessica was born on 27 July 1993.

SCOTLAND

When Jo Rowling eventually returned to Britain in 1994, papers covered with stories about Harry Potter filled half a suitcase. She arrived in Edinburgh, Scotland, with Jessica, well in time for Christmas with her sister Dianne, who worked there as a lawyer and had recently married. There she found Spartan accommodation for herself and her baby, a flat in Leith, to the north of the city near the

Firth of Forth, and set a deadline for herself. Her goal was to complete the novel about the boy wizard before dropping back into work as a French teacher, and to get it published, if she could. She knew that, unless she finished the book quickly, before returning to teaching, she might never complete it. The combination of full-time teaching, including lesson planning and marking, and caring for Jessica as a single mother, would leave her no time at all. She therefore valued every opportunity to write. Whenever Jessica dozed off to sleep in her baby buggy, Jo would rush to a convenient café and write furiously. A favourite tea room for this purpose was Nicolson's, near the Royal Mile, which had been opened by her brother-in-law. Every evening while Jessica slept she also wrote. On top of this she had to type up the whole book without help, living as she was on a single parent's welfare benefit.

When Jo first arrived in Edinburgh she knew no one apart from Dianne. In an early interview she admitted: 'I've never been more broke and the little I had saved went on baby gear. In the wake of my marriage, having worked all my life, I was suddenly an unemployed single parent in a grotty little flat. The manuscript was the only thing I had going for me.' Tiredness made her feelings towards the story ambivalent, sometimes hating it at the same time as she loved it, as the muse drove her remorselessly. She did not forget the needs of her young child and, soon after settling in Edinburgh, had her christened in a Church of Scotland place of worship. In the church she made the acquaintance of Susan Sladden, an older member, who helped Jo out. She would take care of Jessica for an afternoon and urge her to get out, see an art show, window shop or similar. Instead, to Susan's disappointment, Jo would find an empty table at a tea room and write furiously. She felt too insecure about her abilities to show Susan what she had been writing. Susan, however, shares the dedication in *Harry Potter and the Goblet of Fire*, as one 'who helped Harry get out of his cupboard'. In interviews after her worldwide success Jo has occasionally made explicit her Christian faith, which is clearly a thoughtful one. In 2006 she stated: 'like Graham Greene, my faith is sometimes about if my faith will return. It's important to me.' Jo, something of an artist herself, has a favourite painting, 'Caravaggio's *Supper at Emmaus* when Jesus reveals himself to the disciples having risen from the dead. I love it. Jesus looks very likable – soft and rounded – and the painting captures the exact moment when the disciples realise who this man is, blessing their bread'.

At last the final sentences were written:

'Hope you have – er – a good holiday,' said Hermione, looking uncertainly after Uncle Vernon, shocked that anyone could be so unpleasant.

'Oh, I will,' said Harry, and they were surprised at the grin that was spreading over his face. 'They don't know we're not allowed to use magic at home. I'm going to have a lot of fun with Dudley this summer . . .'

Having finished what was, unknown to her, going to be a global bestseller, Jo Rowling drafted a synopsis, which began

Harry Potter lives with his aunt, uncle and cousin because his parents died in a car crash – or so he has always been told. The Dursleys don't like Harry asking questions; in fact, they don't seem to like anything about him, especially the very odd things that keep happening around him (which Harry himself can't explain).

She carefully placed the first three chapters in a smart plastic folder and dispatched them with the synopsis to a literary agent, who returned them immediately. A second agent, however, responded very differently. Christopher Little wrote to Rowling asking to see the whole manuscript, a two-sentence reply that she felt to be the best she had received in her life.

PUBLICATION

A year passed after the writing was complete before a publisher accepted it. Many turned it down, confident that it would not sell. Finally her agent rang her with the news that Bloomsbury in London had made an offer. Rowling describes the moment that she discovered the Harry Potter book would be published as 'one of the best in my life'. In fact, when the phone was put down, she screamed, and jumped in the air, startling baby Jessica, who was happily eating her afternoon meal in her high-chair. At the time she heard the news she was employed as a French teacher at Leith Academy and still haunted by jokes about her surname by students. Now, instead of 'rolling pin' or 'Rolling Stones', the joke was musical, the beginning of a popular theme from the television series *Rawhide*: 'Rollin', rollin', rollin', keep those wagons rollin'.'

The initial print run was 500 copies. This seems stunningly cautious with the hindsight that it was written by someone whose earnings from sales have made her the ninth richest person in the 'celebrity world', slightly behind Dan Brown. Bloomsbury at that time was a small publisher with limited resources. This first edition was in hardback, and 300 of the 500 copies were distributed to libraries. Now these first editions are desperately sought by collectors, some of whom have never sought a rare book before. By contrast, print runs of later books have been in the millions, *Harry Potter and the Deathly Hallows* beating all records with its US print run alone of twelve million. Sales of her books worldwide have been in the hundreds of millions, making her one of the most widely read authors in history.

Some months after her book was accepted for publication in Britain, an American publisher, Scholastic, bought the North American rights. Rowling was delighted by the sum. It enabled her to give up her teaching, and the *Rawhide* theme music, and to start writing full-time. Her life's ambition, formed so early, was fulfilled. The advance also helped Jo and Jessica to move to better accommodation, a house in Hazelbank Terrace, just a couple of miles from Edinburgh's beautiful city centre. The US first edition, which appeared the following year, in 1998, reflected a more fervent faith in the book – 50,000 copies.

Jo Rowling now lives in a comfortable area of Edinburgh called Merchiston, in a Victorian town house, with other houses in rural Scotland and London. On 26 December 2001 she remarried, her new husband being a medical doctor, Neil Murray. When they met he was Senior House Officer in Anaesthetics, but he later went into general practice. Jessica her daughter was fast approaching secondary school age when in March 2003 a son, David, was born, followed by a daughter, Mackenzie, in January 2005. The writing of her more recent instalments of the Harry Potter story has been fitted around the needs of young children, as was the first. Now, however, money is no longer a worry, and Jo is no longer alone as she brings up her children. Old habits die hard for writers, for whom place of composition is very important. Large tracts of *Harry Potter and the Deathly Hallows* were penned in longhand sitting in Edinburgh cafés, customers unaware of her identity. One café became so much a part of her life in 2006 that one night she dreamt of its waiters and waitresses. In the dream they moved around her, 15 feet or more in height, as she searched for Horcruxes in an enormous hall teeming with people. From time to time she promotes her books and engages in charity events. In August 2006 she read with Stephen King and John Irving in New York in such an event. King admitted to her that he found Death Eaters terrifying. She responded: 'I scared Stephen King.'

Since the unexpected success of the first in the series, *Harry Potter and the Philosopher's Stone*, Rowling has given numerous interviews, with many of the questions coming from child fans. These interviews have thrown light on her core beliefs, the books that have influenced her, and her belief in God and Christianity. Indeed, her stories stand in the venerable tradition of Christian fantasy, even if they look nothing like Bunyan's *The Pilgrim's Progress* or Dante's *The Divine Comedy*. This tradition may have originated with medieval tales of King Arthur, and includes recent writers such as Tolkien and C.S. Lewis, and George MacDonald in the nineteenth century. This tradition has a depth and subtlety that are lost on some of her critics. Though fabulously wealthy, perhaps the wealthiest woman in Britain, she tries to live as quiet and ordinary life as possible, shopping in the supermarket, attending church, mothering her children, and with a compulsion to write her books sitting in a café though appreciating the novelty of having her own study.

HARRY POTTER TRIVIA

Interspersed with the happenings of J.K. Rowling's life, as she fights for privacy in a culture obsessed by celebrity, is the trivia of popular culture. This is not merely a matter of children playing Harry Potter games or owning Harry Potter toys. According to the Pentagon, the Harry Potter books in 2006 were the most popular books borrowed by inmates from the library in the Guantanamo Bay detention centre. Furthermore, more Americans know who Harry Potter is than can name the UK Prime Minister. The august International Astronomical Union has named asteroid 43844 'Rowling'. The asteroid was discovered by a Chicago astronomer who is a fan of Harry Potter. Because the initial print run for *Harry Potter and the Philosopher's Stone* in the United Kingdom was astonishingly small, first editions are rare – one sold in 2007 for £7,500 ($15,000).

FIVE

Themes and Features

Friendship, fear, loyalty, betrayal and resistance to evil: these are just some of the themes to be found in the Harry Potter stories. In this chapter we shall explore important themes, particularly as they relate to central characters such as Harry, Hermione and Ron. Then in the following two chapters we shall look at themes that relate especially to the deeper levels and spirituality of the books.

RELATIONSHIPS

Much of the interest of the stories lies in the interrelationships of the main characters. Underlying the books are the friendships and enmities between the school pupils at Hogwarts – such as the core friendship of Harry, Ron and Hermione, and the bitter clashes between Harry and Draco Malfoy, an animosity somewhat overcome by the end of *Harry Potter and the Deathly Hallows*. Gender comes into the relationships: Harry and Hermione are the best of friends; Ron and Hermione eventually fall in love with each other; and Harry must renounce his love of Ginny for a time. Against stereotypes, Hermione is the cleverest of the friends, with her resourcefulness frequently making the difference between success and failure in their many adventures. The pupils have parents and grandparents – or, in Harry's case, an uncle and aunt, and a guardian, Sirius Black. The children have to relate to other adults, good and bad: their professors at Hogwarts, sinister enemies like Voldemort's Death Eaters, and officials from the magical government, the Ministry of Magic.

Friendship and Fellowship

Friendship is celebrated in the stories. The pattern of friends develops and unfolds, and its fellowship is a permanent element in the plot of the seven stories. Its pattern is set in the first year, in *Harry Potter and the Philosopher's Stone*, particularly after Harry and Ron have rescued Hermione from the troll. With this event, in which Hermione gets the boys out of trouble, their friendship is sealed. Thereafter Harry, Ron and Hermione stick together, helping each other and being committed to each other:

> 'I'll use the Invisibility Cloak,' said Harry. 'It's just lucky I got it back.'
>   'But will it cover all three of us?' said Ron.
>   'All – three of us?'
>   'Oh, come off it, you don't think we'd let you go alone.'

Hermione reaffirms their commitment in *Harry Potter and the Deathly Hallows*, when the way Harry has to take is much darker: 'We're coming with you. That was decided months ago – years really.' Hermione and Ron remain on Harry's side in *Harry Potter and the Order of the Phoenix* even when it seems to him that all the school is against him, and when he is in danger from Voldemort. Hermione reminds Harry and Ron about what Dumbledore had said at the feast at the end of the previous term, about Voldemort's great 'gift for spreading discord and enmity'. He had said that they 'can fight it only by showing an equally strong bond of friendship and trust'. The friendship is Harry's main source of strength in persisting with his resolve to oppose Voldemort. After Harry learns in *Harry Potter and the Half-Blood Prince* the awful truth about the prophecy, and the inevitability of a life-or-death encounter with the Dark Lord, he is comforted that Ron and Hermione are still with him.

> A warmth was spreading through him that had nothing to do with the sunlight; a tight obstruction in his chest seemed to be dissolving. He knew that Ron and Hermione were more shocked than they were letting on, but the mere fact that they were still there on either side of him, speaking bracing words of comfort, not shrinking from him as though he were contaminated or dangerous, was worth more than he could ever tell them.

The quality of their friendship is such that it is typical of Ron and Hermione in *Harry Potter and the Prisoner of Azkaban* to stay at Hogwarts over the Christmas vacation to keep Harry company, rather than going home. As events in the stories unfold Harry increasingly relies upon his friends, particularly Ron and Hermione, and later (in *Harry Potter and the Order of the Phoenix*) the larger circle of Dumbledore's Army (DA), in which Luna, Neville and Ginny are an inner circle of friends. Luna, an eccentric and isolated pupil, particularly appreciates the DA, saying in retrospect, in *Harry Potter and the Half-Blood Prince*, 'It was like having friends.' In *Harry Potter and the Deathly Hallows* we learn that she has painted large portraits of Ron, Hermione, Harry, Ginny and Neville on her bedroom ceiling, linked with golden chains made up of the recurring word 'friends'. At the end of *Harry Potter and the Half-Blood Prince*, Ron and Hermione vow to stick with Harry in his ultimate quest to destroy the Horcruxes, and thus Voldemort. Harry has learned enough by now to accept their offer. Dumbledore encourages Harry's friendship with Ron and Hermione. At one point, in *Harry Potter and the Half-Blood Prince*, he advises Harry to confide in them about the contents of the prophecy concerning Voldemort.

In his own inimitable way, the school gamekeeper, Rubeus Hagrid, is as close in the friendship as Harry, Ron and Hermione are to each other. Hagrid (as he is always known) originally befriended Harry, when the half-giant brought Harry his invitation to Hogwarts School of Witchcraft and Wizardry. As well as caring for each other, the three friends look after Hagrid, in *Harry Potter and the Philosopher's Stone* arranging for his beloved pet dragon, Norbert, to be adopted to avoid disaster.

Hagrid is also important to Harry and the others as an adult friend, and the schoolfriends take care to preserve the relationship. In *Harry Potter and the Half-Blood Prince* Hermione is keen to explain to Hagrid why they are not taking classes with him in the Care of Magical Creatures, so that he is not discouraged. Harry has missed him too, and agrees with her that this should be done. But there are other adult friends, in particular Harry's godfather, Sirius, and later the members of the Order of the Phoenix such as Tonks and Remus Lupin.

The friendship between Harry, Ron and Hermione is strong and real. As Dobby the house-elf points out in astonishment in *Harry Potter and the Chamber of Secrets*, Harry is willing to risk his life for his friends. In fact, as it turns out, it is Dobby who actually gives his life for them in *Harry Potter and the Deathly Hallows*. Hermione is also willing to be unpopular with her friends for the sake of her principles, and it is these principles that give them all moral guidance. In *Harry Potter and the Prisoner of Azkaban* she tells Professor McGonagall that Harry has received an anonymous Christmas gift of a Firebolt because of her concern for his safety. Similarly, in the same book, Hagrid intervenes when Ron refuses to talk to Hermione (because her cat, Crookshanks, has attacked his pet rat, Scabbers) and when Harry and Ron rebuff her after she had reported the Firebolt. Hagrid tells off Harry and Ron for putting other things before their friendship with her. They are soon reconciled over the need to respond to Buckbeak's fate. Hermione in turn defends Hagrid by smacking the insulting Draco. When Ron abandons Harry and Hermione in *Harry Potter and the Deathly Hallows*, it takes all their resolve to continue, and many tears are shed.

The Death Eaters provide a significant contrast to the group of friends. They represent a perverted fellowship around Voldemort, whom they serve out of fear rather than love. If any of them think they are close to Voldemort, privy to his inner thoughts and wishes, this is delusion. The Dark Lord sees them only as servants to be exploited; even when he praises Barty Crouch Jr, in *Harry Potter and the Order of the Phoenix*, he calls him 'my faithful servant', not 'my friend'. He similarly calls Snape his faithful servant in *Harry Potter and the Deathly Hallows* immediately before killing him without remorse, so that his power is not jeopardised.

Both Harry and the young Voldemort, Tom Riddle, were originally lonely and friendless, brought up as orphans. Voldemort never had a friend, or wanted one. Their lives at Hogwarts, however, provide a significant contrast. At Hogwarts Harry is delighted to form friendships with Ron and Hermione, in a circle that expands to include Neville, Luna, Ginny and others. The young Voldemort gathers around him future Death Eaters, whom he controls with a sinister power. A secret follower of Voldemort's,

Peter Pettigrew (Wormtail), betrays his supposed friends James and Lily Potter, Harry's parents, to Voldemort, and frames another friend, Sirius Black, so that he is wrongly imprisoned in Azkaban.

Realism and Fantasy

The Harry Potter stories are an intriguing mix of fantasy and realism. Part of the realism of J.K. Rowling's portrayal of friendship is her characterisation of gender and sexuality. In the DA there is a mix of boys and girls training to fight the Dark Arts, in expectation of battles ahead with Voldemort's return. Hermione's resourcefulness and strong role in the group of friends have been noted. In Hogwarts it is the problematic house, Slytherin, that most represents gender stereotypes. (In Harry's first year there are no girls on the Slytherin Quidditch team, although this is not true in later years.) This realism and other more subtle factors help J.K. Rowling to appeal both to boy and girl readers. This is especially impressive, as boys tend to be more reluctant to read than girls. The author has always been careful to attract boy readers; one reason her agent encouraged her to use 'J.K.' rather than 'Joanne' in her name was so as not to put them off.

The realism over sexuality comes naturally from the progression of the stories over the seven school years, a progress reflected in the shifting age range of readers. The first Harry Potter book is for relatively young readers, whereas the latest books are more for mid-teenagers, interested in sexual attraction. J.K. Rowling portrays the tensions, setbacks and progress of the relationship between Ron and Hermione in some depth, though seen mainly from Harry's perspective. Hermione sending her little flock of golden birds to attack Ron in *Harry Potter and the Half-Blood Prince* is particularly memorable. Harry's own awakening, with turbulent but short-lived feelings for Cho Chang, is more directly represented. It is something of a relief when he and Ginny confess their feelings for each other in *Harry Potter and the Half-Blood Prince*, a relationship that cleverly gives depth to the conflict in the plot, where Harry has to sacrifice his own interests in the battle against Voldemort. Harry, typically, is also initially in somewhat of a quandary over Ginny, in case his love for her jeopardises his friendship with her brother Ron. Other interesting relationships that Rowling explores are those between Tonks and Lupin, and Fleur and Bill Weasley (given poignancy by the disfiguring injuries Bill receives from Greyback in *Harry Potter and the Half-Blood Prince*). The marriage of Bill and Fleur is featured in *Harry Potter and the Deathly Hallows*, and their very first home in Shell Cottage provides a refuge for some of those on the run from Voldemort's regime, including Harry and his friends.

Fathers and Mothers

A subtheme of relationships in the stories is that of fathers, many of whom are bad (like those of Tom Riddle, Merope Gaunt and, indeed, Dudley Dursley, Harry's cousin). There are also good fathers, like Arthur Weasley, and James Potter, who died trying to save his wife and baby Harry. Poignantly, in *Harry Potter and the Deathly Hallows*, Lupin at first has doubts about his role in his new family, tempted to abandon Tonks and his infant son, Teddy, because of the danger into which he has placed them. Luna's father is the eccentric editor of *The Quibbler*. Dumbledore is a father figure for many students, including Harry. The Patronus (after the Latin term derived from 'father') is a guardian apparition conjured up by the Patronus Charm – Harry's is a stag, which equals Prongs, his father's Animagus form. Dumbledore revealingly says to Harry that his father is alive in him, and that is why his Patronus is Prongs. Godfathers figure too in the stories. Sirius conscientiously tries to fulfil his role, now that he is free from Azkaban. Harry, too, becomes a good godfather to the orphaned Teddy Remus at the end of *Harry Potter and the Deathly Hallows*. Mother figures in the story are quite varied, from the tragic Merope, mother of Tom Riddle (Voldemort), through the heroic Lily Potter, mother of Harry, to the motherly but formidable Molly Weasley. Lily's action of sacrificing herself for Harry dominates the plot of the entire series of books. Hermione's parents, who are Muggle dentists, make great efforts to participate in their wizarding daughter's life, even visiting Diagon Alley to buy school supplies for her. Neville's parents are tragic figures, whose minds were lost fighting Voldemort and his evil, so that they are condemned to spend their lives in St Mungo's Hospital.

EDUCATION AND GROWTH

The seven Harry Potter stories are dominated by the benign presence of Hogwarts School of Witchcraft and Wizardry, even when it appears to be fully controlled by Death Eaters in the last book. It is not surprising, therefore, that education is an emphatic theme in the stories. Education is empowering, and much of Harry's early story is the discovery of his natural powers of magic. For the first time he is able to take control of his life, which, under the regime imposed by the Dursleys, had hitherto been little different from that of a servant. The true value of Harry's education at Hogwarts becomes sharply evident when it is jeopardised, in *Harry Potter and the Order of the Phoenix*, by the rule of Dolores Umbridge and the Dark Side of the Ministry of Magic, a foretaste of what is to come in *Harry Potter and the Deathly Hallows*. This is particularly highlighted in her ban on practical Defence Against the Dark Arts, leaving the students vulnerable to attack by Voldemort. The fact that a number of students, under Harry's leadership, are forced to develop their own defence classes gives them a greater appreciation of the education offered by Hogwarts.

The importance of education is emphasised by the very existence of Hogwarts, and Dumbledore's commitment to its ethos. It is dedicated to the proper use of magic and is firmly opposed to the use of the Dark Arts. One of its courses prepares its students for attacks by wizards who have gone over to the Dark Side and are prepared to use Unforgivable Curses such as the Cruciatus curse and the Imperius curse, and other Dark Arts to exert their power and to increase their oppression. In theory the values and virtues championed by Hogwarts should be backed up by the Ministry of Magic – the wizarding government that is responsible for enforcing laws governing the proper use of magic. In practice the Harry Potter stories reveal many tensions between the Ministry and the school, centring on the inept leadership of the Minister of Magic, the aptly named Cornelius Fudge. It is with Ministry approval that the sadistic Dolores Umbridge runs a reign of terror at Hogwarts, in which Harry and others are subjected to cruelty and Dumbledore is banished. The culmination of this conflict is the complete takeover of the Ministry by Voldemort's forces in *Harry Potter and the Deathly Hallows*.

The teaching standards of the school vary considerably. In fact the stories could be useful for teacher training! As models, Professor Binns would probably rate badly and Remus Lupin very highly. The methods of some of the teachers (Severus Snape, Gilderoy Lockhart and Sybill Trelawney, for instance) provide, in effect, a satire on secondary school teaching, in all probability based on the author's memories of her schooling and her own experience of teaching.

A child's education, of course, has many more facets than formal learning in the classroom. The stories include much that concerns knowledge and growth. Harry, as might be expected, learns gradually, through his unfolding education in his years at Hogwarts, and through his experiences – not least, confronting Voldemort and his servants. He is not a high-flier academically, his strength being in sports and a natural leadership. The educational process at Hogwarts is traditional, a new step being based on mastering an earlier step. (Thus Hermione – with some bravery – tells Professor Snape that they are not yet ready to learn about werewolves in the Defence Against the Dark Arts classes.) Harry learns partly by instruction and books, and partly by his unusual experiences. Hermione's facility with book-learning and libraries is an important informal part of his educational growth. Growth of knowledge for him is slow and painful, conflicting with his actual experience of having to resist Voldemort even in his first year. It is his actual experience that forces him to grow up fast and make difficult moral choices and decisions.

Harry, like all wizards and witches, has to await his coming of age at seventeen before he can use magic outside school. Because of what Dumbledore acknowledges is a mistake, Harry does not learn the complete meaning of his scar and of the prophecy made before his birth until he is nearly sixteen, leaving him many puzzles and implications to work out before then, as reflected in the narrative point of view of the stories. He has to learn many things for himself the hard way – for instance, the location of the entrance to the Chamber of Secrets and the purpose of the Order of the Phoenix. His struggles to interpret his experiences, a process he shares with his friends, have the result of preparing him better for the last battle between himself and Voldemort in *Harry Potter and the Deathly Hallows*.

As part of this painful growing-up process, and acceptance of moral leadership, Harry has to learn to do without Dumbledore, a reality thrust upon him brutally in *Harry Potter and the Half-Blood Prince*. In the months preceding his death, Dumbledore had deliberately and presciently mentored Harry for the task of defeating Voldemort. Part of this preparation was to ready him to make a terrifying choice to lay down his own life for others, as the only way that Voldemort could be totally defeated. C.S. Lewis's Narnia stories, like other children's stories, have been criticised because the protagonists (it is claimed) always rely on adult authority figures – pre-eminently in this case on Aslan, the lion king of the land. This might be contrasted (it is argued) with the Harry Potter stories, where, for much of the time, the children are forced to rely on their own resources, the intentions of adults actually hindering their struggles with Voldemort's dark forces. In the Narnian stories, however, children, male and female, are often forced to do much on their own, encouraged to do so by Aslan himself, as with Jill and Eustace in *The Silver Chair*, and Lucy in *Prince Caspian*. In the Harry Potter stories, in fact, Dumbledore's guidance is persistent – so much so that his guidance continues after his death in the form of clues, puzzles and mysteries that Harry and his friends must solve, such as those surrounding the Deathly Hallows and the location and identity of the remaining Horcruxes. His mentoring of Harry is the logical conclusion of this guidance. He takes Harry with him like a Sorcerer's Apprentice to the West Country during the summer vacation in *Harry Potter and the Half-Blood Prince* in his quest to persuade Horace Slughorn out of retirement and later, by means of stored memories in his Pensieve, fills Harry in on Voldemort's early history. He recruits Harry in the difficult task of retrieving a deliberately damaged memory in one of the sequences, which holds a vital clue. This means asking Slughorn to divulge his real memory, against his will. Dumbledore believes that Harry can succeed where he has failed. Harry's success in this task proves essential to furthering the defeat of Voldemort.

There is a progression in Dumbledore's mentoring, so that, eventually, he feels able to ask Harry to accompany him on a perilous quest to retrieve one of the Horcruxes containing a fragment of Voldemort's soul. Though the quest ends in apparent failure, the process prepares Harry even more for the task of finding and destroying the remaining Horcruxes, a task he has to do without the aid of his mentor.

Confronting Prejudice

An essential element in the growth and maturity of Harry and his friends is the confrontation of prejudice, a deep and persistent theme of the stories. The children encounter a bewildering variety of prejudice: against werewolves, those without 'pure' wizard blood, Squibs, house-elves, Muggles and even giants. The unscrupulous journalist Rita Skeeter plays on prejudice against giants, for instance, by writing about Hagrid in *Harry Potter and the Goblet of Fire*. Throughout the stories Snape expresses a deep grudge against Harry, a deep-rooted prejudice because Harry is very like his father, James, about whom Snape has bitter memories. There is even prejudice against Slytherin house (shared by Harry, and reflected in his point of view), even though it is clear that there are significant Slytherins who do not, for example, share an antipathy to those who are not 'pure' wizards, such as Horace Slughorn (for whom Lily, Harry's mother, was a favourite pupil) and former headmaster of Hogwarts, Phineas Nigellus Black. Of the children, Hermione is the most active in resisting prejudice, with her campaigning on behalf of the rights of house-elves and her covering-up for Professor Lupin, when she realises that he is a secret werewolf.

The issue of purity of blood is the most serious prejudice explored in the stories. Those with one or both parents who are Muggles are regarded by the prejudiced as impure wizards (even though, ironically, Voldemort himself is a half-blood). The prejudice is especially virulent as behind it lies an ideology, echoing that of twentieth-century Fascism, with its own would-be dictator, the self-styled Heir of Slytherin, Voldemort. The stories make it clear that the ideology goes back to one of the founders of Hogwarts, Salazar Slytherin. Only those with both a wizard mother and father, he believed, should be allowed to study at Hogwarts, to maintain the integrity of the wizard race. His views eventually created a split with the other founders of the school, a division passed down over the centuries since. Draco Malfoy's family regarded itself of pure heritage, as did most members of the family of Sirius Black, and Draco's father was a Death Eater. For those entrenched in the pure-blood ideology, hatred of others is based on blood-line and ancestry. It is this ideology that is responsible for the opening of the Chamber of Secrets in *Harry Potter and the Chamber of Secrets*, and its earlier opening during the schooldays of the young Voldemort, Tom Riddle. The disdain of those claiming racial purity extended to those of lower social classes and economic status. Draco, for instance, continually snipes about Ron's family being hard-up; their poverty overrides their pure-blood status.

Durmstrang, one of the foreign schools participating in the Triwizard Tournament in *Harry Potter and the Goblet of Fire*, is reputed to hold to a pure-blood policy in its selection of pupils. Significantly, its headteacher, Karkaroff, is a former Death Eater. According to Draco Malfoy, it also teaches the Dark Arts. Yet even Durmstrang expelled Grindelwald for his extreme views of wizard superiority.

The ideology of the pure-blood is one of many features in the wizarding domain that has parallels with the Muggle world. When the dog-obsessed Aunt Marge expresses strong prejudices about blood and breeding, comparing Harry to a weak, underbred dog, this expressly parallels the Slytherin mentality. Like most who adhere to such an extreme racist view, she is a bully.

Growth as a Quest

A master image in the stories for education and growth is that of the quest or journey, most emphatically embodied in *Harry Potter and the Deathly Hallows*, as Harry and his friends search both for the last Horcruxes and for clues about the Deathly Hallows. The overall structure of the plot of the seven stories is set by the prophecy that is eventually disclosed to Harry by Dumbledore in *Harry Potter and the Order of the Phoenix*. Sybill Trelawney's prophecy, which was uttered in Dumbledore's presence, was half overheard by Snape. He carried the incomplete version to Voldemort, who, in acting upon its implications, killed Harry's parents and attempted to kill the infant, unwittingly passing on some of his magical powers even as he was disembodied. Voldemort's defining quest is to return to full embodiment and thus power to subjugate others, and to complete the destruction of Harry, whom he fears will kill him. Harry's quest is to resist and ultimately to kill Voldemort, destroying his power and malignant influence. Fulfilling such a quest requires all the resources of his Hogwarts education, the help and guidance of Dumbledore and the resourcefulness of his friends. It also requires his maturity and coming of age at seventeen as a fully-fledged wizard.

Harry's quest takes the shape of the traditional hero's journey, the structure of which is famously charted in Joseph Campbell's *Hero with a Thousand Faces*. Connie Neal, an authority on the Harry Potter books, has applied Campbell's analysis to J.K. Rowling's stories in her book *Wizards, Wardrobes and Wookiees*. Heroes respond to a call to sacrifice and to give their lives. Their lives begin in the ordinary world, where they are summoned to adventure and perilous tasks. This involves, with the help of a mentor, crossing a threshold into another world in which they undergo various trials and encounter allies and foes. There are other elements in the journey, but eventually the hero returns to the ordinary world bearing something of benefit. The journey is an archetypal pattern, and there are myriad ways in which a story may be told and yet display the archetype (Connie Neal's book, for instance, shows the pattern of the hero's journey in the Narnian Chronicles and the *Star Wars* movies as well as in the Harry Potter books). The value of the analysis is that it demonstrates the underlying narrative power and human appeal of the story, and how it may apply in the ordinary world. In particular, Connie Neal shows the pattern in individual books. Harry's great returning gift is that of hope – hope that seemingly implacable evil will be overcome.

Harry's quest and journey can also be described in a Judaeo-Christian manner, which complements the archetypal rendering. He is not in fact strictly a hero in classical terms, but an ordinary boy, mundane and reluctant like the typical biblical hero. Although he has remarkable gifts of magic, he has to rely on moral courage and on his friends to accomplish his tasks. He is not the self-sufficient, individualistic hero. In mythic terms, he is very like the ordinary hobbits Frodo and Sam in *The Lord of the Rings*, whose weakness and small stature accomplish what the great and powerful cannot.

In the Triwizard Tournament, for instance, he is given a great deal of help, unknown to him, by Barty Crouch Jr, disguised as Mad-Eye Moody, whose objective is to get him into the presence of Voldemort. Providentially, Crouch's sinister machinations serve a greater good. What is decisive in subverting the evil aim of Harry's destruction is his moral courage, expressed, for instance, when he rescues Fleur's sister Gabrielle, as well as Ron, in the trial under the lake. Harry's testings and trials prepare him for his ultimate suffering in the last book, which leads at last to healing and peace.

METAPHYSICS

Metaphysics is concerned with the underlying principles of reality, typically asking questions like: Is there a God? What is the nature of reality? What place does the human being have in the universe? What, if anything, happens to me after death? Is the material world essentially evil or good? A number of the themes explored in the Harry Potter books are metaphysical in character, such as death, and appearance and reality. An important setting in the stories – the Department of Mysteries, in the Ministry of Magic – is concerned with areas of life that involve the deeper questions, such as prophecy, dreams, time and the mysteries of the human brain. The existence of magic itself, as an alternative to technology, raises many metaphysical questions.

Appearance and Reality

A theme rich in implications that is worked out in the stories concerns appearance and reality. The reader learns early on that things are very often not what they seem. This is, of course, a basic principle of knowledge. When we notice that a stick appears to bend when half submerged in water, it awakens our curiosity about what is going on in the world. We are very aware also that an apparently three-dimensional picture is printed or painted on to a flat surface. A sudden insight can make us realise that we have been deceived about appearances. Modern science advances on the basis that appearances are not enough. In fact, it is necessary to make imaginative models of many aspects of reality, such as subatomic particles, in order to conceive of them properly and explore their properties. Most of the stuff of the universe is hidden from us, called by names such as dark matter or dust.

In the stories there are numerous examples of things being not what they seem. In *Harry Potter and the Philosopher's Stone* it appears to Harry and his friends that Snape is seeking the Philosopher's Stone. In the same book Professor Quirrell comes across as a nervous and innocuous teacher. In *Harry Potter and the Prisoner of Azkaban* Scabbers seems to be merely Ron's neurotic pet rat, while Sirius Black appears to be a murderer on the loose from Azkaban. In *Harry Potter and the Goblet of Fire* Mad-Eye Moody is apparently a genuine teacher of Defence Against the Dark Arts, not Voldemort's faithful servant assuming his form, complete with swiveling eye. The popular Madam Rosmerta in *Harry Potter and the Half-Blood Prince* presents no clue that she is really under the Imperius curse, her will controlled by Draco Malfoy. Pupils are unaware that the brilliant teacher of Defence Against the Dark Arts in *Harry Potter and the Prisoner of Azkaban*, Remus Lupin, is in fact a werewolf (although Hermione works it out after writing an essay on werewolves). The most profound example of appearance versus reality is J.K. Rowling's exploration of Snape's character as a double agent brilliantly and courageously acting out his cover.

At the very centre of the stories is the fact that the preservation of the wizarding world depends on hiding its reality from Muggles. When non-magical people stumble across Hogwarts Castle in the wilds of Scotland, all that they see are some ruins and a danger sign. All they will see between Platforms 9 and 10 on King's Cross Railway Station is a sturdy barrier. When Muggles are out and about, magical creatures like dragons, unicorns or Blast-Ended Skrewts will appear not to be there.

The all-pervasive contrast between appearance and reality in the fictional stories forces readers to apply judgement to the real world – what is appearance and what reality? As in the world of Harry Potter there are unexplored dimensions of the real world that are likely to hold the key to understanding the true situation. This dialectic is reinforced for the reader by the fact that, in the stories, not only are magical places and items hidden from Muggles, but they choose also to ignore them if they have not been successfully concealed. Interestingly, the Dursleys gradually become more aware of the magical world by having Harry among them. Harry's aunt, Petunia, as sister of Lily Potter, already has some awareness of the magical world and knows its reality. The Dursleys therefore bridge the Muggle and magical worlds.

Time

Another deep metaphysical theme in the stories is that of time. As humans we face the conundrum that we are beings in time, with a beginning and ending, and yet one's inner self apparently transcends the temporal, looking backward, forward or to the present moment. Paradoxes of time enter the plot of *Harry Potter and the Prisoner of Azkaban*. Hermione is allowed to use a Time-Turner so that she can attend a wider range of classes than would be possible on a normal timetable. Through this she almost burns out. At Dumbledore's suggestion, her knowledge of the magical device allows Harry and herself to go back in time several hours to rescue Sirius and Buckbeak the Hippogriff, two victims of injustice. The time travelling raises further issues of how free will can operate in an environment where events must not be changed. An important wizarding law rules that no one should change time. Dumbledore sanctions the breaking of that law, within careful limits, for the sake of Sirius and Buckbeak.

The Department of Mysteries contains a time room, in which the Time-Turners, as used by Hermione, are kept. During the battle at the Ministry of Magic in *Harry Potter and the Order of the Phoenix* a skirmish takes place within the time room, resulting in a Death Eater falling, his head entering a bell jar. The effect is that he keeps repeating a cycle in which his head shrinks to that of a baby's and grows back to its adult form. When he pulls himself out of the jar, with its endless cycle, the baby head's remains fixed on his thick neck, his adult body behaving erratically under infant impulses. His change is part of a whole network of symbolism about babies and infant behaviour, associated with the violation of magic and nature (see Chapter Seven). A locked cycle of events, outside the normal line of time, is also to be found in the beautiful phoenix, in its periodic resurrection from its ashes. On one occasion, in *Harry*

Potter and the Chamber of Secrets, Harry witnesses Fawkes being reborn in such a manner.

Clocks and watches are obvious indicators of time. In the Department of Mysteries the time room is full of them. The Weasleys' home, The Burrow, has a magical clock. Harry notices it when he first visits the house in *Harry Potter and the Chamber of Secrets*, after his rescue from Little Whinging in the flying Ford Anglia. 'The clock on the wall opposite him had only one hand and no numbers at all. Written around the edge were things like "Time to make tea", "Time to feed the chickens" and "You're late".' Dumbledore's golden pocket watch is much more mysterious, described during the reader's first encounter with him in chapter one of *Harry Potter and the Philosopher's Stone*: 'It was a very odd watch. It had twelve hands but no numbers; instead, little planets were moving around the edge. It must have made sense to Dumbledore, though, because he put it back in his pocket and said, "Hagrid's late".' It is clear that magical folk have a very different perception of time from Muggles. As Dumbledore's life span is at least double that of ordinary non-magical people, that is not surprising.

Death

Death is closely related to the theme of time, signifying that what began, and is, is temporal and contingent – one day it will not be. J.K. Rowling stated in an interview for *Newsweek*: 'Death and bereavement and what death means . . . is one of the central themes in all seven books.' Her own loss of her mother, taken from her by MS, added poignancy to the writing of *Harry Potter and the Philosopher's Stone*, deepening the treatment of death in the subsequent stories. Other fantasy writers for whom death is a major theme include Tolkien and George MacDonald.

Harry's own life is overshadowed by death, and ultimately he is called to master it by being willing to lay down his own life for others, as his mother, Lily, did for him. He is brought up as an orphan, his parents murdered by Voldemort. He himself should have died as an infant from the killing curse, but survived only through the Deeper Magic of his mother's sacrificial love. Harry witnesses the death of Cedric Diggory in *Harry Potter and the Goblet of Fire*, the death in battle of his godfather, Sirius, in *Harry Potter and the Order of the Phoenix*, the murder of an elderly man by Voldemort in *Harry Potter and the Half-Blood Prince* (albeit in a precognition), and later in the same story, the sudden murder of Dumbledore from a killing curse of Snape's, and the death of many friends and his beloved owl in *Harry Potter and the Deathly Hallows*. His ability to see the usually invisible Thestrals, the winged horses who pull the carriages from Hogsmeade station to Hogwarts, gives him an affinity with Luna Lovegood, who has also seen death – a condition of seeing the Thestrals. In his fifth year at the school, Harry is made aware that an ancient prophecy concerns his destiny, which suggests he will either kill or be killed by Voldemort. The Dark Lord's very chosen name incorporates death (*mort, mord*), and his servants are called Death Eaters.

Voldemort is obsessed with mastering death, as his name suggests in French (*flight from death*). Before his unexpected disembodiment when his killing curse failed to slay the infant Harry, the Dark Lord had made careful plans to help himself achieve immortality by dividing his soul into several parts, placed into Horcruxes. When he begins to achieve partial resurrection by possessing Professor Quirrell in *Harry Potter and the Philosopher's Stone*, his object is to find the Philosopher's Stone, the elixir of life of the Alchemists. This endeavour fails, and his host, Quirrell, dies. In *Harry Potter and the Chamber of Secrets* he also fails to reconstitute himself through the diary of his younger, schoolboy self, which is a Horcrux, attempting to draw strength from the dying Ginny Weasley. He is forced into a more complex plan in *Harry Potter and the Goblet of Fire*, involving the use of a bone from his buried father, the right hand of his servant, Wormtail, voluntarily given, and blood forcibly taken from the young wizard he fears, Harry Potter. It is not clear how he achieved the hideous embryonic state necessary to carry out this plan, but it partly involved milking the venom from his monstrous pet serpent, Nagini.

The cloud of ghosts who linger around Hogwarts provide a backdrop to the theme of death. In *Harry Potter and the Chamber of Secrets* Harry, Ron and Hermione attend a Deathday Party thrown by Nearly Headless Nick, a spirit from the fifteenth century.

Nick is an affable Gryffindor ghost popular with the pupils. After the death of Sirius Harry asks Nick what happens after death, his thoughts full of his godfather. It turns out that Nick can provide little information. Although wizards can come back after death, as Nick himself has, very few choose to do so. He had chosen a pale imitation of life through fear of death instead of going on, as Sirius had, and Harry has the choice of doing in *Harry Potter and the Deathly Hallows*. Consequently he knows nothing of what happens when people go on after death, rather than lingering like the Hogwarts ghosts with the living, walking 'palely where their living selves once trod'. The most recent Hogwarts ghost is described only as Moaning Myrtle, who inhabits a disused girls' toilet, and was killed by the Basilisk released by Tom Riddle (the young Voldemort) fifty years before the events recounted in *Harry Potter and the Chamber of Secrets*. Her lingering as a ghost included tormenting a fellow pupil who had teased her remorselessly. In *Harry Potter and the Deathly Hallows*, when Harry questions the Grey Lady, the Ravenclaw ghost, he discovers that she is Helena, daughter of one of the founders of Hogwarts, who was murdered by the impetuous Bloody Baron, another Hogwarts ghost, who took his own life after the foolish deed and wore his chains as an act of penance.

Professor Dumbledore makes some sagacious comments about death, comments that take on an increased poignancy in the light of his own demise at Snape's hand in *Harry Potter and the Half-Blood Prince*. In *Harry Potter and the Philosopher's Stone* he remarks: 'To the well-organized mind, death is but the next great adventure.' Later, in *Harry Potter and the Order of the Phoenix*, he observes: 'It is the unknown we fear when we look upon death and darkness, nothing more.' He seems in control of his own death, and there is a Gethsemane-like lead up to it in the story. In search of one of Voldemort's Horcruxes, he takes Harry with him into a huge cave, within which is a huge black lake full of the dead. The setting echoes classical portrayals of the underworld, the region of the dead, complete with a ferry boat. In classical mythology a boat ferries the dead across a grim river, which forms the boundary between earth and the underworld, or Hades. The symbolism in *Harry Potter and the Half-Blood Prince* then becomes more Christian than classical. On the island at the middle of the lake Dumbledore drinks a bitter cup in order to access the Horcrux, a means to the end of destroying Voldemort. The process is a ceremony, almost like Christ's Last Supper, and a trial, like the suffering at Gethsemane, portending his death. Dumbledore is clearly opposing death itself, hideously represented in the inferi who inhabit the lake. Inferi are rotting corpses animated by dark magic, subservient to the will of an evil wizard, described as 'dead guardian[s] of a fragment of Voldemort's shattered soul'. Dumbledore evokes a circle of fire (a symbol of eternal purity and the Holy Spirit) to protect Harry and himself from the encroaching cadavers. The account of Dumbledore's funeral is extensive, his loss affecting magical creatures as well as wizarding folk, merpeople and centaurs, a tribute to the wholeness he desired and championed. For Harry, the 'last and greatest of his protectors had died and he was more alone than he had ever been before'. It was not only that Harry needed Dumbledore, but that now he had to stand against Voldemort and evil without his help. Dumbledore had also appreciated Harry deeply, as his poignant words after leaving the cave make clear:

> 'It's going to be all right, sir,' Harry said over and over again, more worried by Dumbledore's silence than he had been by his weakened voice. 'We're nearly there . . . I can Apparate us both back . . . don't worry . . .'
>
> 'I am not worried, Harry,' said Dumbledore, his voice a little stronger despite the freezing water. 'I am with you.'

Dumbledore's faith in Harry is vindicated in the final book, much of which concerns the Deathly Hallows, three objects that represent the desire to master death, the last enemy. Harry discovers that death is truly mastered only by a willingness to lay down one's own life for one's friends. This supreme act of love on Harry's part evokes the Deeper Magic that underlies all the stories, and makes possible their happy ending.

SIX

Spiritual World View

All human creations, including tales of Harry Potter or the biologist's story of life on planet earth, help to give shape to our world views. These are the varying bedrock beliefs held by individuals and societies about reality, whether concerning the natural world or human life. Our world views give us the confidence to act, to make decisions and to consider some beliefs and not others to be true. Stories – whether coming from the sciences or the media – have traditionally articulated our views about the world, and our very perceptions are shaped by the stories held dear in our lives. J.K. Rowling's tales of Hogwarts are rich in themes that illuminate a very definite world view. In this chapter we shall explore some themes that point to a spirituality that underlies her stories.

WHOLENESS AND PURITY

A vision of wholeness is central to the Harry Potter stories, and this vision is focused upon the ideals of a Hogwarts education – which involves learning, preparation for life and moral education. During the period of the stories – the setting is Britain in the 1990s – a persistent and perennial threat from the use of the Dark Arts (the misuse of magic) has become a dramatic danger with the growing influence of Lord Voldemort, as he seeks to return to power and dominate the world – a wonderfully end-of-millennium theme. The threat has even spilled over from the magical world into the more humdrum domain of Muggles, whom the Dark Lord intends to enslave. A Hogwarts education stresses using magic properly, and aims to prepare its pupils for brutal and inhuman attacks from those who have gone over to the Dark Side. The seven stories are moral tales, even though no didactic aim suppresses J.K. Rowling's love of storytelling. It is clear that, in her view, stories have a right to exist, and do not need an external justification such as the necessity to teach children morality, good though such an aim is in its proper sphere. Whatever we may decide as we look at some central themes in the story, it is clear that Rowling's world view is such that it enables her to create enduring stories loved by people throughout the world, realistically portray the nature of evil, and maintain joy and laughter in the face of great darkness.

The Hogwarts vision of wholeness is not simply expressed in its curriculum. It is also embodied in its four houses to which pupils belong. This house structure is prominent in the lives of the students. The school crest reminds them of it – displaying a lion, an eagle, a badger and a snake. It provokes an image of unity in diversity rather than of discord. The ideal in the school is that the four houses work together to promote wholeness rather than fragmentation, bonded together by friendship and a common purpose. Significantly, Voldemort in *Harry Potter and the Deathly Hallows* wishes to rid Hogwarts of its four houses, having only Slytherin's.

Upon first arrival at the school, an ancient Sorting Hat places new pupils in one of the four houses, depending upon their predominant personal trait, be it courage, intellect and wit, loyalty and diligence, or entrepreneurial cunning and ambition. In creating the houses J.K. Rowling intended them, roughly at least, to correspond to the four elements of classical times, with Gryffindor representing fire, Ravenclaw signifying air, Hufflepuff standing for earth and Slytherin portraying water. Slytherin has a strong reputation for producing Dark Wizards, whether apparent or real – in different generations Voldemort, Severus Snape and Lucius Malfoy were in the house, and Draco was placed in it in the 1990s. This signified a general malaise rather than a fatal flaw – Dumbledore never ceased urging an inclusive wholeness for the houses, and, most controversially, gave his trust to Snape, head of Slytherin house. He also employed a retired ex-head of house of Slytherin as his Potions master in *Harry Potter and the Half-Blood Prince*.

Unity in Hogwarts is complex, a complexity represented in the four houses, which reflects the ancient divisions of the founders. The divisions in themselves do not create disharmony – it is the forces of darkness that exploit divisions. As the stories are told from the perspective of Harry, they give a more favourable view of Gryffindor than of the other houses, particularly Slytherin, but the ideal of unity remains. The Sorting Hat, in its customary song at the opening of Harry's fifth new school year, warns students that they need to stand together.

> For our Hogwarts is in danger
> From external, deadly foes
> And we must unite inside her
> Or we'll crumble from within . . .

In its song the Hat wonders whether dividing the school into houses might further fragment and divide, a concern shared by Hermione. She reckons Quidditch, the school teams of which are based on the houses, creates tensions and bad feelings between them. The Sorting Hat in its song portrays disagreements among the founders as a fall from a happier original state, in which the houses expressed the particular insights and gifts of the founders and worked together in friendship.

The link between the houses and the ancient elements reinforces the magical and alchemical tone of the school. It is also a potent concept in that it ties into the ancient notion of the four humours, which was an extension of the four elements, applied to early medicine and understanding of the human make-up. In effect, the dominant personality trait that determines which pupil goes into what house corresponds in some way to these four ancient humours. There were several schemes in classical times, relating to the four seasons, regions of the body, and bodily fluids – Hippocrates linked the element air with blood, the season of spring and the liver; earth with black bile, autumn and the spleen; fire with yellow bile, summer and the gall bladder; and water with phlegm, winter and the brain and lungs. The resulting characteristics of a dominant element were, in order, being courageous or amorous; despondent or sleepless; easily angered; and calm or unemotional. These corresponded with Galen's famous taxonomy of type: the sanguine, the melancholic, the choleric and the phlegmatic. More relevant, perhaps, are the alchemical types of Paracelsus, each of which seemed to have a corresponding spirit: changeable (the salamander);

industrious (the gnome); inspired (the water nymph or undine); and the curious (the sylph). This is closer to Hogwarts's typology: air as the eagle, championing intellect and wit (Ravenclaw); earth as the badger, encouraging loyalty and diligence (Hufflepuff); fire as the lion, celebrating courage and resourcefulness (Gryffindor); and water as the snake, desiring cunning and ambition (Slytherin). There are modern forms of the taxonomy, notably the Myers–Briggs classification, which has four dimensions of personality, involving a fundamental distinction between the introvert and extrovert. A contemporary educational system that uses the humours or temperament in teaching practice is that of the Waldorf schools, based on the writings of Rudolf Steiner.

What is important is not the precision of these categories but the Hogwarts principle of wholeness, pulling together human diversity in its richness into a community and society. Though the emphasis is on social and communal balance, the stories suggest that the balanced person also has a share of all the house characteristics. Harry is often worried by what he sees as Slytherin tendencies in himself, making him wonder whether he really should be in Gryffindor. His strong ambition to win the Triwizard Tournament is a Slytherin characteristic, as is his risk-taking and a certain disregard for school rules. These tendencies give him frightening affinities with his arch-enemy Voldemort, affinities explained most fully in *Harry Potter and the Deathly Hallows*. Dumbledore, however, reassures him that these characteristics are essentially a good not an evil. It is one's choices that determine one's character for good or ill, not one's make-up. In fact, Harry's own choice was taken into account when he was sorted into the house of Gryffindor upon arriving at the school in his first year.

The principle of wholeness and community based on friendship is at the moral centre of the stories not only because the Harry Potter books are school stories, but also because the events of the entire wizard world are connected into what happens at Hogwarts. This remains true in *Harry Potter and the Deathly Hallows*, where many of the events take place outside the school. In all the stories Hogwarts remains the reference point for events in the wider world, from Voldemort's obsession with the school to Dumbledore's uneasy relationship with the Ministry of Magic.

A main instrument of disharmony is the doctrine of pure-bloods, a form of racism. In *Harry Potter and the Order of the Phoenix* Professor Umbridge brings this divisive force into the institute, which means that pupils have to be protected against internal as well as external evil forces that threaten their education and wholeness. Umbridge deliberately exploits the tensions between Slytherin and the other houses, recruiting its worst elements (Draco and his cronies) to her special Inquisitorial Squad. In contrast, Harry's opposition, the DA, is open to members from Hufflepuff and Ravenclaw as well as Gryffindor (the necessity of secrecy seems to rule out Slytherin members, though the DA could be considered guilty of prejudice against all Slytherins in deliberately not recruiting any members from that house). The doctrine of pure-blood is only one of the contrasts with the ideal of wholeness. The most dramatic is that of fragmentation.

Fragmentation is particularly represented in Voldemort. Rejecting all that is good and whole, Voldemort long ago determined to preserve his life at any cost. He chose to store fragments of his soul in Horcruxes, so that it is eventually divided into what he thought was seven, a powerful number of completeness, but in fact his soul was broken into eight. This was a choice to be less than human. His fragmentation reflects a perversion of goodness and humanity that is astonishingly evil. Voldemort remakes himself, rejecting the divine image in human beings. His ruthless quest for immortality, distorting his soul, is reflected in his followers, the Death Eaters. As a group they contrast sharply with the ideal of wholeness and community reflected in Hogwarts, and embodied most successfully in the core friendship of Harry, Ron, Hermione and Hagrid, and their wider circle of friendship represented in the DA. The service of the Death Eaters to their Dark Master is based on fear, not love, a self-chosen slavery, not friendship. What Hogwarts represents is so powerful that to take up a post at Hogwarts signalled an open allegiance to the Order of the Phoenix, the effective opposition to Voldemort, as Horace Slughorn realised clearly when he abandoned retirement to teach at Hogwarts for a year. Similarly, some of Voldemort's Death Eaters, such as Bellatrix Lestrange, distrusted Snape because he remained in post at the school.

The fragmentation and progressive perversion of Voldemort contrasts also with Harry's moral character. Despite his limitations, flaws and mistakes, Harry remains loyal to Dumbledore, and implacably opposed to the Dark Arts, knowing that his parents had been murdered by the forbidden killing curse. In the course of the stories he remains true to the ideals of Hogwarts despite all his suffering. In the words of Dumbledore he remains pure and whole. The headmaster points out to Harry that Voldemort 'cannot possess you without enduring mortal agony . . . I do not think he understands why, Harry, but he was in such a hurry to mutilate his own soul, he never paused to understand the incomparable power of a soul that is untarnished and whole.' In speaking of a soul that is whole he is referring to what he had said to Harry just before: 'In spite of the temptation you have endured, all the suffering, you remain pure of heart, just as pure as you were at the age of eleven, when you stared into a mirror that reflected your heart's desire, and it showed you only the way to thwart Lord Voldemort, and not immortality or riches.'

THE DEEPER MAGIC

J.K. Rowling has been familiar with C.S. Lewis's Narnian stories since childhood. In interviews she has referred to them, particularly relishing Lewis's idea of the Wood between the Worlds, where each of the various ponds might give access to another world. For her, that captures the essence of reading books, in that they take you into alternative worlds. An important element in the Narnian tales is the idea of Deep Magic and a Deeper Magic. The Deep Magic represents the moral order obeyed (or disobeyed) by the magical creatures of the Narnian world. The Deeper Magic, however, represents an even more fundamental principle that resembles the Christian New Testament notion of grace, the deepest form of love, which brings to maturity and fulfils the older law. Thus, in Narnia, the Deeper Magic allows a willing victim to die in the place of a traitor (as Aslan does for the boy Edmund). There is a rather similar principle underlying the Harry Potter stories. The principle is highlighted in the sacrificial love of Harry's mother, Lily, dying for her infant son. Her death protects Harry, the first evidence of which is that Harry fails to die under the killing curse administered by Voldemort. Hitherto, this curse had been thought inviolable, but the deeper principle of Lily's love allows Harry to survive, albeit with the lightning-shaped scar on his forehead. The deflection of the curse also causes Voldemort's disembodiment, meaning that it takes him many years to reconstitute himself. It also causes his soul to fragment further. Voldemort confesses in *Harry Potter and the Goblet of Fire*: 'His mother died in the attempt to save him – and unwittingly provided him with a protection I admit I had not foreseen . . . His mother left upon him the traces of her sacrifice . . . this is old magic, I should have remembered it, I was foolish to overlook it.'

Self-sacrificial love runs as a dominant theme through the stories. Not only does Lily's sacrifice for Harry indirectly shape the plot of all the stories – Harry, for instance, acquired some of Voldemort's powers in the attack on him – but there are many other acts of self-sacrifice. Harry is willing to die for his friends – a fact remarked upon by Dobby the house-elf in *Harry Potter and the Chamber of Secrets*. He reveals the reality of this willingness at the decisive moment in *Harry Potter and the Deathly Hallows* that turns out to resolve all the dangers to his friends from Voldemort, the moment he comes to the Dark Lord in the forest as the sacrifice. He is not alone in being sacrificial, however. Ron risks his life in *Harry Potter and the Philosopher's Stone*, as the three friends go through various trials in their quest to prevent the Philosopher's Stone falling into evil hands. On the enormous chessboard, where the giant animated figures show no mercy, Ron allows himself to be taken by the Queen to get Harry and Hermione out of danger. To their protests he had yelled: 'That's chess. . . . You've got to make some sacrifices! I take one step forward and she'll take me – that leaves you free to checkmate the king, Harry!' Sirius takes it as given that people would die for their friends when he castigates Wormtail for his treachery in *Harry Potter and the Prisoner of Azkaban*. He gives his own life defending Harry and his friends in the battle within the Department of Mysteries in *Harry Potter and the Order of the Phoenix*. In *Harry Potter and the Half-Blood Prince*, Dumbledore acquiesces in his own killing to protect Harry. Dumbledore remains convinced to the last that love is more powerful than Voldemort's kind of magic.

The magical laws of self-sacrifice are complex. The bond between wizards when one saves another runs very deep, which means that Wormtail must feel some sense of obligation to Harry for saving him, compromising his allegiance to Voldemort. In *Harry Potter and the Deathly Hallows* this obligation results in a moment of pity for Harry that swiftly costs Wormtail his life. In the case of Lily Potter, she was both magician and mother in saving Harry, providing a double bond for Harry. Dumbledore tells Harry in *Harry Potter and the Order of the Phoenix* that the force of the Deeper Magic is captured in a room within the Department of Mysteries. It is a power, Dumbledore says, that Harry has and Voldemort lacks. The room is always kept locked and 'contains a force that is at once more wonderful and more terrible than death, than human intelligence, than the forces of nature. It is also, perhaps, the most mysterious of the many subjects for study that reside there.'

The Deeper Magic of love and sacrifice is one of the many themes in the stories that has a Christian parallel, the strongest in fact. Perhaps because of a widespread condemnation of the Harry Potter books in some Christian circles, most pronounced in parts of the USA, a number of high-quality studies have appeared demonstrating Christian values and virtues in the stories. Much of the condemnation of the stories as promoting black magic, the Satanic and the occult came as a result of an article in the popular satirical online magazine the *Onion*. The article was widely circulated on the Internet as factual evidence of the diabolical influence of the stories, senders and recipients not realising that it was satire. In the years following that article the Harry Potter books have been high on the list of banned books, or of books some parents and others wished to be banned from school and public libraries. At least such protestors were willing to present arguments for their concerns. Some groups, in contrast, have held public burnings of the books. As John Milton commented, 'As good almost kill a man as kill a good book; who kills a man kills a reasonable creature, God's image; he who destroys a good book, kills reason itself, kills the image of God.'

The first to appear, in 2001 in the UK and 2002 in the USA, was Francis Bridger's *A Charmed Life: The Spirituality of Potterworld*, which is particularly effective in expounding the moral values and theology of the stories. It also explores philosophical issues relating to J.K. Rowling's fantasy, as it challenges a rationalist approach to reality. Bridger is a theologian and pastor, and Principal of a leading evangelical theological college in Bristol. He argues that, far from promoting Satanism, the Harry Potter books are firmly based upon Christian values and offer vital insights into relationships, human character and spirituality. In fact, the stories, he believes, are a potent resource for understanding the morality and theology of the Christian faith. The secret that allows Harry and his friends to triumph over evil is not wizardry and magic as such, but their goodness, love and friendship. Bridger's book covers the first four of the Harry Potter stories. While Christianity is not explicit in Potterworld, he argues, 'the values it espouses resonate at critical points with Christian morality: loyalty, fidelity, honesty (in the deepest sense), courage, trust and, above all, love are prominent virtues worked out in the lives of our heroes, while the reality of evil and wrongdoing are clearly brought out and condemned. In book after book, evil fails as goodness triumphs.' He sees the compassion and wisdom of Dumbledore evoking 'the kind of wisdom we find in the book of Proverbs, with its combination of ethical realism and virtuous behavior'.

Hard on the heels of Bridger was the publication of John Killinger's *God, the Devil, and Harry Potter*, in 2002. This is subtitled 'A Christian Minister's Defense of the Beloved Novels'. The book is a tough, non-nonsense apologia for the stories, which sees J.K. Rowling as 'a mistress of wonder'. Her books capture 'the sheer wonder of existence, the magic of being'. Harvey Cox commented on the book, 'At last! . . . A sensible Christian reading of Harry Potter . . . Remember, even Jesus himself was accused of necromancy by his enemies!' Killinger believes that 'the world of Harry Potter would be inconceivable apart from the structures of Judeo-Christian theology and a very traditional Christian conceptualisation of human existence and the way it should be approached by every follower of Jesus.' Killinger's careful reading of the books covers the first four of the stories.

Connie Neal has a much more popular touch than Bridger and Killinger, but displays equal insight into the stories. Her study of Harry Potter also came out in 2002, and covers the same books as

Bridger and Killinger. *The Gospel According to Harry Potter: Spirituality in the Stories of the World's Most Famous Seeker* finds an extraordinary number of themes that can be seen as glimmers of the Christian Gospel. Her book is partly provoked by those who have scrutinised the Harry Potter books for references to the occult and Satanic practices in order to condemn them as a wicked influence. Neal sees this attitude as confirming a comment J.K. Rowling once made in an interview: 'People tend to find in books what they look to find.' What is different in Neal's quest for parallels from the demon-hunters is that she loves the Harry Potter stories, and seeks to read them attentively, sharing her insights with others on the assumption that they too are careful, attentive readers who will appreciate from Neal's alternative reading the dangers of *reading into* the stories one's assumptions.

A Parent's Guide to Harry Potter is more recent. Published in 2005, it takes into account the first five books, and looks at them from the perspective of the child reader, and his or her moral development. As both parent and educator, Gina Burkart has an invigorating take on the stories, showing how children can learn from specific situations and emotions in Harry Potter's world, such as fear, anger, bullying, diversity and choosing good over evil. She also points out how the books can enrich relationships not only between children, but also between children and adults who care for, love and support them. Gina Burkart's guide grew out of her own reading of the books with her children. 'I shared with and learned from them,' she says, 'just as much as they shared with and learned from me.' Far from seeing the Harry Potter books as a danger to children, she sees them as a unique good.

John Granger's *Looking for God in Harry Potter: Is there a Hidden Meaning in the Bestselling Books?* was originally published in 2002, with an updated second edition in 2006 that now includes discussion of the first six stories in the series. It is an unusual and stimulating study that unravels a kind of 'Harry Potter Code', centring on the many allusions to ancient alchemy in the stories. These coded elements, in his view, point to underlying orthodox Christian themes. His approach is much more convincing than it might appear, although the alchemical elements in the stories are rather overstated. Magic and alchemy is very much a literary device rather than a believed element in the Harry Potter books. Nevertheless, his study is full of starting points for a richer awareness of what is going on in the stories. At the heart of his analysis is that readers – from whatever culture around the world – are wired to appreciating the greatest of stories (the Gospel narratives of God becoming a human being) by virtue of the fact that each of us concretely bears God's image. The Harry Potter stories embody imagery, themes and stories that beat to the same drum as that master story, he believes, and this is the deep secret of their global appeal. Granger's view has similarities with the belief of Tolkien and C.S. Lewis that great stories prefigure and anticipate, or refer in some other way, to the master story of the Gospels. Granger tries to read the Harry Potter stories in the context of the tradition of English Literature, which for most of its life, he points out, has been predominantly Christian in ethos.

All the books I have mentioned were written before the publication of *Harry Potter and the Deathly Hallows*, a story that draws very clearly upon Christian meanings, in particular alluding to the death and resurrection of Jesus Christ. As with Tolkien and C.S. Lewis, who draw upon the spell of the New Testament Gospels, this does not spoil the storytelling, but rather enhances it. Tolkien argued, in his seminal essay 'On Fairy Stories', that the Gospel accounts bring into sharp focus the patterns and insights of great stories: myth becomes fact as the tale is told in real history.

One instance of the pattern that he gives is what he calls 'eucatastrophe', the good catastrophe, when there is a sudden reversal of fortune after deepest darkness and greatest calamity. *Harry Potter and the Deathly Hallows*, like Tolkien's *The Lord of the Rings*, exhibits this kind of satisfying eucatastrophe when Harry makes his way willingly to the Forbidden Forest as a result of Voldemort's ultimatum. The Dark Lord has gambled that Harry would be foolish enough to come, out of concern for his friends. Harry knows that he must die in order that his friends and all who have helped him and actively resisted the tyrant at the Battle of Hogwarts can live. Voldemort's killing curse takes Harry to a between-world. The splinter of Voldemort's soul that has been within him since an infant has been wrenched out of him. In that place of vision, what seems to be the Dark Lord himself is a wounded naked small child who is helpless and beyond all help. Harry, however, is allowed to return to the world of the living if he so chooses, which he does, and helps in the final defeat of Voldemort.

Parallels between the Gospels and Harry's chosen sacrifice are not literal, but more as in a parable, just as in the Christian parallels in Tolkien. The meaning of the concept of sacrifice is superbly illuminated. Because the reference to the Gospels of the story of Harry's dying and return is by allusion and not by strict correspondence, his sacrifice can apply in various ways to different readers. This variety of application is characteristic of all good stories. A Jewish reader of *Harry Potter and the Deathly Hallows*, who loved the book, tried to apply the account of Harry's sacrifice and resurrection within his own faith. He saw it

as a strong sign of the author's xian religious background . . . Throughout the series there was the theme of Harry's having received magical protection from his mother's having died trying to save his life . . . I'd like to read Deathly Hallows as continuing the same theme. Harry's being willing to sacrifice himself out of love for his friends and out of committment to fighting evil led to everyone else's receiving magical protection at the end of the fight with Voldemort. I think that the story works perfectly well that way.

Another of the many parallels of this kind with the Gospels exists in the complex relationship between Harry and Dumbledore, his mentor. Christian theology from its earliest period has acknowledged the mystery of the Trinity, the three persons of the one Godhead. A tantalising aspect of this is the relation of God the Father to his Son, who became a human being at a definite time and place in human history. This relationship is at the heart of Christian teaching. The Son willingly came to die for the sins of the world. The Father willingly sacrificed his Son. Presumably, in his self-chosen limitations as a human being developing from infant to child to boy to man, Jesus gradually became aware of what he had to do. As a parable, not as a literal correspondence, the relationship between Dumbledore and Harry is more fully revealed in *Harry*

Potter and the Deathly Hallows than in the earlier books, and has parallels with the Father and Son in the Gospels. Dumbledore realises almost from the beginning, after the infant Harry survives Voldemort's killing curse, that one day he would be faced with the choice of sacrificing himself as the only way to destroy Voldemort and to save the world. The burden of that knowledge gives a profound complexity to Dumbledore's relationship with his protégé. It also superbly illuminates this central feature of Christian theology, the relation of Father and Son, a feature that has been elaborated by some of the greatest minds in history.

Like Snape, Dumbledore is one of the most complex and enigmatic characters in children's fiction, sharing the fascination people have with his imaginative forebears, Merlin and Gandalf.

PROPHECY, PREDICTIONS AND PROVIDENCE

'The consequences of our actions are always so complicated, so diverse, that predicting the future is a very difficult business indeed . . .' In *Harry Potter and the Prisoner of Azkaban* Dumbledore characteristically says this to Harry in the light of issues raised by time travelling. Harry and Hermione had travelled three hours into the past in a desperate rescue attempt. In theory, Harry and Hermione were free to change events that had become fixed in the past, events that were now history. Tampering with such events, however, could have catastrophic consequences, and yet, in order to save two innocent parties – Sirius and Buckbeak the Hippogriff – it was necessary for them to intervene in a past world where every event was already the result of a network of cause and effect that went back, as it were, to the beginning of the universe. (Even in a fictional work the causes of events are very complex: even though its causality is enormously simplified, at the very least the creation of the work itself and any consistency that it has is caused from the real world outside the fiction.) Part of the complexity of Harry and Hermione's time travelling is that Sirius's rescue turns out to be dependent upon them successfully rescuing Buckbeak from execution. It additionally involves Harry saving, in the past, both Sirius and himself from the Dementor's Kiss, which is worse than death.

The limits to the freedom the two friends can exercise require great resourcefulness in the rescues. Hermione, who has had a great deal of experience of time-turning from extending her timetable, is more aware than Harry of the dangers. This is why she stops Harry grabbing his Invisibility Cloak to prevent Snape finding it. Every change they make to the past increases the complexity of what might happen, jeopardising their aim of saving Sirius. As Dumbledore points out afterwards, the complexity of events makes prediction of the future very difficult. So of course does freedom of action.

Providence in events implies a divine hand shaping what is going on, taking into account free human actions and the processes of natural causes. The term comes from the Latin *providens*, 'to see before', or 'foresee'. Providence implies that events are ultimately patterned by design and intention, not, in the final analysis, by chaos, randomness and chance. Such a theological view of things is implicit in the Harry Potter stories.

Dumbledore, more than any other figure, represents providence in the books, both as a reassuring figure for those fighting the Dark Arts and as a spokesman for such a hopeful view. He is ever confident that there is a benevolent purpose behind things, and that evil is not ultimate and everlasting. Such a hopeful view of life is revealed in his characteristic reassurance directed to the hidden Harry and Ron in *Harry Potter and the Chamber of Secrets*, when he is given notice of suspension from the school by Lucius Malfoy: 'You will find that I will only *truly* have left this school when none here are loyal to me. You will also find that help will always be given at Hogwarts to those who ask for it.' Dumbledore seems to know and interpret events, and is a protective force that even Voldemort fears. His assertion that help would be forthcoming is borne out when Harry specifically asks for it on one occasion in *Harry Potter and the Deathly Hallows*. His yell for help in the dungeon of Malfoy Manor is effectively a prayer. His cry of desperation comes when he sees what he thinks is Dumbledore's eye in his mirror, but which turns out to be Aberforth's. Aberforth responds by sending him the help of Dobby the house-elf.

A world shaped by providence is one in which prophecy as well as prayer is possible. Not surprisingly, therefore, prophecy plays a pivotal role in the shape of events in the Harry Potter stories. From the beginning of the first story we are introduced rather incidentally to prophecy. Referring to the infant Harry's unprecedented escape from Voldemort's killing curse, Professor McGonagall in *Harry Potter and the Philosopher's Stone* remarks to Dumbledore: 'He'll be famous . . . there will be books written about Harry – every child in our world will know his name!' Her words turn out to be prophetic. Though she talks of Harry's future fame in the magical world, by a strange irony her words would turn out to be true in the real world outside fiction. In the early years of the twenty-first century, children around the globe know the name of Harry Potter.

The pivotal prophecy, however, is that given by Professor Trelawney the year before the birth of Harry. It is given to Dumbledore and, crucially, overheard by Snape. Even more crucially, Snape conveys only part of the prophecy to Voldemort. Dumbledore points out to Harry in *Harry Potter and the Half-Blood Prince* that the Dark Wizard himself had activated the prophecy concerning him and Voldemort. Like many stored in the Department of Mysteries, it would have remained unfulfilled. It became significant only

> because Voldemort made a grave error, and acted on Professor Trelawney's words! If Voldemort had never murdered your father, would he have imparted in you a furious desire for revenge? Of course not! If he had not forced your mother to die for you, would he have given you a magical protection he could not penetrate? Of course not, Harry! Don't you see? Voldemort himself created his worst enemy, just as tyrants everywhere do! . . . He heard the prophecy and he leapt into action, with the result that he not only handpicked the man most likely to finish him, he handed him uniquely deadly weapons!

The prophecy did not mean Harry was fated to act on its predictions. It was his choice to act. Harry realised that this was 'the difference between being dragged into the arena to face a battle to the death and walking into the arena with your head held high'. The world of Harry Potter is not like that perceived by Astrology, in which events are ruled by fate. Nor is it like the view of materialism, in which mechanistic forces determine all events. It is instead a world ruled by providence, in which choices are truly significant in the complex outcome of events, and in which prophecy is possible despite that complexity.

Although in many respects Professor Trelawney is, in Hermione's words, a 'huge fraud', there are other examples of prophecies inadvertently uttered by the 'sibyl'. These are not of the magnitude of the prophecy of Harry and Voldemort, which determines so much of the plot. One is her prophecy about Voldemort's servant (Wormtail) in *Harry Potter and the Prisoner of Azkaban*, who would return to his Dark Master before midnight on the day of the prophecy, and would help him come back to power. In this case Wormtail does not hear the prophecy, and so his choice to escape and return to Voldemort is not shaped by it. Another prophecy occurs in *Harry Potter and the Half-Blood Prince*, foretelling, on the basis of a Tarot card, the catastrophe on the lightning-struck tower. At the time of the prophecy, all the factors that cause Dumbledore's death are in place and the event is not shaped by anyone acting on the prophecy. Both these prophecies underlie the fact that the hand of providence is shaping the events, taking in the effects of the choices of the various players, such as Wormtail, Draco Malfoy, Harry, Dumbledore and numerous others.

The prophecies are major pointers to providence in the stories – to the hope that goodness will ultimately triumph over wickedness as implacable of that of Voldemort's. There are many minor signals of hope. One is the behaviour of Mr Weasley's magically enhanced Ford Anglia. The magic not only gives the car the property of flight, but it somehow actively connects it into the forces of goodness. Most dramatically, in *Harry Potter and the Chamber of Secrets*, it rescues Harry and Ron from an unspeakable fate at the hand of the acromantula, the gigantic flesh-eating spiders of the Forbidden Forest. Another example of magical properties of things being larger than their practical function is that of the Felix Felicis charm. Far more than simply bringing good luck, it puts the charmed person in touch with a benevolent force. Thus, in *Harry Potter and the Half-Blood Prince*, Harry under the influence of the Felix Felicis charm is able to obtain the true memory of the conversation that had passed long before between Slughorn and Tom Riddle (Voldemort). This is a vital step in understanding Voldemort's motives and strategy.

Harry is even helped unwittingly by the Dark Side in *Harry Potter and the Goblet of Fire* (by the fake Mad-Eye Moody, Barty Crouch Jr), strongly indicating that evil is not ultimate. Crouch intended his machinations to place Harry in the clutches of Voldemort and be destroyed. Instead Harry achieves a significant victory over the Dark Lord and learns essential information for later battles. Another indicator of hope is that skills acquired by Harry, Ron and Hermione later prove providential in events (Harry's ability as a Seeker, Ron's brilliance at Chess, and Hermione's acumen in scholarship, to name some).

A more mysterious pointer to the presence of providence in the world of Harry Potter is the music, the healing and other qualities of the phoenix, Fawkes. The phoenix plays a complex and poetic role in events. Its music, for instance, provides a symbol that help is always there for those who need it. 'Piping its weird music,' Fawkes's song accompanies Dumbledore's sending of the Sorting Hat to Harry as he confronts Tom Riddle in *Harry Potter and the Chamber of Secrets*.

> The music was growing louder. It was eerie, spine-tingling, unearthly; it lifted the hair on Harry's scalp and made his heart feel as though it was swelling to twice its normal size. Then, as the music reached such a pitch that Harry felt it vibrating inside his own ribs, flames erupted at the top of the nearest pillar.

In *Harry Potter and the Half-Blood Prince*, Fawkes seems to express Dumbledore's wordless emotion at Harry's faithfulness to him, when Harry told him of Rufus Scrimgeour's accusation that he was 'Dumbledore's man through and through'. The phoenix had given a 'low, soft, musical cry' as the wizard's eyes had watered. Later, Fawkes laments his lost master by his fallen body while, as once before, in the Chamber of Secrets, Harry feels the music is inside him – 'it was his own grief turned magically to song that echoed across the grounds and through the castle windows'.

The effect of the phoenix's dirge parallels the healing properties of his tears. Harry, in *Harry Potter and the Chamber of Secrets*, had experienced the healing in the Chamber of Secrets, after being fatally bitten by the Basilisk. He benefited again from Fawkes's tears after the final trial of the Triwizard Tournament. The phoenix 'was resting its beautiful head against Harry's injured leg, and thick, pearly tears were falling from its eyes onto the wound left by the spider. The pain vanished. The skin mended. His leg was repaired.'

My favourite demonstration of the mysterious presence of hope and providence is when Harry time-travels from the immediate future in *Harry Potter and the Prisoner of Azkaban*. At the lakeside he uses the Patronus Charm to disperse the Dementors attacking Sirius, Hermione and himself. The stag is his dead father's presence with him. He actually sees it from two viewpoints: as one of those benefiting from its presence, as the ghostly stag routes the Dementors; and as the person who sends it. He sees the stag, as white as a unicorn, gallop in dazzling light through the darkness across the lake and then canter back after the Dementors flee.

The Dementors are one of J.K. Rowling's compelling images of evil. Her exploration of this theme and its relation to magic is the subject of the next chapter.

SEVEN

Images of Good and Evil

It may come as a surprise to learn that J.K. Rowling denies believing in magic, as portrayed in her stories, and equally surprising to discover that her stories emerge out of a recognisable Christian faith. Before the publication of *Harry Potter and the Deathly Hallows* made her faith clear, this revelation was buried in the enormous number of interviews she has given since Harry Potter became a household name. The reason for this scarcity is that very few interviewers actually have asked her if she believed in God, or, more specifically, in Christ. One interviewer asked her if she believed in magic. Rowling responded: 'Magic in the sense in which it happens in my books, no, I don't believe. I don't believe in that. No. No.' Another interviewer, in Canada, asked her directly about her spiritual beliefs, particularly if she was in fact a Christian. Her reply was equally direct:

> Yes, I am . . . Which seems to offend the religious right far worse than if I said I thought there was no God. Every time I've been asked if I believe in God, I've said yes, because I do, but no one ever really has gone any more deeply into it than that, and I have to say that does suit me, because if I talk too freely about that I think the intelligent reader, whether 10 or 60, will be able to guess what's coming in the books.

At the time the interview in Canada was given, four of the books were published, so Rowling was referring to events in the last three books particularly, as being shaped in plot by a Christian influence on her work.

The Harry Potter books are perceived in strikingly different ways. Some who are Christians, for instance, see them as promoting the occult and Satanism, and have tried, sometimes successfully, to ban them from libraries and schools. Other Christians, more discerning, such as Jerram Barrs of The Francis Schaeffer Institute of Covenant Theological Seminary, St Louis, see them as morally unambiguous about the nature of good versus evil, promoting the good. He writes of J.K. Rowling's 'very clear moral universe'. A pagan witch finds herself bemused by arguments that the Harry Potter stories are full of accurate and true information about witchcraft, and by accusations of Satanism. She writes that the 'only "real" witchcraft elements in the books are the real stereotypes that have dogged witchcraft for decades. Flying around on broomsticks, pointed witches' hats, and the shooting of lightning from magic wands, to name a few'. She points out that Wicca is a religion with a god and goddess. But 'there is no spirituality', she claims, 'in these books and movies at all!' In contrast, a Jewish Rabbi asserts, 'The "Harry Potter" books are not just novels. They are modern fairy tales with predominant spiritual themes. They describe the struggle between good and evil and the ultimate triumph of the good through courage and ingenuity of the human spirit, and the power of human love.' The Rabbi Noson Weisz points out that 'Evil as presented in the Harry Potter books – whose ambition is to destroy the good for the sake of its own hegemony – is not innate to the universe. In reality, evil only comes about through the corruption of the good.' The Harry Potter stories, with the attendant movies, have been phenomenally successful around the globe. The fantasies of Tolkien and C.S. Lewis have enjoyed a similar planet-wide success. Though there are important differences in the fantasies of Tolkien, Lewis and J.K. Rowling, there are dramatic similarities in the values embedded in their works. This is no more apparent than in their depictions of evil in story form, in a manner that a contemporary readership and audiences find topical and relevant.

J.K. Rowling's portrayal of evil in the Harry Potter stories is complex and many-layered, reflecting a rich tradition of fantasy literature. Fantasy for both adults and children has become increasingly important in contemporary literature, reflecting the tumult of social change in modern society in the twentieth century, with two global wars and numerous other conflicts with apocalyptic casualties. As we have seen, in the Harry Potter stories people and things are often not what they appear, which has the effect of engaging the reader in reflection on the nature of evil. Evil, focused upon the Dark Lord, Voldemort, contrasts with qualities and virtues like love, self-sacrifice and courage, prized and defended by Harry and his friends. A society based on fear (the Death Eaters) contrasts with the supportive friendship of Harry, Hermione, Ron, Hagrid and others. J.K. Rowling's portrayal of evil is orthodoxly Christian, in the tradition of St Augustine, rather than Gnostic or materialistic, demonstrating that this ancient tradition is relevant and applicable to a modern world. The stories have a clear moral structure, in which the Dark Arts (representing evil) are explicitly condemned, as well as opposed in the unfolding events.

THE NATURE OF MAGIC IN THE WIZARDING WORLD OF HARRY POTTER

The fantasy of the stories is tied up with the existence of magic. This magic is seen as part of the goodness of reality, but, as in the non-magical world, evil exists as a perversion of what is good. The scope of magic in the stories is extensive. It can be illuminated, first, by showing its affinity with the high magic of the pre-Enlightenment sixteenth century; second, by strong parallels that exist between magical practice in the stories and modern technology – arguably the modern manifestation of magic; and, third, by considering the nature of magic in relation to religion.

The High Magic of the Sixteenth Century

Magic is a central organising principle of the Harry Potter stories. Fundamentally the population of the world is divided between the majority Muggles and the wizarding community. J.K. Rowling is drawing upon a concept of magic that is pre-Enlightenment, belonging to a pre-modernist society. Tellingly a bust of Paracelsus is prominently displayed in a corridor of Hogwart's School. Paracelsus (1493–1541) was a prominent alchemist of the sixteenth century. The subject of the first Harry Potter story – *Harry Potter and the Philosopher's Stone* – further emphasises the symbolic presence of an ancient concept of magic. The philosopher's stone is the distinctive quest of the alchemist, the ingredient that would enable the transmutation of base metals into gold and prolong life. Albus Dumbledore, headmaster of Hogwarts, is practised in the science and friend of the historic alchemist Nicolas Flamel, who appears as a character in the first Harry Potter book.

In his Oxford *History of Sixteenth Century Literature*, C.S. Lewis gives a vivid picture of this old white or 'high' magic, which he sharply distinguishes from goeteia or Satanic magic – what is called the Dark Arts at Hogwarts. In the sixteenth century, observes Lewis, there was an 'animistic or genial cosmology', where nature was perceived as 'a festival not a machine'. It was not until towards the end of that century that the beginnings of the scientific movement 'delivered nature into our hands'. This mechanistic perception of nature, in contrast to a cosmos full of life, impacted on both thought and emotion – effectively, to use different words, it created a different consciousness that lost an essential harmony and wholeness. Lewis argues:

> By reducing Nature to her mathematical elements it substituted a mechanical for a genial or animistic conception of the universe. The world was emptied, first of her indwelling spirits, then of her occult sympathies and antipathies, finally of her colours, smells, and tastes. . . . The result was dualism rather than materialism. The mind, on whose ideal constructions the whole method depended, stood over against its object in ever sharper dissimilarity. Man with his new powers became rich like Midas but all that he touched had gone dead and cold. This process, slowly working, ensured during the next century the loss of the old mythological imagination: the conceit, and later the personified abstraction, takes its place. Later still, as a desperate attempt to bridge a gulf which begins to be found intolerable, we have the Nature poetry of the Romantics.

If C.S. Lewis is right, the Muggle population depicted by J.K. Rowling was born with this dualism of a mechanised view of nature. In Chapter Nine we shall look at the roots of her vision of wholeness and harmony in the Romantic Movement that Lewis mentions.

Lewis has fascinating insights into the high magic, where, in his words, 'there is no Satanism or Faustian compact'. This high magic can be studied, he says, in people like Picodella Mirandola (1463–94), Ficino (1433–99), Paracelsus, Agrippa (1486–1535), Dr John Dee (1527–1608) and Henry Moore, in his *Philosophical Works* (1662). They held to a kind of 'Platonic theology' where Plato represented a common wisdom of the ancients. Interestingly, Lewis himself made imaginative use of this idea of an ancient common wisdom, focused in a sixteenth-century view of Platonism, in his *Chronicles of Narnia*, much admired by J.K. Rowling.

Magic in the Muggle World: Technology and Applied Science

For both C.S. Lewis and Tolkien, the modern form of magic is technology. In *The Lord of the Rings*, the central image, the ring, is a kind of ultimate machine into which the Dark Lord has poured his soul. (Here Tolkien makes use of an ancient element of fairy stories – placing the soul in an external object – that is also employed by Rowling in her Horcruxes. Both writers have brilliantly transformed the ancient device for the purpose of their stories.) When technology is misused, it takes on a life of its own, and a whole society can become technocratic, ruled by a machine mentality, as argued by Jacques Ellul, in his study *The Technological Society*. Literary critic Alan Jacobs seems to have been the first to notice an important parallel between the correct use of magic in the wizarding world of Harry Potter and the proper use of technology in the Muggle world. The ethical lessons in the stories of the proper use of magic are parallel lessons in the crux question of handling technology and its awesome power so that our lives are enriched rather than enslaved and ruined. Following the lead given by Jacobs, Benjamin Lipscomb and Christopher Stewart argue, in 'Magic, Science, and the Ethics of Technology', that the categories of bad and evil apply as much to technology as to magic.

This is not merely a matter of ruling out bad 'uses' of essentially neutral powers. The Unforgivable Curses are not simply hurtful uses of essentially neutral powers. They are bad spells. The basic implication of Rowling's ethic contrasts sharply with the conventional piety that 'technologies are neutral between our possible uses of them, and what we must do is use them well; no kind of power should be rejected by people outright'.

Technology, like magic, is a power, and hence can be used or misused. Just because a power exists does not make it right. This principle is as true in the wizarding as in the Muggle world.

Magic and Religion

At Hogwarts students are taught not only to use magic but also to control it – they learn the morality of magic. It is not seen as neutral. Both Harry and Tom Riddle are aware when young that they have special powers, but it is their invitation to Hogwarts School that makes each realise that these are magical gifts. This is likely to have been a common experience for those brought up in non-magical families. In entering the magical world, those attending Hogwarts have to accept the moral laws of that world. Hogwarts can expel and the Ministry of Magic can punish.

Parallel to natural magical ability in J.K. Rowling's fictional world is the human ability to think and imagine in the real world. Neither ability can be explained adequately by material causes. Unlike the gift of magic, all human beings have the gift of thought and imagination. Only some, however, go on to higher study in the sciences or humanities, or to use their imaginations in creative arts. Such parallels raise the question of how magic relates to religion.

Magic in the Harry Potter stories and religion in the real world are clearly not the same. In the world of Harry Potter its magic does not call on supernatural beings like angels or devils to intervene, nor does it make supplication to a divine creator. However, the Deeper Magic in the stories – involving love, self-sacrifice, the bonds of friendship and the phenomena studied in the Department of Mysteries – can be said to equate with the religious and the transcendent. All magic within the Harry Potter stories is subject to moral law, being therefore either good or dark and evil. Deeper Magic equals the religious and the transcendent (including the theological element in the books).

Why, we might ask, are there no religious ceremonies in the stories if the Deeper Magic is so central to it? Admittedly, Christmas is celebrated at Hogwarts, and carols sung, but there is no explicit Christian reference other than that it indicates the Christian feast. The answer for this absence is quite simple. Though it is not an alternative world in the same way as Narnia or Middle-earth, the magical world of Harry Potter is a subcreation. Its consistency and credibility come from the potency of imaginative laws, symbols and a literary decorum. Inserting this-worldly elements such as familiar religious ceremonies or other didactic elements would spoil the magic. It would also hinder or put off readers who do not have similar religious beliefs (and a good number who do). Even when J.K. Rowling uses seminal quotations from Jesus and St Paul in *Harry Potter and the Deathly Hallows*, the source is not disclosed, and they are an integral part of the story. Writers of fantasy have always realised this, going for what has imaginative and storytelling appeal. There is no explicit religion as such in Tolkien's *The Lord of the Rings*, or even in C.S. Lewis's *The Chronicles of Narnia*, despite sometimes rather obvious parallels in the latter with Christian teaching. The fact is that atheists can enjoy good fantasies written by Christians, as Christians can savour good fantasies written by atheists. Readers of fantasy can step inside and thus receive worlds that are very different from their own. As C.S. Lewis said, such stories help us steal past 'watchful dragons', allowing us to perceive reality in a fresh or different way. Through such stories we can be subverted and challenged, undeceived and awakened from slumber and delusion. Christ's own preferred method of teaching, evidently, was through stories, parables that deliberately provoked a response and demanded an application from his audience. He also left his portrait and message in four historical narratives, rather than in a treatise or collection of abstractions.

EVIL IN THE HARRY POTTER STORIES

Like the fantasies of C.S. Lewis and Tolkien, the Harry Potter stories have evil as a central theme, embodied in plot and a rich symbolism. The images of evil and goodness in the stories are now part of the vocabulary of children of the world. In terms of education alone, this must count as a remarkable effect. In a world seemingly often dominated by a secular cast, a traditional understanding of good and evil is successfully embodied in a powerful and staggeringly popular story. To adapt Professor McGonagall's prediction in the first book, children throughout the world know Harry's name.

Evil as Corruption and Perversion

St Augustine's enormously influential Christian view of the nature of evil is strikingly similar to that of J.K. Rowling. His view is expounded in his *Confessions* (written in AD 397). At one point Augustine looks back to his thirty-first year. He realised then that the cause of sin lies in free will, and rejected the Manichean heresy, with its eternal dualism of good and evil. Though he had abandoned belief in astrology by then, he was perplexed and miserable about the origin of evil. He had found in the Platonists the seeds of the doctrine of the divinity of the Word, but not of his Incarnation. Finally he discovered the truth about Christ through the study of Scripture, especially St Paul's letters. He saw that it follows from the incarnation – God taking on the flesh of a human being – that the world and humanity are good, and that the evil that exists is a corruption of what is good. Evil cannot exist of itself; it has no substance.

> It was manifested unto me, that those things be good which yet are corrupted . . . So long therefore as they are, they are good: therefore whatsoever is, is good. That evil then which I sought, whence it is, is not any substance: for were it a substance, it should be good. For either it should be an incorruptible substance, and so a chief good: or a corruptible substance; which unless it were good, could not be corrupted. I perceived therefore, and it was manifested to me that Thou madest all things good, nor is there any substance at all, which Thou madest not; and for that Thou madest not all things equal, therefore are all things; because each is good, and altogether very good, because our God made all things very good.
>
> And to Thee is nothing whatsoever evil: yea, not only to Thee, but also to Thy creation as a whole, because there is nothing

without, which may break in, and corrupt that order which Thou
hast appointed it . . .

. . . And I enquired what iniquity was, and found it to be no
substance, but the perversion of the will, turned aside from Thee,
O God, the Supreme . . .

Evil understood as corruption and perversion of good is exactly how
evil is represented in the Harry Potter stories. As we explore the
nature of evil in following Harry's years at Hogwarts, we are also on
the same ancient pilgrimage as St Augustine.

Some Images and Personifications of Evil in the Stories

Many characters in the stories clearly express opposition to or
acceptance of Dark Arts by word or deed, or both.

Dumbledore is pre-eminent in opposition, his antipathy to evil
being enshrined in the ethos of Hogwarts.

Harry's father, James, hated the Dark Arts – in *Harry Potter and
the Prisoner of Azkaban* Harry realised clearly that his father would
not have wanted his friends to become killers by doing away with
Wormtail, even though they were motivated by anger at his betrayal
of and culpability in the deaths of James and Lily Potter.

In *Harry Potter and the Order of the Phoenix* Professor Umbridge
was willing to use the Dark Arts, arguing that ends justified means.

When Defence Against the Dark Arts teacher Snape speaks of
forbidden magic as representing principles that are eternal and
indestructible, Harry, with his heightened awareness of evil, reacts to
Snape's use of the phrase 'unfixed . . . indestructible'. Snape had
claimed: 'The Dark Arts . . . are many, varied, ever-changing and
eternal. Fighting them is like fighting a many-headed monster,
which, each time a neck is severed, sprouts a head even fiercer and
cleverer than before. You are fighting that which is unfixed,
mutating, indestructible.' As it turned out, Snape did not actually
believe that evil could not be destroyed, though he may have had
doubts at times.

Standing as the antithesis of first Dumbledore and later Harry,
Voldemort expresses the ultimate belief of the Dark Wizard. His
philosophy, as expressed by his servant Professor Quirrell, is

summed up in the words: 'There is no good and evil, there is only power, and those too weak to seek it.' After falling to Voldemort's forces, the Ministry sports the slogan 'Magic is power'. The wizard Grindelwald, Voldemort's continental counterpart, excuses all kinds of wickedness with his sound-bite 'for the greater good'. This reliance on might and superiority is the attitude of those seeking to dominate and to possess, the supreme bullies. This mentality can apply to the use of technology as well as to magic, as we saw.

Voldemort, the Dark Lord of the stories, is a former brilliant pupil at Hogwarts called Tom Riddle, who turned to evil, seeking immortality. His main strategy is to divide his soul into pieces, embodied in objects called Horcruxes. This allows him to survive, albeit at first in a disembodied state, after his killing curse against the baby Harry went wrong. Harry quickly recognises Voldemort as the supreme manifestation of evil and as his enemy. As early as *Harry Potter and the Philosopher's Stone*, Harry realises that stopping Voldemort is more important than being expelled from Hogwarts. He spells out to his friends the implications of Voldemort getting hold of the Stone. By the end of *Harry Potter and the Half-Blood Prince*, he realises that the task of destroying the Dark Lord must take precedence over his studies at Hogwarts, and Ron and even Hermione agree, standing with him in the task.

Voldemort was originally the handsome star pupil at Hogwarts, who became Head Boy. His inward process of perversion and corruption is expressed in his changing physical appearance. In *Harry Potter and the Philosopher's Stone*, his face, which has taken shape at the back of Quirrell's head, has red eyes and slits. He has become a 'mere shadow and vapour' – a wraith. He gets his strength from drinking the blood of innocent unicorns he has had slain. After Quirrell's death, Voldemort re-forms into a hideous embryonic figure, a perversion of human birth, who is sustained by the 'milk' of his monstrous pet serpent, Nagini, who is also a living Horcrux, carrying a portion of his severed soul. After he re-embodies with Wormtail's help, he is terrifying and inhuman in appearance. In *Harry Potter and the Deathly Hallows*, as he faces defeat, Voldemort is portrayed unsentimentally in Harry's between-worlds vision as a wounded child to be pitied, but beyond help. He early displayed instincts for 'cruelty, secrecy and domination'.

According to Dumbledore, he is 'the most dangerous Dark Wizard of all time'.

Voldemort's discovery and exploitation of the Horcrux, upon which he misplaced his faith, is one of the strongest indicators of his character. To make a Horcrux the soul has to be sundered, rupturing its original wholeness. The consequence is that, even if a magician's body is destroyed, that person cannot die while the Horcrux remains, for a part of the soul remains embodied in the object. The soul can be divided only as a result of the magician committing murder, which splits the soul, as it is a gross violation of nature. An unknown spell is used to encase the split portion of the soul in the external object. Dividing the soul not once but six times, to have seven parts, appeals greatly to the young Tom Riddle (Voldemort). The Horcrux is a banned subject at Hogwarts, a place whose mission is wholeness. In *Harry Potter and the Chamber of Secrets* Tom Riddle's diary is a Horcrux that has a life of its own, as possessed by a part of his soul, and becomes a weapon used against Harry as well as a guarantee of Riddle's survival. In the final two volumes Horcruxes feature strongly – one is destroyed by Dumbledore, whose hand is withered in the process, and one has already been found, believed destroyed, leaving the others to be eliminated by Harry before he can attempt to kill Voldemort. As Harry seeks to destroy the Horcruxes, he discovers what Dumbledore knew all along: that Harry himself accidentally became a Horcrux when Voldemort's killing curse failed to kill him as an infant, and that he himself must therefore die. The Horcruxes were usually trophies, heirlooms or other valuables with a rich magical history, although one was a living creature, Nagini. It appealed to Voldemort to have Horcruxes that were associated with the history of Hogwarts, particularly its four founders. His intention was that the school would follow his principles rather than those championed by Dumbledore, and by its founders at the very beginning.

In George MacDonald's short story 'The Giant's Heart', a giant's strength is stored in his heart, which is hidden apart from his body, his heart being rather like a Horcrux. In his essay 'On Fairy-Stories', J.R.R. Tolkien refers to an ancient idea that is very widespread (J.K. Rowling draws upon it in her notion of the Horcrux, as does Tolkien in his symbol of the One Ring). This is the notion, he says, 'that the life or strength of a man or creature may reside in some other place or thing; or in some part of the body (especially the heart) that can be detached and hidden in a bag, or under a stone, or in an egg'. He refers to MacDonald's story as well as a millennia-old Egyptian tale preserved on a papyrus. He quotes from this Egyptian *The Tale of the Two Brothers*, where the younger tells the older brother:

> I shall enchant my heart, and I shall place it upon the top of the flower of the cedar. Now the cedar will be cut down and my heart will fall to the ground, and thou shalt come to seek for it, even though thou pass seven years in seeking it; but when thou has found it, put it into a vase of cold water, and in very truth I shall live.

CONCLUSION

Hogwarts, Harry and their enemies give concrete expression to the age-old discussion of good and evil, giving fresh metaphors and renewed perception of these themes. J.K. Rowling's stories are popular and contemporary, and also embody ancient and perennial values. Though Rowling's series of stories reflects end-of-millenium uncertainties in Harry's bewilderments and doubts (as we shall see in the next chapter), hers is a universe of moral clarity that does not seem twee or unreal for her readers throughout the world. She offers a deeply thought-out traditional understanding of the nature of evil as privation, perversion and parasite. Evil is not something that exists independently or has always and inevitably existed, and that will exist for ever.

EIGHT

The Great Tradition of Children's Literature

The world of wizardry invented by J.K. Rowling is not a distinct other-world of the same kind as Middle-earth or Narnia; instead, it is a world that constantly interconnects with and interpenetrates the world we know. In fact, it is part of the same world, but hidden from it. Nevertheless, like the Faerie and fantasy tradition to which it belongs, it has strict rules of being. In the case of the wizarding world of the stories, its imaginative reality depends on supposing the existence of magic.

The hero of J.K. Rowling's stories, Harry Potter, attends Hogwarts School of Witchcraft and Wizardry between 1991 and 1998, and each of the seven books corresponds to a year in the life of that secondary school. The school and its existence is hidden from Muggles, that is, non-magical people, who make up most of the population. Harry grows from an eleven- to a seventeen-year-old (the year of coming of age for a wizard or witch) during his eventful school career. The books cleverly combine a number of established genres: the classic boarding-school story in the tradition of Tom Brown (though Rowling's is a co-educational comprehensive), the *Bildungsroman* (novel of growing up and rites-of-passage), fantasy (Christian and perhaps epic fantasy), and even science fiction of sorts (given the parallels between the natural magic of the wizarding world, and the applied science or technology of the Muggle world – the world of materialistic modern people, shaped by the scientific revolution). J.K. Rowling's books also belong firmly to the literary context of the 1990s and end of millennium. According to Colin Manlove, in his recent study of children's literature, the narrative point of view of the stories is particularly significant. The stories are nearly always told from Harry's point of view, even though they are in the third person. This strongly affects the structure, making it rather different from a children's tale told from an adult perspective.

J.K. Rowling's handling of the point of view in the stories reflects a general cultural shift over issues of identity and authority. Rowling's narrative prose therefore increases the topicality and relevance of the books for a contemporary reader.

The stories did not arise in a vacuum. When the author originally conceived the basic ideas for the series on a delayed train journey, she was widely read in children's literature, and literature in general, including works from other languages, particularly French (almost certainly including the classic tale of *Gargantua and Pantagruel*, by François Rabelais, and written between 1532 and 1564, a comic fantasy full of giants and of the joy of living, like the Harry Potter stories). Her degree in French included the study of such historic literary works, and she took minor subjects in classics, developing some knowledge of Latin. The magic in the stories does not come from a scholarly knowledge and interest in historical magic, and alchemy in particular – it is instead a literary device, used rather as science is in science fiction. Nevertheless, she is widely read in history, referring to actual alchemists such as Agrippa and Nicolas and Perenelle Flamel, and no doubt would have interesting things to say about the relationship between Sir Isaac Newton's alchemy, his scientific contribution and his Christian beliefs. Her portrayal of injustice and slavery in the stories has a context in her work for a time as a research assistant with Amnesty International in London.

If the Harry Potter stories are considered in context, therefore, their richness and creative blending of several genres can be better appreciated in the light of the tradition of literature for children. Some knowledge of this tradition would, I think, answer much of the criticism of the stories – from those who think them morally harmful to children and those who consider them poor writing (and therefore, presumably, unworthy of reading). Their reception by children (and adults) is also worth considering. Worldwide sales for the first six books alone are estimated around 325 million in well over 50 languages, including ancient Greek and Latin, sales over such a brief spell probably unique in children's literature (those of the hugely popular Lewis Carroll, over a period approaching a century and a half, have proved to be incalculable). These sales represent many more than the estimated world population in the first century, or the equivalent of the population of the USA and

Canada today! The diverse ethnic backgrounds and types of reader rule out a passing fad. The pattern of sales has been sustained over the seven books. The fact that sales have been sustained suggests that readers consuming the book merely out of fashion make up only a proportion – perhaps a minor one – of the unprecedented reception – though, of course, sales would have been dramatically lower without the massive marketing and publicity the books have received. There are other excellent writers, such as Diana Wynne Jones, who have not received this kind of exposure and whose sales appear tiny in comparison with J.K. Rowling's. A much better explanation than mere fashion is likely to be that the main appeal of the books is that they satisfy expectations of children's literature (a tradition of high pedigree), they have the appeal of a good story, and they have an incipient spirituality that attracts a generation steeped in a technology and materialism which perhaps realises deep down an absence of true magic and meaning in modern living.

The history of children's literature has always been tied up with a society's changing perception of childhood. The following is necessarily merely a sketch, not intended to skate over the richness and complexity of this history, and largely concerns literature in Britain – given that J.K. Rowling is a British writer, and that Britain has the richest tradition of children's literature. There have always been real children, of course, but a discovery of childhood (a necessary factor in the existence of a diverse literature for children) seems to have been comparatively recent. There are exceptions. A notable one is the place and respect Jesus Christ gave to children in their own right. He drew attention to their essential humility, and even made reference to their games. His observation of childhood is remarkable in the context of the first-century world – indifferent to 'childhood' generally – and probably most of world history.

Awareness of childhood is tied up historically with a growing scientific interest in the world, affecting educational theory. A milestone is 1659, the year of the publication of *Orbis Sensualium Pictus* (*The Visible World in Pictures*) by Jan Amos Comenius. Though its illustrations seem crude to the modern eye, it was the first known picture book for children. The combination of picture and text was an innovative teaching device. It marked a change in consciousness over the world of the child as someone to be considered in his or her own right, revolutionary like Jesus's inclusion of children. Comenius was an outstanding thinker and educator, a native of what is now the Czech Republic, who influenced the Royal Society in England, the engine of the new scientific movement. Comenius's example was not quickly followed, but another creative innovator, his contemporary John Bunyan, author of the famous *The Pilgrim's Progress*, wrote meditations directly for children in a little book, the earliest title of which is not known for certain, but may have been *A Book for Boys and Girls, or Country Rhymes for Children*. Though written for adults, interestingly, his *The Pilgrim's Progress* (1678) was before long adopted for children's reading, along with *Robinson Crusoe* (1719) by Daniel Defoe. Soon after Defoe, John Newbery (1713–67) became the first effective British publisher of children's books, the prestigious Newbery Medal, established in America in 1922, being named after him.

Even with a growing awareness of children, as a fit audience for their own literature, they still tended to be regarded as mere adults in the making, for whom a didactic literature was appropriate, a view that persisted until well into the nineteenth century. This reflected a very long-standing view of the human being, whose emotions and physical attributes needed to be moderated and controlled by reason, a view going back to Aristotle in particular. Perception of the world of childhood as something valuable and significant in its own right – inhabiting a world of wonder – is tied up particularly with the rise of the Romantic Movement in the arts and literature. (Insights into a child's view of reality are, however, anticipated by the seventeenth-century poet Henry Vaughan, in his poems *Childhood* and *The Retreate*, Comenius, and no doubt others.) The philosopher and educationalist Jean Jacques Rousseau (1712–78) provided another important element in the changing perception of childhood. To pick out a further significant moment in the development of children's literature, the poet and writer Robert Southey of Keswick, England (1774–1843) wrote 'The Story of the Three Bears' for his and Coleridge's children (whom he called the 'little people'), published in his long compilation *The Doctor*. The story has the distinctive features of the version familiar to us, a notable difference being that a vagrant old women rather than

Goldilocks enters the house of the three bears. Southey was an associate of William Wordsworth, who explored new insights into the special nature of childhood in his *The Prelude* and elsewhere, famously writing that 'The Child is father of the Man'. In a connected poem he wrote:

> There was a time when meadow, grove, and stream,
> The earth, and every common sight,
>   To me did seem
>   Apparelled in celestial light,
> The glory and the freshness of a dream.

The period of the discovery of childhood, with the writing of literature specifically for children, had many complex strands (like the social changes of the Industrial Revolution) as well as the growth of the Romantic Movement. A rapid fragmentation of human knowledge led to a persistent quest, which is still with us, for a unifying principle outside science – such as a spiritualised nature, the primitive world of the noble savage, a collective or unconscious mind, and the more spiritually attuned world of childhood. The discovery of childhood was becoming established when an interest in collecting folk tales, myths and traditional fairy stories began in earnest. Celtic and northern mythology was popularised, the results translating readily into children's reading. Tales and myths gathered by the brothers Jacob and Wilhelm Grimm (published between 1812 and 1822) and Henry Longfellow's *Poets and Poems of Europe* (1863, including translations of Icelandic poetry based on northern mythology) became well known.

J.K. Rowling's Harry Potter stories draw upon the world of the child and adolescent, based on her remembered experience of these years. She brilliantly pulls in magical creatures from northern and classical mythology, loved by children, as well as her own inventions, in an accomplished eclectic mix reminiscent of C.S. Lewis and Edmund Spenser. There is a *mélange* of magical and ordinary worlds, giants, centaurs, dragons, Bowtruckles, and the bully down the street. Her plots, too, are superbly constructed, with seemingly trivial twists turning out later to be of intense significance. But her invention does not stop at magical beings and richly fashioned plot. As suggested earlier, the stories seamlessly integrate a number of familiar genres found in traditional children's literature, arousing and satisfying reader expectations of the genres, while at the same time taking them in new directions and evoking allusions at many levels. Genres include the school story, the *Bildungsroman* (the tale of spiritual development and education of a character and coming of age), the series, fantasy and fairy tale, and the mystery and adventure story. Each of these genres played their part in the development of children's literature. This can be illustrated, for example, by the history of the school story, works of humour and word-play, and the tale of fantasy and fairy story, including their distinctive forms in the 1990s – the period in which the stories are set, and in which the first four in the series were written.

THE SCHOOL STORY

The school story originated around the middle of the nineteenth century, particularly with Thomas Hughes's *Tom Brown's Schooldays*, set in an English public school, the famous Rugby School, during the period when the charismatic headmaster Dr Thomas Arnold ruled. (A public school is one endowed for providing a liberal secondary education for those who can afford the fees, involving the students boarding during term-time.) The story is set in the 1830s, though published in 1857 (a US edition appearing that same year). Hughes wrote it intentionally and unapologetically as a moral tale, with his son in mind, who was about to go off to public school. He decided that the best way to put over his fatherly advice was in the form of the story. Dad Hughes based his story on his vivid memories of his own school life, replete with wise headmaster and school bully. The book is a classic of children's literature, entertaining even with its heavy didactic purpose. When J.K. Rowling began her school stories, set in the 1990s, the school story was in radical decline. Ten years earlier, in fact, Isobel Quigly concluded: 'The genre was finished . . . it was impossible to keep it going.' Like *Tom Brown's Schooldays*, a strong morality undergirds Rowling's story, even though her purpose, unlike that of Hughes, is first and foremost to tell a good story, and the dominant school game is Quidditch rather than Rugby football. When Hughes wrote his story many of his readers were public-school pupils. The vast majority of J.K. Rowling's readers have no experience of a boarding school and have read no other story that features a boarding school. The appeal of the school story, a genre that had been considered in general to be in terminal decline, has proved to be as strong as ever, the genre alive and well, thanks to the bespectacled Harry Potter, and his Hogwarts chums.

What is the appeal of the school story? To quote from Isabel Quigly again:

> The public school turned out to be a remarkably convenient setting for fiction. It was an enclosed community, self-contained, self-sufficient, concentrated, dramatic; a place where people could either be seen as 'humours' rather than individuals, acting out their roles in the way expected of them, arousing partisan feelings for and against; or else treated as fiercely individual, in contrast to their narrow surroundings and rule-ridden existence. Isolated communities have always attracted novelists, and in its isolation the public school was comparable only with prison or monastery, with both of which it had a good deal in common . . . [H]uman relations are the raw material of fiction and, again to a high degree, they matter particularly in small, self-contained groups; groups that, at a public school, were concentrated further by close proximity and adolescence.

Though Hogwarts is not a public school, *per se*, it is a boarding school and, as such, provides a world-within-a-world that provides a convenient structure for storytelling, with the temporal pattern of the academic year, punctuated by vacations at Christmas and summer, tension heightened by exams and homework, while offering all the possibilities of events and adventures in classrooms, in the castle in the evenings, late at night and during the weekends. The focus is intensified further in that the boarding-school world of Hogwarts Castle is within the magical world – itself a world-within-the-world of ordinary Muggle existence.

In the history of school stories a number stand out, illustrating the range and diversity of the essential genre. Twenty-five years after *Tom Brown's Schooldays* a comic treatment of school life appeared,

Vice Versa (published in 1882), in which a father, against his will, is magically switched with his son at boarding school, which presented rich humorous possibilities for its author F. Anstey. C.S. Lewis and his brother Warren, who a generation later had suffered at an appalling English boarding school run by a headmaster going insane, appreciated immensely its picture of schoolboy tribulations. Lewis even took the name of the father, Paul Bultitude, calling a lumbering bear in his novel *That Hideous Strength* Mr Bultitude. In Anstey's work the father exactly assumes the form of his son, Dick, just as if he had taken the Polyjuice Potion of the Harry Potter stories, while Dick enjoys life as a London City gentleman. In fact, the magical switch had taken place as a result of the power of an oriental talisman.

Seven years later one of the most outstanding examples of the school story was published, championing the values of the British Empire. It was Rudyard Kipling's *Stalky and Co.* (1899), set in a public pchool in north Devon, in the west of England, and drawing on the author's remembered experience as a pupil at the school at Westward Ho! The opening is a good taster of its tone and world:

> In summer all right-minded boys built huts in the furze-hill behind the College – little lairs whittled out of the heart of the prickly bushes, full of stumps, odd root-ends, and spikes, but, since they were strictly forbidden, palaces of delight. And for the fifth summer in succession, Stalky, McTurk, and Beetle (this was before they reached the dignity of a study) had built like beavers a place of retreat and meditation, where they smoked.
>
> Now, there was nothing in their characters as known to Mr Prout, their house-master, at all commanding respect; nor did Foxy, the subtle red-haired school Sergeant, trust them. His business was to wear tennis-shoes, carry binoculars, and swoop hawklike upon evil boys. Had he taken the field alone, that hut would have been raided, for Foxy knew the manners of his quarry; but Providence moved Mr Prout, whose school-name, derived from the size of his feet, was Hoofer, to investigate on his own account; and it was the cautious Stalky who found the track of his pugs on the very floor of their lair one peaceful afternoon when Stalky would fain have forgotten Prout and his works in a

volume of [novelist Robert Smith] Surtees and a new briar-wood pipe. Crusoe, at sight of the footprint, did not act more swiftly than Stalky. He removed the pipes, swept up all loose match-ends, and departed to warn Beetle and McTurk.

Notice Foxy, who has something of the future Argus Filch of Hogwarts in him, and the rule-bending – in this case building dens and smoking pipes rather than sneaking into Hogsmeade through a secret tunnel. Though the school here is an all-boys' one, and for the privileged classes, it is recognisably of the same family of books as the Harry Potter series.

Parallel to the school story is the phenomenon of recording childhood in adult biography and autobiography. Such records in general came into existence around the same time as as imaginative children's literature. Wordsworth's poem of his life and development as a poet, *The Prelude* (1850), includes his childhood and adolescence. C.S. Lewis's autobiography, *Surprised by Joy* (1955), concerns only his early life and features his childhood in great detail. This book owes a great deal to Wordsworth's *Prelude*, in his quest for an elusive experience he called joy. Lewis's record of his traumatic school experience is longer, and told with more pain, than his experiences in the trenches of the First World War. Almost every adult biography or autobiography since the middle of the nineteenth century is likely to include a great deal about the subject's early life, as the key to the later person. George MacDonald wrote for children *Ranald Bannerman's Boyhood* (1871), which draws heavily upon his own experience growing up in Huntley, Aberdeenshire. His adult novel, *Wilfred Cumbermede* (1872), is partly inspired by the experiences of his friend John Ruskin, and covers part of the childhood of its hero, Wilfred. The world of childhood appeals to the modern adult reader as much as to the child reader. This fact would have seemed strange in the centuries and millennia before the comparatively recent discovery of childhood.

This post-Romantic fascination with childhood and the processes of growing into adulthood is captured by Alain-Fournier (Henri Alban-Fournier, 1886–1914) in his *Le Grande Meaulnes*. Before writing it he confessed: 'Childhood is my creed in both art and literature; and to render it and its mysterious depths without childishness. Perhaps my future book will be an endless and imperceptible moving to and fro between dream and reality. By "dream" I mean the vast, vague world of childhood hovering over the adult world, and forever perturbed by its echoes.' He believed that memories of childhood made his 'deepest being what it is'.

CHILDREN'S FANTASY AND FAIRY STORY: THE ROMANTIC TRADITION OF GEORGE MACDONALD, C.S. LEWIS AND OTHERS

The importance of the Romantic Movement to children's literature – in which wonder has its place, in all the moral teaching – is far too complex to treat fully here. By the middle of the nineteenth century stories began to appear in which the imagination was more evident, changing the tone of stories from the merely moral, and better reflecting a distinct world of childhood, characterised by wonder. In the stories of Harry Potter, dominated as they are by the wizarding world and Hogwarts School, magic actually represents the imagination, and its power in human life for good and evil. In the words of Colin Manlove about Rowling's use of magic in her stories, 'magic . . . in one way is the wild imagination actualised'.

The Romantic tradition in children's literature (and its counterparts in adult fantasy and science fiction) comes out of a profound reflection on the relationship between thought and imagination, and how imagination relates to reality and to truth. Laying the foundation for many of the ideas that shaped later writers for children, including George MacDonald, Tolkien and C.S. Lewis, was the Romantic poet and thinker Samuel Taylor Coleridge (1772–1834). At the centre of Coleridge's radical view of the imagination was 'the perception of similitude in dissimilitude', and the effect of the imagination upon the very way we see the world. Imagination takes in the subjective and the objective, because it is active in making sense of the world. Its power to organise and make sense of our perceptions was, in his words, 'magical.'

Coleridge's writings were edited by his daughter, Sara Coleridge (1802–52). She was a poet, but also wrote for children. She composed the first fairy-tale novel written in English. It was called *Phantasmion* (1837), drawing upon Edmund Spenser's *The Faerie Queene* (1589–96), the sixteenth-century poem that was later to be part of the inspiration for C.S. Lewis's *The Chronicles of Narnia*. Interestingly, Sara Coleridge was brought up in the household of Robert Southey in Keswick, which means that she very likely enjoyed his story of 'The Three Bears'.

George MacDonald (1824–1905) reflects many of Coleridge's ideas, and emphasises that when the imagination shapes perception, it is working with meanings placed there by God, whose imagination shares some of the nature of the finite and necessarily limited human imagination. The hallmark of the human imagination is therefore meant to be wonder and holiness. This view of the imagination proved intensely liberating to MacDonald, as it was in the twentieth century for his disciple, C.S. Lewis. One of his greatest stories is the short *The Golden Key* (1867). It concerns Mossy and his companion Tangle. Mossy lives with his great-aunt in a little house on the edge of fairyland and a great forest. Mossy loved a story his great aunt told him of finding a golden key at the end of the rainbow. He feels the forest calling him and goes in search of the golden key, which he soon finds. Tangle has run away from her home, where she is neglected, as her mother is dead, and meets Mossy. Together they seek a lock the key will open, and the country from which the shadows fall.

The Golden Key is a perfect example of MacDonald's distinctive magic, a magic that is only what it is by being full of holiness and goodness. The mystery it embodies looks towards a world we do not usually see, the supernatural. Its story centres on light, and bright shadow, ultimately expressed in the rainbow. The light falling from a hidden country is found in MacDonald's other stories, which, like *The Golden Key*, explore the theme of death – a central theme in later writers of fairy story like Tolkien and J.K. Rowling. MacDonald, however, was not writing for a world in which belief had departed, and the real divine presence unacknowledged, so he could openly say, 'all that is fully real is Heavenly'; that is, true reality is heaven itself.

A story that has never been out of print, and is a classic of the tradition of wonder in children's literature, has a very different setting from *The Golden Key*. It is a fantasy that does not look like one, set in the 'real' world of Victorian London. The power of MacDonald's *At the Back of the North Wind* (1869–70) lies in what his son, Greville, called 'its two world consciousness'. Into its London events constantly flows another real world we do not normally see, bringing out the essence of everyday events, people and things. That other world is epitomised in the mysterious figure of the North Wind. As G.K. Chesterton wrote: 'George MacDonald did really believe that people were princesses and goblins and good fairies, and he dressed them up as ordinary men and women. The fairy story was the inside of the ordinary story and not the outside.' Consequently, he makes 'all the ordinary staircases and doors and windows into magical things'. According to Greville MacDonald again, *At the Back of the North Wind* appeals to 'the imaginative seeing of a truth'. Two main truths that are presented in this way are the importance and presence of death in human life, and the fact that suffering and evil do not mean that evil has the ultimate victory. The story deals with these issues, moreover, without sentimentality.

Writing in what is a different universe to the one known by MacDonald, J.K. Rowling, one of his heirs, similarly has a 'two-world consciousness' in her stories – the magical and the ordinary – and comes afresh to the great themes of death, suffering and the reality of evil, like MacDonald, without sentimentality. The wonder is there, too, but in a form appropriate to a very different readership over more than a century of enormous changes later, but still one largely made up of children and drawing upon a distinctive experience of childhood. She cannot assume a widespread belief on the part of her readers in the theological themes and motifs that dominated the West for a vast period.

Other writers of the nineteenth century were involved in writing stories specifically for children that were highly imaginative in their own right, and were not justified solely in terms of their moral teaching. Elements of wonder, fairy and folk story reflected a perception of the world of the child that was endued with a similar wonder. One such writer was George MacDonald's friend John Ruskin, who published *The King of the Golden River* in 1851. It was written ten years previously, when Ruskin was in his twenties, long before he was famous, and is one of the earliest fantasies in England written especially for a child. Ruskin himself did not rate it highly, and yet it has remained popular with children since its publication, and was certainly a favourite of mine as a child.

He thought it 'a fairly good imitation of Grimm and Dickens, mixed with some true Alpine feeling of my own'. The hero, Gluck, is twelve, and 'kind in temper to every living thing', unlike his ugly, bullying two brothers, who get their comeuppance when they are visited by the South-West Wind, Esquire. They owned a small alpine valley that they misused as they farmed it, greedily intent on gain. It is a kind of Cinderella story, like that of Harry Potter; in this case, through the King of the Golden River, the two brothers are turned into black stones, and a new river restores the valley for Gluck – which comes to life again, a little as Narnia magically emerges in C.S. Lewis's *The Magician's Nephew*.

Ruskin's mention of Grimm (the Grimm brothers, Jakob and Wilhelm) is significant, as the discovery of mainly orally transmitted folk stories played an important part in the growth of fantasy and the wonder tale. Another important influence, transmitted through George MacDonald and others, was that of continental writers such as Novalis, Baron de la Motte Fouqué and Hans Christian Andersen.

Other writers were important in this burgeoning of fantasy for children, such as William Thackeray, with his *The Rose and the Ring* (1853), Charles Kingsley, with his *The Water Babies* (1863) and Oscar Wilde, with his collection *The Happy Prince* (1888). Even with the innovations, Lewis Carroll's *Alice in Wonderland* (1865) was revolutionary, and continues to captivate young readers today throughout the world. Elements he added to the 'cauldron of story,' as Tolkien calls it, find their way into the Harry Potter stories.

J.K. Rowling acknowledges Edith Nesbit (1858–1924) as an important influence on her. As in MacDonald's *At the Back of the North Wind*, the enchantment and magic flows into the real world of contemporary society, with dramatic and, in Nesbit's case, comic effect. Nesbit created the Bastable family in *The Story of the Treasure Seekers*, and also composed a sequence of fantasy tales, *Five Children and It*, *The Phoenix and the Carpet* and *The Story of the Amulet*. The *Treasure Seekers* and its sequels about the family, though not fantasy, are notable for their employment of a child narrator, a device that had been used already by Dickens and his contemporary Mrs Ewing, and that is handled with such important effect by J.K. Rowling.

The decades between Edith Nesbit and J.K. Rowling have a continual ebb and flow but never absence of fantasy stories, tales of wonder, for children. The genre includes (to name just some in the rich and varied tradition) Kenneth Grahame, Tolkien, Elizabeth Goudge (her *The White Horse* had a formative influence on Rowling), C.S. Lewis, T.H. White, Mary Norton, Diana Wynne Jones, Alan Garner, Ann Pilling and Philip Pullman.

To pluck one name from this wealth of authors, Mary Norton, with her stories of *The Borrowers*, illustrates an element from the 'cauldron of story' that emerges, with a different skew, in J.K. Rowling. In Mary Norton's stories, a family of miniature people – Pod, Homily, and Arrietty – live under the ancient floors of a country mansion and subsist by secretly 'borrowing' items from the inhabitants of the old house. There is an imaginative similarity between Norton's creation of a miniature world of the Borrowers under the grandfather clock and the wizarding world of Harry Potter. Both are worlds-within-worlds, one hidden from the other, dominant one. According to the *Encyclopedia Britannica*, 'All that follows from this premise [of Norton's] is logical, precisely pictured, and carries absolute conviction' – just like the wizarding world. A similar milieu of diminutive people, who provide a mirror for the ordinary modern world, is found in the Lilliputian survivors portrayed by T.H. White in his *Mistress Masham's Repose* (1947). There, the descendants of the Lilliputians of Jonathan Swift's *Gulliver's Travels* retain the behaviour and dress of the eighteenth century in their secretive existence, rather as the members of the ancient magical community in Harry Potter live an existence alternative to a technological society and wear distinctive robes and other wizarding paraphernalia.

STORIES OF MAGIC

Magic dominates the Harry Potter books so much that it tends to eclipse the other genres used by J.K. Rowling, such as the school story. Stories involving magic have played an important part in children's literature, and are squarely a species of fantasy. Successful children's stories have never been written to promote the occult and the practice of real magic. Magic in children's literature normally uses magic as a fictional convention – it has to, in order to work – as does much adult use of magic in fantasy. On rare occasions a writer might have first-hand knowledge of real, primary-world magic. In the adult fantasies of Charles Williams, a member of the literary circle of C.S. Lewis and Tolkien, he may have drawn upon a real knowledge of the Order of the Golden Dawn, a Rosicrucian society, via his membership of A.E. Waite's breakaway Fellowship of the Rosy Cross, but in none of them is his purpose to be informative of real magic. In his *The Greater Trumps*, for instance, the plot centres around the Tarot pack, but this is merely a literary device. His last novel, *All Hallows' Eve*, concerns Simon, a dark magician, and benefited from discussion by Lewis, Tolkien and other Inklings as it was read to the group. Rather like some of the characters in Lewis's *The Last Battle*, two of the central protagonists die before the novel opens.

The magic in children's stories is not, therefore, a simple matter. There is, however, a striking amount of agreement among its writers about this magic. Though, within the fantasy, magic involves impossibilities (like flying, or turning a stone into gold, or gaining immortality), it has to obey rules that are fitting to its often undefined and implicit nature. According to J.K. Rowling, what is most difficult for the writer is deciding what is *not* possible in the world of the story. As Tom Shippey and Peter Nicholls point out: 'Much of the amusement of worlds-where-magic-works stories lies in developing the possibilities of a small number of magical rules.' The imaginative possibilities of the magical rules work only because the reader knows that it is fantasy and not reality – rather as a metaphor works only if we are aware that it is not identical with its reference. We would get rather confused, for instance, if we thought that love had eyes, and was actually blind. The agreement among writers of stories of magic is based on several assumptions.

According to children's writer Diana Wynne Jones, the basic assumption is that magic can happen within the world of the fantasy, even if the setting is this world – the primary world – rather than a secondary world like Narnia or Middle-earth. I take her to mean that, if the setting is this world, as in J.K. Rowling's stories, the magic flows in (rather as the supernatural makes its presence felt in the everyday world in writers who believe in God, gods or spirits). If the setting is a secondary world, the magic resides there, and not in the primary world, as in Lewis Carroll's *Alice in Wonderland* or C.S. Lewis's *The Chronicles of Narnia*. Indeed, Lewis rejected his first draft of *The Magician's Nephew* precisely because in it magic occurred in the primary world – Digory at first was able to understand the languages of trees and animals. In either type of world, however, the distinctive nature of the magic shapes the story. Diana Wynne Jones describes the process of magic in a secondary world in *Alice in Wonderland*:

> The way this influence [of magic] works is most easily seen in one of the best-known worlds of magic: the wonderland of *Alice's Adventures in Wonderland* (1866) by Lewis Carroll. Because Carroll was a mathematician, he started the book with ideas of logic (in the form of logic-chopping) and concomitant wordplay. Before the book has gone very far, we have the bread-and-butterfly and Humpty Dumpty busy with words. *Alice* illustrates . . . [that] magic inheres in a particular secondary world or universe, but not in our own; Alice returns to mundane life at the end.

In J.K. Rowling, in contrast, the magic resides in the supposed primary world, our familiar Muggle world from which the magical community and magical creatures and objects are carefully hidden. In the same way, in George MacDonald's *At the Back of the North Wind* the magical element represented by the North Wind breathes, blows and gusts into the everyday world of Victorian London. In C.S. Lewis's *That Hideous Strength* (for illustration – it is in fact a 'fairy story for grown-ups') the wizard Merlin of Arthurian legends participates in events in the modern English Midlands.

What is true of both types of narrative – a setting in the primary or a secondary world – is that it is the imaginative possibilities of supposing magic that shape the story.

A second assumption in stories of magic is that the realms of science (or at least technology) and magic have substantial affinities. Such an assumption is underlined, for instance, by J.K. Rowling's many references to alchemy (drawing on a strong literary tradition). In the early years of modern science there was no sharp distinction between science and alchemy. In the writings of Tolkien and

C.S. Lewis there is a conviction that technology is the modern form of magic. A similar attitude is encapsulated by the science-fiction author Arthur C. Clarke, in his 'Third Law', in *Profiles of the Future*: 'Any sufficiently advanced technology is indistinguishable from magic.'

The writing of magical stories in children's literature mirrors a distinct tradition in science fiction (Philip Pullman's *His Dark Materials* in fact might be seen, simultaneously, as a children's magical fantasy and an adult science-fiction sequence of stories). This is not surprising, given the marked presence of fantasy in much science fiction – for some readers it is the fantasy element and wonder of other worlds that is the attraction of science fiction, rather than simply its technology. The technology in fact is a device – a supposal – that creates imaginative possibilities.

Tolkien sees magic as at the very heart of the fairy story, writing:

> Even fairy-stories as a whole have three faces: the Mystical toward the Supernatural; the Magical toward Nature; and the Mirror of scorn or pity toward Man. The essential face of Faërie is the middle one, the Magical. But the degree in which the others appear (if at all) is variable, and may be decided by the individual story-teller.

In such a story a tree (say, the Whomping Willow) may move, an owl may be given instructions, a snake or a spider may speak, a piece of wood may make a flying broomstick or a wand, and herbs may heal or add properties to an object.

More specific than the presence of magic in much children's literature is the role of witches and wizards. In this there are many forerunners to J.K. Rowling, from Jill Murphy's *Worst Witch* stories (the first of which appeared in 1974) to Ann Pilling's *The Witch of Lagg* (1985), including John Masefield's *The Midnight Folk* (1927), Alan Garner's *The Weirdstone of Brisingamen* (1960), C.S. Lewis's *The Chronicles of Narnia* (1950–6), Diana Wynne Jones's *Charmed Life* (1977) and *Howl's Moving Castle* (1986), Susan Cooper's *The Dark is Rising* series (1965–77) and T.H. White's *The Once and Future King* (1958). The last opens with a syllabus reminiscent of Hogwarts:

On Mondays, Wednesdays and Fridays it was Court Hand and Summulae Logicales, while the rest of the week it was the Organon, Repetition and Astrology. The governess was always getting muddled with her astrolabe, and when she got specially muddled she would take it out of the Wart by rapping his knuckles. She did not rap Kay's knuckles, because when Kay grew older he would be Sir Kay, the master of the estate. The Wart was called the Wart because it more or less rhymed with Art, which was short for his real name . . .

The Wart, of course, is the young Arthur, as yet unaware of his powers and not yet acquainted with Merlyn, the most famous wizard in literature, forerunner of Tolkien's Gandalf and Rowling's Dumbledore.

HUMOUR AND NONSENSE

There is playfulness and a comic structure in J.K. Rowling that is sustained throughout the dark themes of death and opposition to the Dark Arts, behind which lies a Dark Lord. As with the terrifying Boggart, who assumes the shape of one's worst fears, the remedy is laughter – the charm to utter is 'Riddikulus!' Even the wraiths called Dementors, who wear dark and despair like a robe, and suck the happiness out of a person, are repelled by the bright Patronus, created by a charm combined with a deeply happy memory, followed by a healing process of eating chocolate. Her comic invention is effortless and constant, not at all clashing with her serious themes of sacrifice, courage and death. When Harry escapes the ghastly Aunt Marge, who is staying with the Dursleys, he is given a room in the Leaky Cauldron, a London inn that guards the entrance to the wizarding shops of Diagon Alley. In his room Harry

caught sight of himself in the mirror over the basin. . . . He raised his hand automatically and tried to make his hair lie flat.

'You're fighting a losing battle there, dear,' said his mirror in a wheezy voice.

The humorous vein in these stories picks up another tradition in British children's literature, the comic, from Lewis Carroll's *Alice* stories and humorous verses, Edward Lear's nonsense poems, Anstey's *Vice Versa* discussed above, right through to Roald Dahl's children's stories, including *Matilda* (1988), about a hyper-talented little girl whose grotesque parents make Harry Potter's Uncle Vernon and Aunt Petunia seem almost tolerable. Like these authors, Rowling is a very funny writer, even merely on the level of her richly invented names, such as that of the decrepit and seedy wizard, Mundungus Fletcher (called 'Dung' for short). 'Mundungus' means 'foul-smelling tobacco'. Some of her magical creatures, like the Blast-Ended Skrewt, Bowtruckle or the Flobberworm, compare with the best of Lewis Carroll or Edward Lear, as when Alice asks Humpty Dumpty,

> 'and what are '*toves*'?'
> 'Well, '*toves*' are something like badgers – they're something like lizards – and they're something like corkscrews.'
> 'They must be very curious-looking creatures.'
> 'They are that,' said Humpty Dumpty; 'also they make their nests under sundials – also they live on cheese.'

The comic tradition is alive and well in the stories of Roald Dahl. In *Matilda*, her winsome teacher, Miss Honey, asks the little girl to tell her a children's book she likes (Matilda had read all the volumes in her local public library).

> 'I liked *The Lion, the Witch and the Wardrobe*,' Matilda said. 'I think Mr C.S. Lewis is a very good writer. But he has one failing. There are no funny bits in his books.'
> 'You are right there,' Miss Honey said.
> 'There aren't many funny bits in Mr Tolkien either,' Matilda said.
> 'Do you think that all children's books ought to have funny bits in them?' Miss Honey asked.
> 'I do,' Matilda said. 'Children are not so serious as grown-ups and they love to laugh.'

There is no doubt that Matilda would have relished the Harry Potter stories for their sustained humour, even though she is wrong about there being none in Narnia and *The Hobbit*.

Humour emphasises the importance of writing for children without a justification, such as a moral one – such stories and poems are a good in their own right. Humour celebrates the joy of being alive and human, acknowledging a great gift, even in the face of very real darkness and evil.

THE UNCERTAINTY OF THE 1990s

Ironically the perception of childhood as a distinctive period – so integral to the existence of children's literature – may be in danger of dying, as its traditional awe and wonder belong to a transcendent world marginalised by a prevailing materialistic culture. Children are once more becoming seen as mini-adults devoid of any magic, their world embodying no spell to enchant an adult made grey and colourless by the age of the machine. The Muggle world of gadgets and the modern magic of technology have left out a world of natural magic, in the terms captured in the Harry Potter books, which includes the Deeper Magic of love, friendship and self-sacrifice. The modern panacea for all difficulties is often, in practical terms at least, to kill off God, and to give children a supposedly adult view of a world that is without qualities, and is only about biological replication, a consumer's life, scepticism about any narrative to account for the human and no explanation for evil. Interestingly, the Harry Potter stories are brilliantly successful in embodying the contrary: a transcending perspective, providing hope that human beings are not two-dimensional and can fight for beauty, goodness and truth. It is significant that the popularity of the stories worldwide coincides with globalisation, modernity and the spell of technology, where millions turn aside to paganism, gnosticism and new religions in a quest for spirituality, and very many to existing world religions.

The decade in which J.K. Rowling wrote four of the stories, and which provided the setting for them, was characterised by uncertainty about human identity, God, institutions like marriage and education, and any other important certainties. Her narrative appropriately reflects the postmodern context: the stories are mainly told from Harry's point of view, reflecting his limited but developing perspective. It raises the important age-old dilemma of reality behind appearance. Within these chosen limitations, however, she brilliantly combines elements of fairy story and social-realistic writing (in respect of psychological depth) in a number of chosen characters – part of her ability to combine genres inventively.

In his study of children's fantasy in England, Colin Manlove observes of the Harry Potter stories:

> This is a different kind of literature. It expresses a child's ideal world and a child's way of seeing, because that is the unique ability J.K. Rowling has. Her books sometimes seem not so much written *for* children, in the sense of an adult writing about remembered childhood, as in a way *by* them . . . If we can see these books as part of the new mode of 1990s children's fantasy, written wholly from a child's point of view, then we will not try to put them besides those of say Philippa Pearce or C.S. Lewis, or ask them for conventional literary methods when those they use are real enough in their own terms.

J.K. Rowling's inventive mix of a 1990s approach and the traditional fantasy, contemporary questioning and age-old values and virtues, marks all her writing. It is strikingly evident in her interesting mix of archetypical or stock characters – the bully (Draco; Snape; Uncle Vernon), the hero (Harry), the prig (Percy), the swot (Hermione), the accident-prone (Neville; Tonks) – and maturing, well-rounded, organic characters. She combines personality type (derived from the classical four humours, and reflected in the four Hogwarts houses) with three-dimensional characters – those who are in the foreground, like Harry, Ron, Hermione, Snape, and who also have stock elements to their make-up. In the background are characters who are flatter and often the object of satire, such as the Dursleys in particular, though Aunt Petunia displays more depths to her person as the stories develop. The psychological depth of some of Rowling's children reflects development in social-realistic children's literature, and particularly the heritage of the writings of Edith Nesbit, whom she admires.

But we need to get deeper into the qualities of the stories that make them work as literature, now that we have seen something of their rich context.

NINE

The Storyteller's Craft

J.K. Rowling is first of all a storyteller, and in her stories the imagination is represented pre-eminently in magic – particularly the existence of an extraordinary world of wizards and magical creatures hidden from the sight of Muggles, that is, the majority world of ordinary folk who inhabit the planet and who have a limited vision of what makes up reality. ('Bless them,' Mr Weasley no doubt would add.) Her craft is shaped by her evident joy in the imagination. It is therefore well-nigh impossible to disconnect her literary invention from her spirituality and world view. This chapter may therefore be seen as complementing Chapter Six as part of the same exploration. Novelist Alison Lurie, of Cornell University, believes that magic – what she calls 'secret powers' – in the Harry Potter stories represents something even wider than the imagination as such. In the stories, she says, magic 'can be seen as a metaphor for the special powers of childhood: imagination, creativity, and especially humour – as well as being exciting, her books are often very funny'.

The affinity between J.K. Rowling's fiction and her spirituality becomes evident when we consider her writing as part of a tradition that goes back to the Romantic movement. (We touched on this in the previous chapter, but will go more deeply into its features here.) Though we know little from the author herself about her theories of her craft, it does illuminate her work to see a kind of theology of Romanticism (or, to use another term, theology of fantasy), however theoretically unformulated, in her stories. We shall explore the themes, symbols and preoccupations of her fantasy in the light of this Romantic tradition. There are signposts to this belief-system in some of the interviews she has given over the years, which are reinforced by her actual practise as a fantasy writer. If we look at the convictions of some of the early Romantics we can see how they lay foundations for the Harry Potter books. This will help us appreciate some of the central literary features of the stories.

To clarify slightly, the term 'Romantic' when talking of the Romantic movement of Wordsworth, Coleridge, John Keats and others comes from a use of 'romance', taken from a longstanding medieval genre. Many stories of romantic love much in evidence in bookshops and libraries today present only an aspect of 'romance' in this sense – they may or may not authentically capture the actual state or quality of being in love that would be the quest of the Romantic tradition. In this tradition stories of romance are concerned with a variety of states or qualities such as love, courage, honour, mercy, sacrifice and joy, and they relish wonders and marvels, the awesome and the uncanny, the magical and the supernatural, the sublime in nature, as well as horror, terror and other responses to evil. They feature adventures and quests, where the appeal lies in the kind of danger or attraction a hero may face – such as dragons, giants, underworld journeys and encounters with other worlds or non-human beings, each with its own quality of danger or fascination. They draw upon 'the far away and long ago', as a basic longing of the human heart, and seek the whole in human experience, rather than only parts. As fantasy writing for both children and adults has developed, the seminal idea of fairyland or Faerie, from fairy stories, has extended into the invention of secondary worlds like Middle-earth, Earthsea, Narnia or the magical places of the Harry Potter stories like Diagon Alley, the Forbidden Forest or Hogwarts Castle.

THE ROMANTIC TRADITION

The Spiritual Imagination: Samuel Taylor Coleridge and George MacDonald

The imagination is an integral part of our mental make-up. With it we create languages, metaphors and models, tools and technologies, and it helps us to be able to put ourselves into another person's position (empathy), as well as to pray to a being we can no more see than the wind that bends the tree in a storm. With it we can paint a green sun in the sky or capture the tones of joy or sadness in music.

The human mind, believed Samuel Taylor Coleridge (1772–1834), is active in making sense of the world. It organises and unifies our hearing, seeing, touching, smelling and tasting, so that our experience is of wholes rather than an overwhelming torrent of separate and alien details. The mind imposes itself on reality, having a central role in knowledge, shaping and adapting it. Drawing on our mental powers, the poet is like a magician, using a 'synthetic and magical power' that Coleridge calls imagination. He was reacting against a growing domination of scientific rationalism, driven by the Enlightenment, which reckoned both the human reason and imagination were passive in knowledge, finding truth as it submitted to material causes. He saw the imagination as the key to an organic rather than a mechanistic knowledge. '[Coleridge's] face,' Owen Barfield wrote, 'was turned . . . in the opposite direction to the one which natural science was taking in his time and, in spite of his efforts and those of a few others like him, has continued to take since his death. For it was his firm conviction that, if knowledge was to advance, there must be a science of qualities as well as quantities.'

For Coleridge the imagination as a power of the mind is 'esemplastic', unifying and shaping its material. He sets out its pattern in a famous passage in his *Biographia Literaria*. Notice his observation that the imagination unites the general and the concrete, and reconciles many other realities that are seen by the abstract mind as irreconcilable opposites. He is pointing towards the different but complementary functions of theoretical reason and imagination.

This power, first put into action by the will and understanding, and retained under their irremissive, though gentle and unnoticed control . . . reveals itself in the balance or reconcilement of opposite or discordant qualities: of sameness, with difference; of the general with the concrete; the idea with the image; the individual with the representative; the sense of novelty and freshness with old and familiar objects; a more than usual state of emotion with more than usual order; judgement ever awake and steady self-possession with enthusiasm and feeling profound or vehement; and while it blends and harmonises the natural and the artificial, still subordinates art to nature; the manner to the matter; and our admiration of the poet to our sympathy with the poetry.

Just as Tolkien would attempt in his seminal essay 'On Fairy Stories', Coleridge tries to distinguish a primary and secondary imagination.

> The Imagination then I consider either as primary, or secondary. The primary Imagination I hold to be the living power and prime agent of all human perception, and as a repetition in the finite mind of the eternal act of creation in the infinite I AM. The secondary Imagination I consider as an echo of the former, co-existing with the conscious will, yet still as identical with the primary in the *kind* of its agency, and differing only in *degree*, and in the *mode* of its operation. It dissolves, diffuses, dissipates, in order to recreate: or where this process is rendered impossible, yet still at all events it struggles to idealise and to unify. It is essentially *vital*, even as all objects (*as* objects) are essentially fixed and dead.

The primary imagination is concerned with, and operates in, the primary world, which is external to us and fixed – it is objective. The secondary imagination, employing language, image and metaphor, reworks and reshapes this primary world. Functioning to a higher degree as God's divine image in us, it imparts the breath of life.

Coleridge captures the significance of imagination in his famous poem *The Rime of the Ancient Mariner* – the story of a sailor who, during a voyage, offends all that is good by gratuitously shooting an albatross with his crossbow. Killing the albatross, which then hangs dead around his neck, alienates the Mariner from God and all that is benevolent. He consequently sees without feeling and under-standing: for instance, 'slimy things did crawl with legs / Upon the slimy sea'.

Later, he begins to see with feeling, that is, with awakened imagination, and is able to wonder and to perceive anew. This change helps to redeem him from the curse upon him. A proper vision is restored. He consequently sees the ocean deep and its creatures, which had previously been repulsive, in a new way. The water-snakes 'moved in tracks of shining white, / And when they reared, the elfish light / Fell off in hoary flakes . . .'. He found himself loving and blessing them, and also able to pray. The curse lifts and the dead albatross falls from his neck. He begins to live a full human life again. Coleridge's seeing-with-feeling is perception that participates in the world, rather than being passive and mechanical. The world is perceived by way of God's gift of human imagination.

George MacDonald, like Coleridge, explored the concept of the imagination in great depths, following the Romantic pattern so brilliantly articulated by Coleridge. His ideas are found particularly in his essays 'The Imagination: Its Functions and its Culture' (1867) and 'The Fantastic Imagination' (1882). His views there remarkably foreshadow those of Tolkien and C.S. Lewis, and are an important development of insights similar to Coleridge's. He put his views into practice as he wrote for children, writings in which wonder and holiness are central themes, and only sometimes the desire to teach intrudes. W.H. Auden observed: 'To me, George MacDonald's most extraordinary, and precious, gift is his ability, in all his stories, to create an atmosphere of goodness about which there is nothing phony or moralistic. Nothing is rarer in literature.' He is of enormous importance in shaping fantasy in children's literature. Macdonald also continued a Christian element in fantasy, and the understanding of imagination, that was there in Coleridge's Romanticism and would be there in the future with varying emphasis in the writings of C.S. Lewis, Tolkien, J.K. Rowling and others.

MacDonald sees the human imagination as living and moving and having its being in the imagination of God. 'The imagination of man,' he writes, 'is made in the image of the imagination of God. Everything of man must have been of God first.' The human being is therefore not creative in a primary sense. 'Indeed,' says MacDonald, 'a man is rather *being thought* than *thinking*, when a new thought arises in his mind . . . He did not create it.' Even the forms by which a person reveals his or her thoughts are not, in a primary sense, created by him or her; they belong to nature.

A central function of the imagination (an idea that would also be developed by C.S. Lewis) is the making of meaning, evidenced for instance in storytelling. This making is strictly subordinate to the primary meanings put into created reality by God. However, in 'the new arrangement of thought and figure . . . the new meaning contained is presented as it never was before'. MacDonald writes:

> Every new embodiment of a known truth must be a new and wider revelation. No man is capable of seeing for himself the whole of any truth: he needs it echoed back to him from every soul in the universe; and still its centre is hid in the Father of Lights.

He sees the operation of the imagination as choosing, gathering and vitally combining the material of a new revelation.

MacDonald's view of the imagination is thus squarely based on the view that their primary creator, God, puts all meanings into reality. All meaning refers to him, and thus points beyond and outside of the human maker. MacDonald explains:

> One difference between God's work and man's is, that, while God's work cannot mean more than he meant, man's must mean more than he meant . . . A man may well himself discover truth in what he wrote; for he was dealing all the time with things that came from thoughts beyond his own.

Such a view is highly conducive to fantasy literature. It also instils a confidence in writers whose beliefs are not widely shared by their society. As far back as the 1930s, for instance, Tolkien and C.S. Lewis, who were close friends, realised that a Christian view of the world could be expressed in stories without any obvious cultic or ritualistic elements. In fact, they believed, the West had become post-Christian, so much so that there was a widespread ignorance of core Christian teaching. It would not even be recognised as such when it appeared embodied in stories. They believed that Christian faith was fact (i.e. based on actual historical events) and that well-told and well-invented stories by their nature drew upon the same fountain of facthood as the Christian story, though in unfocused form. Modern fantasy has proved to be remarkably powerful in embodying not only Christian belief, but other world views such as Gnosticism or even a religious and devout kind of atheism like that of Philip Pullman. Modern fantasy is, arguably, subversive, its formative authors implicitly or explicitly challenging status quos like modernism, monolithic institutions (the 'Church', according to Pullman), dreary materialism (the Muggle world) or post-Christianity (the modern world as seen by Tolkien and Lewis). J.K. Rowling is closer than many contemporary writers to the central virtues and values championed by Lewis and Tolkien. This is because she is an heir of a theological Romanticism shaped by Coleridge and MacDonald, and characteristically expressed in the medium of fantasy.

The Inklings and Romanticism in the Modern World: C.S. Lewis and Tolkien

The place of the imagination in the thought and writings of C.S. Lewis and Tolkien is perhaps best encapsulated in manifesto essays they wrote, both included in a memorial to another of their literary group of friends, the Inklings, a collection called *Essays Presented to Charles Williams* (1947). Williams had died suddenly in 1945, to the grief of his friends. Tolkien's was called 'On Fairy Stories' and Lewis's was simply 'On Stories'.

Originally given as a lecture in 1939, 'On Fairy Stories' reveals Tolkien's thinking and theology behind his creation of Middle-earth and its stories. It also gets to the quick of fantasy, a mode of literature he has influenced enormously. Tolkien sees humanity as being in the image of its divine creator, and therefore able to create in the image of God's creation, that is, the primary world – making secondary worlds or subcreations.

Fairy tales, he points out, are stories about the world of faerie: 'the realm or state where fairies have their being.' Fairy tales are fantasy, allowing their hearers or readers to move from the details of their limited experience to 'survey the depths of space and time'. The successful fairy story in fact is 'subcreation', the ultimate achievement of fantasy, the highest art, deriving its power from human language itself. The successful writer of fairy story 'makes a

Secondary World which your mind can enter. Inside it, what he relates is "true": it accords with the laws of that world.' In addition to offering a secondary world, with an 'inner consistency of reality', a good fairy tale has three other key structural features. In the first place, it helps to bring about in the reader what Tolkien called recovery – that is, the restoration of a true view of the meaning of ordinary and humble things that make up human life and reality, such as love, thought, trees, hills and food. Second, the good fairy story offers escape from one's narrow and distorted view of reality and meaning. This is the escape of the prisoner rather than the flight of the deserter. Third, the good story offers consolation, leading to joy (what C.S. Lewis liked to call *Sehnsucht*, from German Romanticism).

The consolation, argued Tolkien, has meaning only because good stories point to the greatest story of all. This story has all the structural features of a fairy tale, myth or great story, with the additional feature of being true in actual human history. It loses neither its historicity nor its imaginative power by being both myth and fact. This is God's Spell (God's Story), the Gospel – the story of God himself coming to earth as a humble human being, the greatest storyteller entering his own story. The incarnate God is a king, like Aragorn, in disguise, in *The Lord of the Rings*, and a seeming fool, like Frodo and Sam.

C.S. Lewis's essay 'On Stories' focuses upon the ability of stories to capture, however imperfectly, states or qualities. These might be joy or sacrifice, but the essay concentrates upon the creation of a convincing fictional or a secondary world – how stories can embody atmosphere, country, weather and a sense of actually being in a place. This is true of stories that have a this-worldly setting as well as those that have an other-worldly one. The domain of an other-world fantasy is constructed according to a consistent and strict logic. Readers are usually interested in more than the excitement of the plot, demonstrated as the story is reread, where surprise, but not surprisingness, is necessarily eliminated (rereading is a trait, for Lewis, of good readers). The attraction of a story rather is the elusive something it catches, however fleetingly – a state or quality. In the fairy story of Jack the Giant Killer, there is not merely danger, but a distinctive danger from giants. The danger has a quality of giantness to it. Stories of romance – fantasies – may present access to profound experiences that might otherwise be rejected by a reader (if, for instance, they were presented as religious). Stories might also make concrete a reality that to the abstract mind is contradictory – such as the relationship between free will and destiny, or prophesised events and free agency. The plot of a story, says Lewis, is a net for capturing, even if only for a moment, an elusive something – a quality or state that has become tantalisingly tangible and concrete. The story as such, believes Lewis, may even surpass poetry in this ability.

J.K. Rowling's Romanticism

In J.K. Rowling's world of Harry Potter, the controlling principle is magic. This is what her fantasy centres around, and it is the magical domain of wizards and astounding creatures that is her consistent secondary world, or subcreation. More correctly, it is a world-within-a-world because the this-worldly setting of Muggle folk is, of course, also a literary invention. As this chapter will show, her stories display features of Romanticism, and theological features in particular, akin to the tradition of Coleridge, MacDonald, Lewis, Tolkien and others.

In her magical world, events, creatures and people can be controlled directly by mind and word, thought and declaration. Wizards and witches do not call upon external occult powers, such as spirits and demons, to implement their spells and curses, but draw upon natural magical abilities. These abilities can be trained and controlled. In fact, always in the foreground of the stories is an emphasis on education, underlining the centrality of mind and word. Hogwarts School of Witchcraft and Wizardry dominates events, even when they take place in other parts of Britain, particularly in *Harry Potter and the Deathly Hallows*, or even abroad. Epitomising the school's ethos of goodness is the benign figure of Albus Dumbledore, the white wizard.

Romanticism has traditionally been associated with idealism, a philosophical movement in which the mind – whether divine or human – has the primacy in the universe. The wizarding world reflects such idealism. Romanticism characteristically is opposed to realism, which in recent times has often been expressed largely in a mechanistic and materialistic view of reality. This is even though there are forms of critical realism that acknowledge the importance of mind and word in knowledge. In the Harry Potter stories, it could be said that Muggle society, in its sharp contrast to the magical world, reflects such a modern realism – dealing with things, pushing and pulling levers, and pressing buttons – the kind of activities that endlessly fascinate Arthur Weasley. A division between idealism and realism goes back to early philosophy, conveniently symbolised in Plato (427–347 BC) and Aristotle (384–322 BC). The contrast is expressed in a painting by Raphael (1483–1520) entitled *The School of Athens*. In the fresco Raphael has Plato pointing one finger upwards, gesturing towards a heavenly world of forms and ideals, while Aristotle spreads his fingers wide, indicating the earth with his hand, pointing towards the individual and tangible.

The ideals of Hogwarts School are practised in its teaching and lie at the moral centre of the stories. They include the school's fervent refusal to train its pupils in the Dark Arts, teaching only defence against evil wizardry. The natural gifts of its students are brought out and honed, with the aim of preparing them for life in the world. At the centre of concern is the proper use of magic even in extreme circumstances. Their minds are educated, and they are taught charms and other spells to add qualities to objects, so that something can be summoned to a wizard by a word, or his or her body can be instantly transported to another place. The technology of the Muggle world, amusingly, is seen as a way of making do without magic.

Stories in the Romantic tradition – romances – draw upon an ancient link between story and magic. In early English a spell and a story are one and the same word, *spel*. We could say that J.K. Rowling's stories of Harry Potter have cast a spell around the globe. Children are often spellbound by them. Aware of this ancient link, C.S. Lewis and Tolkien deliberately wrote stories that they believed might break the spell of materialism and unbelief in modern Western society. They felt that technology, in the absence of values to sustain humanity, had developed a life of its own and was the modern form of magic, even its technological weapons of catastrophic destruction casting their seductive spell over us. In the Harry Potter stories, the way Hogwarts students are taught not to misuse magic is very relevant to the morality of handling technology.

HARRY POTTER, FANTASY AND FAIRY TALE

The first Harry Potter story, *Harry Potter and the Philosopher's Stone*, is something of a Cinderella story, as many commentators have observed. The orphan Harry is brought up with his ugly cousin, Dudley Dursley, by an aunt and uncle who treat him as a chattel. Despite the disadvantages of his upbringing, he is essentially an attractive and good character who discovers that his strange powers can be explained by the fact that he really is a wizard. In this variant of the Cinderella story, the magical helper is Dumbledore, watching over him and inviting him to Hogwarts. The rags-to-riches element (echoed in real life events in Harry's author) involves his discovery that he has what seems like limitless wealth stashed away for him by his dead parents. It would be a mistake, however, to consider the first, and the other stories, simply as fairy story. At least, if they are fairy story, it is in the sense developed by Tolkien in his essay 'On Fairy Stories', which is really a classification of fantasy. Here Tolkien pointed out the presence of an alternative or secondary world – a subcreation – in the fairy story. When the secondary world is significantly developed – as it is in Middle-earth or Narnia – then it belongs to fantasy as such, which utilises fairy story but is larger than it. In fairy story, the magic happens in the secondary world as a domain that is alternative to the primary world. In fantasy, the strange, uncanny and magical can happen in the primary and in a secondary world, but at all times obedient to the inner logic of the fantasy. The logic springs from the story's basic supposal. In C.S. Lewis's Narnian Chronicles, the supposal is that there exists a world of talking animals within which its divine maker appears as a talking king of the beasts, a lion. There the magic occurs in Narnia, not in the primary world of wartime England and after, even though there exist portals between the worlds. In J.K. Rowling, the supposal is that there is a world of wizards and magical creatures carefully hidden from the eyes of Muggles in the ordinary world. The logic of that supposal allows magic more easily than in Lewis to intrude into the ordinary world – such as the suburban world of Little Whinging near London, the village of Little Hangleton, or even the Prime Minister's office at 10 Downing Street. Indeed, the rise of the Dark Lord Voldemort threatens both the wizarding and the Muggle worlds. Hogwarts School exists in the actual world, in a wild part of Scotland, albeit visible only as ruins to Muggle eyes. The domain of wizards and magical beasts is a world-within-worlds in Rowling's fantasy.

The supposals that give rise to imaginative literature are extraordinarily potent. Lewis's Narnia stories originally sprang out of a dream of a faun in a snowy wood, carrying parcels and an umbrella – a dream that haunted him for years before he started writing the Narnian stories. John Bunyan's inspiration for *The Pilgrim's Progress* came to him suddenly in prison as he thought of life, and the Christian life in particular, as a road or journey. In his 'Author's Apology' he tells us that as he 'fell into an allegory' it developed 'Like sparks that from the coals of fire do fly'.

> Thus I set pen to paper with delight,
> And quickly had my thoughts in black and white,
> For having now my method by the end,
> Still as I pull'd, it came; and so I penn'd
> It down; until at last it came to be,
> For length and breadth, the bigness which you see.

When J.K. Rowling's inspiration for the Harry Potter stories came she was trapped on a held-up train but, unlike Bunyan, she lacked a pen to jot down her teeming thoughts as the basic plot quickly emerged in essence fully-formed, rather as in Bunyan. It was immediately evident to her also that the idea had a built-in potential for comedy. In an interview, Rowling remembered: 'From the moment I had the idea for the book, I could just see a lot of comic potential in the idea that wizards walk among us and that we are foolishly blind to the fact that the reason we keep losing our car keys is that wizards are bewitching them for fun.'

FRESH METAPHORS AND RENEWED PERCEPTION

Stories write large the ability of symbolic language to help us to see the world in a fresh way or to restore ways of seeing that have been lost. They help to create, in a receptive reader, a new consciousness, or felt thought, where abstract concepts are perceived in a concrete form. Good stories generalise, illuminating themes and qualities like evil, sacrifice, death, love and even the pleasure of a meal, while remaining particular. The Harry Potter stories, I believe, have given a whole generation of children throughout the world – dubbed by a *Time* journalist Generation Hex – a restored vision of ancient virtues and values. The stories are not simply yet another fantasy treatment of the war between good and evil employing a well-worn theme. The tales of Hogwarts School present a highly imaginative and plausible understanding of the nature of evil as corrosive of something good, rather than something that has to exist, and will exist for ever.

Change of Consciousness

We see the world in a different way through reading the Harry Potter stories. This is nowhere more obvious than in the word that Rowling has bequeathed to the English language – 'Muggle'. The word 'Muggle' in her sense is gradually entering new editions of English dictionaries such as the *Oxford English Dictionary*, where, as well as the meaning in the Harry Potter stories – a person who possesses no magical powers – its sense is extended to include a person who lacks a particular skill or skills, or who is regarded as inferior in some way. What is interesting about the word 'Muggle' is that it represents the perspective of the fictional wizarding community on ordinary, non-magical folk. So we are seeing ourselves from an outsider's perspective!

Another example of an imaginative shift in perception, a change of consciousness, comes about through the reader's exposure to the wizarding world, and in particular to life at Hogwarts. In place of a normal modern scientific view of things, we see the world through the lens of a way of life not based on technology. We even get a taste of sixteenth-century Alchemy, with a bust of Paracelsus in a Hogwarts corridor, herbal remedies, charms and potions, and Dumbledore having a friend – Nicolas Flamel – who is over 600 years of age, having discovered the elixir of life. Even wizards like Dumbledore have a greatly extended lifespan, like the Numenoreans in *The Lord of the Rings*. The very attire of wizards, with long robes and tall pointed hats, is strikingly different from our familiar Muggle habits of dress. There is much to amuse us when a wizard attempts to dress like a Muggle. Harry meets two wizards attempting to look like Muggles as he attends the Quidditch World Cup: 'Both were dressed as Muggles, though very inexpertly; the man with the watch wore a tweed suit with thigh-length galoshes; his colleague, a kilt and a poncho.' Another, elderly wizard wore a 'long flowery night-gown', not realising that these were worn by Muggle women, not men.

Harry has been brought up in a Muggle family, but his friend Ron Weasley is from a large wizarding family. Ron constantly provides a wizarding perspective on Muggle ways, as when he attempts to ring Harry on what is to him an unfamiliar telephone, shouting down the receiver to Uncle Vernon. His father, Arthur Weasley, is constantly fascinated by Muggle gadgets such as cars and escalators. But most of all, what is most obvious from a wizarding perspective is a lack of magic among Muggles. Photographs and paintings do not move, and mirrors do not engage you in conversation. There is a serious edge to this comic contrast between the wizarding and Muggle worlds, which is that there is something seriously lacking in Muggle life, which makes it two-dimensional.

Recognition

The serious side of how fantasy, as a product of imagination, can engender a significant shift in consciousness is underscored by changes in perception undergone by several characters. We might call such change 'recognition' – a common element in fantasy. This element is based upon an understanding that we live in a story-shaped world. Within a fictional world characters might recognise that they are within a story of some kind. Aristotle saw such recognition as pivotal in a story; it signalled movement from a tangle of ignorance to knowledge. A protagonist recognises that somehow the story has been telling them – a narrative structure precedes the event they are in, and will reach a conclusion subsequent to that event. This raises questions about the role of providence and free agency. An important point in the stories for

Harry is when he makes two discoveries, both related, one of his past history and the other of his future task. Concerning his past, he discovers that Voldemort attempted to kill him as an infant, but failed because of the self-sacrificial love of his mother, Lily. He also discovers why Voldemort wanted to kill him in the first place – it was because of a prophecy that the Dark Lord knew in part, which pointed to Harry as his potential nemesis. Concerning his future, Harry learns he is the Chosen One, whose destiny is to destroy Voldemort, or to be killed by him, again from the prophecy. With this discovery of his past and future story, Harry understands that he is not a pawn in events, but that his choices (and also Voldemort's) shape events and outcomes. The voice of wisdom in the stories, Dumbledore, had already explained to Harry at the end of *Harry Potter and the Chamber of Secrets* why he is fundamentally different from Voldemort: 'It is our choices, Harry, that show what we truly are, far more than our abilities.'

Undeception

Closely related to recognition, and one aspect of it, is a shift in perception that can be called 'undeception.' It is a quality or state that has theological or philosophical implications – it might result in the redemption of a character, or it might raise the ancient question of the difference between appearance and reality, a question very central to the Harry Potter stories. C.S. Lewis gave the name 'undeception' (with 'awakening' as an alternative) to a feature of Jane Austen's novels. He observes: 'the undeception, structurally considered, is the very pivot or watershed of the story. In *Northanger Abbey*, and *Emma*, it precipitates the happy ending. In *Sense and Sensibility* it renders it possible. In *Pride and Prejudice* it initiates that revaluation of Darcy, both in Elizabeth's mind and in our minds, which is completed by the visit to Pemberley.' Learning from Jane Austen, undeception is a constant feature of C.S. Lewis's own fiction. Many of his characters experience it. These include Mark Studdock over the sinister NICE in *That Hideous Strength*, Prince Rilian in the Narnian story *The Silver Chair*, and Queen Orual, the narrator of *Till We Have Faces*. Like Lewis, Rowling is a great admirer of Jane Austen, and it is therefore fitting that the quality of undeception features in the Harry Potter stories. There are numerous examples, but the following are typical.

In *Harry Potter and the Prisoner of Azkaban* we learn that for twelve years, while Sirius Black has been incarcerated in Azkaban, his former friend Remus Lupin has believed that Sirius was culpable in the death of Harry's parents. The moment of undeception comes when Lupin realises that the Marauder's Map has shown the footsteps of Peter Pettigrew, who was believed to have been killed by Sirius. That Pettigrew lives led to the unmistakable conclusion that Sirius had been wrongly imprisoned – he was innocent. It was Pettigrew who was guilty, and in league with Voldemort.

Pettigrew was an Animagus, capable of taking animal form, in his case a rat, giving him the nickname Wormtail. For the years of Sirius's imprisonment Pettigrew had lived as the Weasley family pet rat, Scabbers, ending up as Ron's pet. In Ron's case it was hard for him to be undeceived about Scabbers – he loved his pet, and the idea that all the time he had been harbouring a murderer who had had a part to play in the death of Harry's parents was unthinkable. He was forced by the evidence to accept the unpleasant truth, and his love for Scabbers turned to hatred of Pettigrew.

The most labyrinthine example of undeception involves the changing perceptions of Severus Snape, who must rank as one of the most complex characters in children's literature. His allegiance, or lack of it, to Dumbledore was discussed by children and adult readers throughout the globe, as the books appeared. The subtlety of Snape is compounded by the fact that the stories are largely told through Harry's eyes, reflecting his limited but growing understanding and perception. From the very beginning of Harry's schooldays at Hogwarts, Professor Snape bullies Harry and treats him despicably. He looks like a classic villain, with black robes, greasy hair and sallow skin. In *Harry Potter and the Philosopher's Stone* Harry and his friends, understandably, suspect him of being up to no good and seeking the Philosopher's Stone. All the evidence seems to point that way. At one stage it appears that Snape is trying to kill Harry by making him fall from his broomstick during a Quidditch match. (It later turns out that it was another professor, Quirrell, who was hexing Harry at the game – Snape was in the process of saving Harry with a counterspell.) A moment of undeception for Harry comes when he encounters Quirrell, not Snape, in an underground chamber. The undeception is complete (though short-lived) when Quirrell is revealed as being partly possessed by Voldemort. In fact Snape's behaviour, even his bullying, is brilliantly compatible with his being a double agent employed by Dumbledore, as it was preserving his cover. A truly revelatory moment is when the beautiful Patronus of a doe, which appears in the Forest of Dean to guide Harry to the sword of Gryffindor, eventually turns out to be that of Snape's, a Patronus shaped by his life-long devotion to Lily Potter, his original love.

OTHER LITERARY FEATURES

We have already discussed J.K. Rowling's skilful blending of several genres from the rich tradition of British children's literature. Her skilful eclecticism is characteristic of much modern fantasy, such as Lewis's *The Chronicles of Narnia*, T.H. White's *The Sword and the Stone* and the writings of Terry Pratchett. Like these writers, her stories, though eclectic and teeming with diverse elements, integrate into a generally satisfying and harmonious whole – there is unity in diversity, even though the unity may be a rather baggy one in J.K. Rowling's case, because of the considerable lengths of the last four volumes. Her books are school stories; tales of coming of age, following Harry's life from age eleven to seventeen; a brilliantly constructed serial of seven stories, making a larger whole; tales of magic and the fantastic; and mystery stories. They deal head-on with formidable themes like death and implacable evil, yet their humour does not destroy the tone. The reader is carried along by Rowling's seemingly effortless invention of memorable characters, places and plot. Her greatest strength is in her storytelling, which grips her readers through many rereadings.

The Harry Potter Stories as a Secondary World

As we saw earlier in this chapter, Tolkien believed that the art of true fantasy or fairy story writing is subcreation. The ideal for Tolkien – a view that has influenced many subsequent writers of fantasy – is to make an imagined other world that is thoroughly consistent and plausible on its own inner terms. With a well-imagined world as a context for the story, its symbolic geography and history are able to heighten the events, adding tone and depth. Tolkien's view, and the expression of it in *The Lord of the Rings*, was Lewis's inspiration for the creation of Narnia. Pre-Tolkienian fantasies or symbolic stories often have a rudimentary but discernible secondary world, as in John Bunyan's *The Pilgrim's Progress* (1678) or George MacDonald's *Phantastes* (1858). C.S. Lewis's Narnia is an outstanding example of a successful secondary world, created with Tolkien's views in mind.

J.K. Rowling is familiar with the fantasies of Tolkien and Lewis, and many others besides. While she has not written about her craft in the way that Tolkien and Lewis have done, it is clear from her stories that she has expended great care in making her fictional world compelling and plausible. So great is her attention to the details of her creation that numerous attentive readers have been able to find few inconsistencies. Even a mistake can seem like the kind of quirk you would find in the real world, as when Marcus Flint remains captain of the Slytherin Quddich team when he should, by then, have left school. He might well have failed his advanced examinations (NEWTs) and stayed on another year to complete them.

When writing the stories, the author herself tells us, she took great pains to make the stories self-consistent. As her basic supposal is a world of wizards and magical creations carefully hidden from the eyes of Muggles, it was important, of course, to establish the rules of the magic within the stories. J.K. Rowling revealed in an interview, 'The five years I spent on *Harry Potter and the Philosopher's Stone* were spent constructing The Rules. I had to lay down all my parameters. The most important thing to decide when you're creating a fantasy world is what the characters *can't* do.' These same magical rules, so long in framing, created rich imaginative possibilities, as we can see from the existence of the stories. This example from *Harry Potter and the Prisoner of Azkaban* shows how the sense of a magical world is so beautifully maintained:

The journey to King's Cross was very uneventful compared to Harry's trip on the Knight Bus. The Ministry of Magic cars seemed almost ordinary, though Harry noticed that they could slide through gaps that Uncle Vernon's new company car certainly couldn't have managed. They reached King's Cross with twenty minutes to spare; the Ministry drivers found them trolleys, unloaded their trunks, touched their hats to Mr Weasley and drove away, somehow managing to jump to the head of an unmoving queue for the traffic lights.

The plausibility of the magical world is helped by its simple contrast with how an ordinary event like being driven to the railway station through busy London streets would normally take place. There is nothing arbitrary about how the Ministry cars move through the traffic. Everything accords with the nature of magic as present consistently in the stories. The fantasy, like all successful fantasy, abides by a strict internal logic.

A secondary world presupposes a relationship of some kind with the primary world – the world we inhabit, and touch, taste, smell, hear, see, investigate and think about. This is as true of a world-within-a-world like that of wizards and magical creatures in the Harry Potter stories. A portal into a secondary world is a common feature of fantasy literature and is more specific than a threshold or borderland between worlds (like the Wood between the Worlds in *The Chronicles of Narnia* or the spiritual King's Cross in *Harry Potter and the Deathly Hallows*). A portal could be a mirror, a door, a gate, a tunnel, a picture, a labyrinth, a film or television screen, or (in science fiction) a wormhole in space-time. Portals in the Harry Potter stories include the back of the Leaky Cauldron public house, on London's Charing Cross Road. This leads into Britain's main wizarding shopping area, Diagon Alley (with its sinister side street, Knockturn Alley). Another portal is the barrier between Platforms Nine and Ten on London's King's Cross Railway Station. This gives access to Platform 9¾, and the Hogwarts Express. Another important portal is an insignificant looking telephone box in a London Street, which provides magical entry to the Ministry of Magic. Also in London, a derelict Department Store once called Purge and Dowse Ltd hides the entrance to St Mungo's Hospital for Magical Maladies and Injuries. Access is gained through stepping into one of the windows. A common feature of portals in the world of Harry Potter is that they hide the domain of wizards and magical creatures from Muggles. Portals are at the imaginative centre of the stories; in *Harry Potter and the Philosopher's Stone* the portals into Diagon Alley and onto Platform 9¾ particularly have a strong attraction. They mark a transformation from the humdrum ordinary world, associated with Muggles, to the world of wizards, spells and magical creatures. The idea of the portal is central to the conception of Harry Potter's world of magic, and an important part of the appeal of the stories. When someone goes through a portal, the reader can be sure that he or she must face wonders and strangeness, and new dimensions of reality.

Talking Animals and Magical Creatures

Animals and animal stories have been a staple of tales told to or read by children. Animals such as Peter Rabbit, Paddington Bear, Reynard the Fox, Timmy the dog (one of the Famous Five) and Dumbledore's pet phoenix, Fawkes, are an indelible part of children's literature. Many of the animals have the ability to speak. Some of the inspiration for talking animals may have come from once-familiar Bible narratives. The speaking serpent of Genesis in the Garden of Eden, and Balaam's talking ass of a later period of history, are powerfully attractive to the imagination.

Talking animals have a long tradition in literature, mythology and folklore. The ancient tales of Aesop are still read today, along with the stories of Narnia, which concern a veritable world of talking beasts. More recently, Philip Pullman has created the great figure of Iorek Byrnison, the armoured bear in his *Northern Lights*. In a this-world setting, talking animals are animals that are strikingly unusual in their ability to speak. In this world, the norm is the dumb beast. In a secondary world, the ability to speak is part of the nature of at least some animals. In Tolkien's *The Hobbit* it is not only Smaug the dragon who speaks, as one would expect of a dragon, but also the ordinary birds of the air – who may be friends to travellers, or spies for the enemy. C.S. Lewis's *Chronicles of Narnia* makes much of a distinction between animals who speak, and those which do not. Those who do are the equals of the humans who find themselves in that world. There is a similar affinity in Tolkien – Treebeard the Ent is a creature that can keep company with humans and elves if he wished. In the Harry Potter stories, the ability to understand the speech of animals is a magical one, possessed by wizards and witches. The ability to understand the speech of snakes is uncommon, however, and is associated with the descendants and heirs of Salazar Slytherin, one of the founders of Hogwarts, or those having an affinity with him. Even in that company, Parselmouths are extremely rare. Harry Potter's ability both to speak and to understand the speech of snakes plays an important part in the plot of several of the books. In J.K. Rowling's stories, the speech of animals is not the mark of what C.S. Lewis in his science fiction called *hnau* – that is, personality and rationality akin to that of humans. It is only an attribute of the magical nature of some animals.

There is a variety of talking animals – magical creatures, all of them – in the stories, with a corresponding richness or poverty of discourse. One of the most distinctive is the gigantic Aragog, much loved by Hagrid, who is an Acromantula, a spider monster originating from Borneo that has eight eyes and can speak. Aragog plays an important part in *Harry Potter and the Prisoner of Azkaban*, and his funeral takes place in *Harry Potter and the Half-Blood Prince*, officiated by Hagrid and witnessed by Harry and Horace Slughorn, who desires his precious venom. J.K. Rowling skilfully introduces Harry's ability as a Parselmouth in the very first book. Before Harry is aware that he is a wizard he finds himself unwittingly discoursing with a bored Brazilian snake on a trip to the zoo with Dudley and the Dursleys, with comic results. In later stories, from *Harry Potter and the Chamber of Secrets* onwards, Harry's encounters are much darker. Hideous serpents play their part – the giant green Basilisk in *Harry Potter and the Chamber of Secrets*, and Voldemort's giant pet Nagini in *Harry Potter and the Goblet of Fire* and *Harry Potter and the Order of the Phoenix*. Though there is no evidence of speech, Fawkes, Dumbledore's pet phoenix, sings hauntingly at his death and at his funeral in *Harry Potter and the Half-Blood Prince*. In the earlier story, *Harry Potter and the Chamber of Secrets*, his beautiful and numinous song brings salvation from the clutches of Tom Riddle (Voldemort). Merpeople use a sophisticated language called Mermish and have organised communities. More minor magical beasts are able to speak, notably the gnomes reluctantly turfed out of the Weasleys' garden in *Harry Potter and the Prisoner of Azkaban* and perhaps the Mandrakes in *Harry Potter and the Chamber of Secrets*. The grunts uttered by most trolls are believed to belong to a crude language.

Transformation

At the very centre of fantasy, and of the stories of Harry Potter in particular, is transformation or metamorphosis. (Technically, the two terms are sometimes distinguished, with transformation implying an external agent of change, as when Dudley Dursley is partly transformed into a pig by being given a tail by Hagrid in *Harry Potter and the Philosopher's Stone*.) The term 'metamorphosis' comes from ancient Greek, translating as 'change of shape'. The shape-shifting, however, in fantasy is usually meant quite radically, as transforming from one kind of being to another, as when Sirius Black assumes his Animagus of a large dog in *Harry Potter and the Prisoner of Azkaban*. According to *The Encyclopedia of Fantasy*, in Western myths, when metamorphosis happens, the events involve magic. In the Harry Potter stories, therefore, transformation is doubly important, for they are both fantasies and have magic at the centre of the narratives.

Ovid's first-century *Metamorphosis* helped to define Western fantasy. His compendium of myths from the creation of the world to his present moment in Roman history – mainly taken from Greek sources – is skilfully linked together by the theme of metamorphosis. In the next century Apuleius' *The Golden Ass*, the plot of which centres on the adventures of a man transformed into an ass, was also immensely influential.

Transformation is so important in the Harry Potter series that expounding the theme could very well mean retelling all the stories. In several of them the Polyjuice Potion plays its part, allowing a person to take on the appearance of another. With it Harry and Ron in *Harry Potter and the Chamber of Secrets* are able to metamorphose into Crabbe and Goyle, Draco Malfoy's lackeys, in order to find out if Draco is the heir of Slytherin. More importantly, Barty Crouch Jr employs the Polyjuice Potion in *Harry Potter and the Goblet of Fire* to masquerade as Mad-Eye Moody, the Defence Against the Dark Arts teacher. This allows him to manipulate the Triwizard Tournament, so that finally Harry falls into the clutches of Lord Voldemort. Animagi are significant to many of the events in the stories, particularly in *Harry Potter and the Prisoner of Azkaban*, where it emerges that Harry's dead father, James, was an Animagus, assuming at will the form of a stag, while his schoolfriends Sirius Black and Peter Pettigrew could take the shape of a large dog and a rat respectively. They learned the difficult skill of becoming an Animagus to help their friend, Remus Lupin, who was a werewolf as a result of a bite while a child. He transformed into a werewolf when the moon was full. The shape of the Animagus reflects character – Pettigrew, who betrayed Harry's parents to Voldemort, is a rat; amusingly, Rita Skeeter's form as an Animagus is a large beetle. At the very beginning of book one, *Harry Potter and the Philosopher's Stone*, we are first introduced to Professor McGonagall in her Animagus shape, that of a cat, the markings around its eyes echoing the teacher's spectacles. Professor McGonagall teaches the important subject of Transfiguration at Hogwarts, once taught by Dumbledore. In the first lesson that Harry and his friends have in the subject she tells them: 'Transfiguration is some of the most complex and dangerous magic you will learn at Hogwarts.' Their first exercise was to transform a match into a needle, but soon they were doing much more advanced transfiguration. One of the most vivid examples of transformation in the stories involves Boggarts, who take the shape of a person's worst fears. In *Harry Potter and the Prisoner of Azkaban* Professor Lupin (one of the best teachers at Hogwarts) creatively employs a Boggart to help Harry learn how to fend off the dread-inducing Dementors. All in all, shape-shifting in the stories reinforces the important theme of contrast between appearance and reality.

A prolific writer on the Harry Potter books, John Granger (no relation of Hermione) makes much of the alchemical allusions in the stories – for example, the Philosopher's Stone of the first book's title – revealing a rich literary ancestry for them. Transformation is at the crux of alchemy, for example, in the transforming of base metal into gold, which stood for a deeper transformation, that of the human spirit from its fallen to its redeemed state.

Naming

Names in fantasy are very important. Many stories are ruined by the names chosen. In contrast, in Tolkien's stories, names reflect his invented languages, and help to create a particular tone. J.K. Rowling is highly inventive in her naming of characters, objects and creatures. Sometimes she makes new names (e.g. 'Horcrux') or transforms existing names (e.g. Nurmengard). Many she has collected from a variety of sources, such as tombstones. The tone she creates with particular names is sometimes comic and sometimes serious, depending exactly upon the intended effect. The contrast can be seen in the names Mundungus Fletcher, on the one hand, and Lord Voldemort on the other. The name 'Harry Potter' is chosen to reflect that Harry is an ordinary boy, even though he has extraordinary wizarding gifts. Professor Albus Dumbledore has names that indicate 'the white' (Latin, *Albus*, i.e. symbolising his goodness) and his grand quirkiness respectively – 'Dumbledore' is an early English name for a Bumblebee. J.K. Rowling is said to have chosen this name as she imagined him flitting around the corridors of Hogwarts, humming to himself. Among the hokum one finds on the Internet is a belief, asserted with implacable conviction, that J.K. Rowling is a reincarnation of Charles Dickens. What is true is that Rowling shares with Dickens a facility in naming (and also in the plenitude of her character creation).

Narrative Voice

A story is always told from a point of view, even if, within that, it incorporates a variety of perspectives from characters or the author. Indeed, the point of view may be the author's. A point of view in a story is the perspective adopted by the author in presenting characters, actions, setting and events that make up the narrative. J.K. Rowling has chosen to tell the stories largely from Harry's perspective, even though she employs the third person. There are only a few exceptions – such as the first, scene-setting, chapter of *Harry Potter and the Philosopher's Stone*, and the beginning chapters of *Harry Potter and the Half-Blood Prince*, when the reader learns of Severus's vow to help and protect Draco Malfoy as he seeks to accomplish the task set him by Voldemort. Mostly events unfold through Harry's eyes, the knowledge of what is happening limited by the lad's stage of understanding.

This choice of a Harry-centred point of view has far-reaching implications for the telling of the story. For one thing, it is beautifully appropriate for a coming of age story, as we move from Harry's childhood to adolescence, with attendant questions of identity and self-knowledge. For another, the choice of perspective introduces a curious note of realism into the fantasy – this is what life is like; as we live from one day to the next, events unfold and the overall story only gradually opens up. Harry and the reader are constantly engaged in interpretation, puzzling, for example, about the intentions and devices of Dumbledore. The story is inherently complex and many-layered.

One important implication of the chosen point of view is structural: a story told from Harry's slowly developing perspective is necessarily more baggy and unformed than one told from the author's perspective, who, God-like, knows beginnings and ends and can be crisp and polished. The enormous length of the last four books can be seen in fact as a function of being in Harry's perspective, reflecting the increasing complexity of his life as he progresses through Hogwarts. Whatever the correspondence between length and the narrative voice, however, it does seem true that J.K. Rowling finds structuring the story more of a problem as the series extends. This is especially so with books six and seven, which are two parts of one story, making *Harry Potter and the Half-Blood Prince* less self-contained than the other stories.

To overcome some of the limitations in Harry's perspective and experience, J.K. Rowling skilfully feeds in information from beyond Harry's knowledge via characters such as the adults Dumbledore and Professor Lupin (as when Lupin, in *Harry Potter and the Prisoner of Azkaban*, explains to Harry about Dementors, and why they affect him so badly), and the studious Hermione, who is constantly referring to the history of Hogwarts and other authorities to enhance Harry's knowledge. Hagrid, an adult friend of the children, plays an important role in the stories in revealing much to Harry. This is particularly effective because Hagrid is an outsider among the Hogwarts staff, a half-giant who was wrongly expelled during his schooldays, and because he is relatively inarticulate. Information comes out from him in a non-linear way, rather than from an information-dump. Harry and company often have to pump and trick him into revealing something, an action that reinforces the dynamics of their friendship. Often he reveals an important fact or clue without intending to do so – 'Shouldn't 'a said that' is a characteristic comment of Hagrid's. Hagrid is a friend who is also in the adult world (first as gamekeeper and then later as a teacher as well), yet child-like, retaining a child's wonder at magical creatures. He provides a bridge to the adult world for Harry, Ron and Hermione. A further effective device to supplement Harry's limited perpective on things is the Pensieve, which allows Harry to see others' memories objectively. The device is used extensively in *Harry Potter and the Half-Blood Prince*, where a lot of backstory has to be presented, particularly the history of Voldemort. In *Harry Potter and the Deathly Hallows* the Pensieve becomes an integral part of the plot, rather than simply a device (however effective) to provide information. The fact that the story is told from Harry's point of view can also be used for comic effect, relying on the reader knowing more than Harry, as when he is baffled by the behaviour of girls:

> Parvati positively beamed. Harry could tell that she was feeling guilty for having laughed at Hermione in Transfiguration. He looked around and saw that Hermione was beaming back, if possible even more brightly. Girls were very strange sometimes.

Because it is told from Harry's point of view the story requires interpretation. Both characters and events are often ambiguous. The reader is drawn into the process of interpretation (people all over the world, for instance, debated Snape's moral orientation as the volumes appeared, the new ones often adding to the ambiguity until the final revelation of his character in *Harry Potter and the Deathly Hallows*). Help, however, is provided from within the world of the story. Dumbledore, like Gandalf in Tolkien's *The Lord of the Rings*, serves as an interpreter of events, as when, in *Harry Potter and the Prisoner of Azkaban*, he tells Harry that the time may come when he is very glad that he was responsible for sparing Pettigrew's life. Ron and Hermione also serve as interpreters for Harry, as he shares astonishing or puzzling adventures or discoveries with them, or as they discuss events that they have all been drawn into. Much of the ambiguity, requiring interpretation, comes from characters who surprise us as readers. Even when we reread the books, and there is no longer the initial surprise element, there remains an element of the unexpected to these characters. Such complex characters include Snape, in his role as double agent, Professor Quirrell (who seems a timid man with a stutter, but turns out to be a 'man of two faces' in both a literal and a metaphorical sense), Professor Lupin, the brilliant teacher of Defence Against the Dark Arts at Hogwarts who is revealed to be a secret werewolf, transforming each month at full moon, and Sirius Black, introduced as an escapee from Azkaban prison intent on murdering Harry for Voldemort, who emerges as an innocent man, and godfather and protector of Harry.

ASSESSING J.K. ROWLING

The early Harry Potter books made their debut to critical acclaim, and won numerous literary awards. By 2001 the first film of the series had appeared, increasing the popularity and sales of the books. *Harry Potter and the Philosopher's Stone* won the Gold Medal in the prestigious Smarties Book Prize in 1997 – the year of its publication – and several other awards, including children's Book of the Year by the British Book Awards. The next year J.K. Rowling again won the Smarties prize, this time for *Harry Potter and the Chamber of Secrets*. That book won several other awards, and Rowling was heralded the *Bookseller* Author of the Year for 1998 by the Booksellers Association. In 2000 *Harry Potter and the Prisoner of Azkaban* achieved the Whitbread's Children's Book of the Year, the Smarties Book award and other awards. The awards have continued, but some more recent critics have been less favourable to the stories. A heavyweight literary critic, Harold Bloom, was critical from the very first, saying of *Harry Potter and the Philosopher's Stone* that it represented a dumbing-down of literary culture. It is true that J.K. Rowling is characteristically over fond of using adverbs, but Bloom's claim that the first book is cliché-ridden is surprising, and does not reflect the usual care behind his great scholarship. He claims, for example:

I went to the Yale University bookstore and bought and read a copy of 'Harry Potter and the Sorcerer's Stone'. I suffered a great deal in the process. The writing was dreadful; the book was terrible. As I read, I noticed that every time a character went for a walk, the author wrote instead that the character 'stretched his legs'. I began marking on the back of an envelope every time that phrase was repeated. I stopped only after I had marked the envelope several dozen times. I was incredulous. Rowling's mind is so governed by clichés and dead metaphors that she has no other style of writing.

I was surprised at Bloom's claim, because I could not remember J.K. Rowling using this expression for walking. It is true that Rowling does not overwrite for the sake of literary polish – she has the ability to keep the narrative pace going and so does use colloquial expressions where appropriate. She usually writes very well, using a style fitting for her purpose. Her work can be appreciated best in some of the literary features outlined in this chapter, rather than taking a reductive approach to style like that of Dr Bloom. I went back to *Harry Potter and the Philosopher's Stone* and carefully looked right through it for the expression 'stretched his legs' or variants of that expression. If Bloom was right it should appear every few pages. I did find an example of the usage in chapter one, where we are taken into the thoughts of Vernon Dursley: 'He was in a very good mood until lunchtime, when he thought he'd stretch his legs and walk across the road to buy himself a bun from the bakery.' There were no other examples that I could find in the remainder of the book, in any variation.

I thought I would look in the next book, *Harry Potter and the Chamber of Secrets*, for examples of the expression. They were likely to be there if Rowling used it so much, and if her mind was so wired into dead metaphors and clichés, as claimed by Bloom. I did find a variant, which comes just after Harry has been rescued by Ron and the Weasley twins and is sitting in the flying Ford Anglia: '"Let Hedwig out," he told Ron. "She can fly behind us. She hasn't had a chance to stretch her wings for ages."' Later in that book, after much searching, I found a reference to the many legs of the young giant spider, Aragog (whom Harry later meets in its old age):

If, as a boy, Hagrid had heard that a monster was hidden somewhere in the castle, Harry was sure he'd have gone to any lengths for a glimpse of it. He'd probably thought it was a shame that the monster had been cooped up so long, and thought it deserved the chance to stretch its many legs; Harry could just imagine the thirteen-year-old Hagrid trying to fit a leash and collar on it.

This seems an entirely valid, and humorous, variation on the staid expression. I could not find any more uses, in any variation, in *Harry Potter and the Chamber of Secrets*. When I looked carefully in *Harry Potter and the Prisoner of Azkaban*, the next book, I could find no examples at all. My conclusion is that Harold Bloom had not read *Harry Potter and the Philosopher's Stone* carefully and attentively enough, perhaps because he took a dislike to it from the onset. His misgivings may reflect a tension in fiction writing between the more colloquial style of a storyteller (like Tolkien in *The Hobbit* and Rowling in Harry Potter) and a more self-conscious literary approach, which has its eyes to the academy.

In discussing the Harry Potter books, it is important (and courteous) to focus on qualities appropriate for fantasy and storytelling. The stories are what they are, and not something else. Similar mistakes are made if we wrongly identify the magic in the stories as demonic and as promoting and celebrating evil, which is not warranted by the stories themselves, standing as they do in a venerable tradition of fantasy and stories of magic.

Appendix: A Brief Chronology of J.K. Rowling

1965 31 July: J.K. Rowling born near Chipping Sodbury, England.

1976 Enters Wyedean Comprehensive School, near her home village of Tutshill, close to Chepstow.

1983 Begins a four-year French language degree at University of Exeter, Devon.

1985 Begins a year in Paris as part of her course, in order to experience French culture, teaching English part-time in a French School.

1987 Moves to London to seek work.

1990 The idea of a series of stories about Harry Potter falls into her mind on a delayed train journey from Manchester to London. 30 December: the death of her mother, Anne.

1991 Moves to Oporto, Portugal, to teach English as a Foreign Language. Continues writing the first Harry Potter book.

1992 16 October: Marries a Portuguese journalist, Jorge Arantas.

1993 27 July: Birth of first child, Jessica.

1994 The marriage having failed, J.K. Rowling returns to Britain with her daughter, settling in Edinburgh, Scotland.

1996 February: She sends a synopsis and the first three chapters to Christopher Little, a Literary Agent, who requests to see the whole manuscript. It is turned down by Penguin and eleven other publishers until finally it is accepted by the independent house Bloomsbury.

1997   July: Publication of *Harry Potter and the Philosopher's Stone* by
         Bloomsbury of London. Wins Nestlés Smarties Book Prize (one of
         many book awards).

1998   September: US publication of *Harry Potter and the Sorcerer's
         Stone* by Scholastic. J.K. Rowling later regretted the title change.
         July: publication in the UK of *Harry Potter and the Chamber of
         Secrets*, which wins the Nestlé Smarties Book Prize.

1999   June: US publication of *Harry Potter and the Chamber of Secrets*.
         July: UK publication of *Harry Potter and the Prisoner of
         Azkaban*. October: US publication of *Harry Potter and the
         Prisoner of Azkaban*.

2000   July: Publication of *Harry Potter and the Goblet of Fire* in the UK
         and USA. Awarded honorary degree of Doctor of Letters from
         Exeter University.

2003   June: Publication of *Harry Potter and the Order of the Phoenix* in
         the UK and USA.

2005   July: Publication of *Harry Potter and the Half-Blood Prince* in the
         UK and USA.

2007   July: Publication of *Harry Potter and the Deathly Hallows* in the
         UK and USA.

Notes

Abbreviations

PS *Harry Potter and the Philosopher's Stone* (USA: *Harry Potter and the Sorcerer's Stone*)
CS *Harry Potter and the Chamber of Secrets*
PA *Harry Potter and the Prisoner of Azkaban*
GF *Harry Potter and the Goblet of Fire*
OP *Harry Potter and the Order of the Phoenix*
HBP *Harry Potter and the Half-Blood Prince*
DH *Harry Potter and the Deathly Hallows*

Because of the variety of editions of the Harry Potter books, references are given for chapters rather than specific pages.

PART ONE: QUICK REFERENCE GUIDE

Chapter One: The Plot

Page 27   'The sword of Gryffindor was hidden': DH, ch. 15.

Chapter Three: An A–Z

Page 45   *Harry's birth number yields the master number 11*: from George Beahm, *Fact, Fiction, and Folklore in Harry Potter's World: An Unofficial Guide* (Charlottesville, Va: Hampton Roads, 2005), p. 148.

Page 65   'Dumbledore's benevolent but strict theology': A.O. Scott in online *Slate* magazine, 24 August 1999, quoted by Alison Lurie, *Boys and Girls Forever: Children's Classics from Cinderella to Harry Potter* (London: Random House, 2003), p. 118.

Pages 86–7   *Latin in the Harry Potter stories*: for more on the Latin in the stories see http://www.pyrrha.demon.co.uk/spot.html.

Page 104   'Phoenix song is magical': Newt Scamander (a.k.a. J.K. Rowling), *Fantastic Beasts & Where to Find Them* (London: Bloomsbury, 2001), p. 32.

Page 106   'the triumph of good, the power of innocence': DH, ch. 22.

Page 107   the Prime Minister in that period of the 1990s would have
            been John Major: John Major was PM 1990–7, and was
            succeeded by Tony Blair (PM 1997–2007).

Page 119   'a very flawed hero. An anti-hero': OnLine interview with
            J.K. Rowling,
            http://www.bloomsbury.com/harrypotter/default.asp?sec=3.

Page 120   spells: J.K. Rowling revealed her working theory on her
            official website: www.jkrowling.com/'extrastuff'.

Page 127   'The gently smiling Dolores Umbridge': review of OP by
            Stephen King, Entertainment Weekly, 11 July 2003.

Page 130   'wand that chooses the wizard': PS, ch. 5.

PART TWO: J.K. ROWLING AND THE WORLD OF HARRY POTTER

Chapter Four: A Life

Page 141   'what looked like a large beach ball': PS, ch. 2.

Page 142   'We spent about three quarters of our childhood':
            'Biography', official website, www.jkrowling.com.

Page 143   Hermione Granger's character is partly a combination of
            herself and her sister: television interview with Richard and
            Judy, Channel 4, July 2006.

Page 143   he and Jo would dress up as wizards, a story denied by
            Rowling: interview with J.K. Rowling, 'Biography', official
            website, www.jkrowling.com.

Page 144   Chepstow 'is a town dominated by a castle on a cliff, which
            might explain a lot': Lindsey Fraser, An Interview with
            J.K. Rowling (London: Egmont Books, 2002), p. 4.

Pages 144–5 Peter Francis's memories of Tutshill: personal
            communication by email, Thursday 10 August 2006.

Page 146   'They stuff people's heads down the toilet the first day at
            Stonewall': PS, ch. 3.

Page 151   'Harry's feelings about his dead parents had become much
            deeper': 'Biography', official website, www.jkrowling.com.

Page 151   directly inspired by the death of her mother: see Eddie Gibb,
            'Tales from a Single Mother', Sunday Times, 29 June 1997.

Page 152   'I've never been more broke and the little I had saved':
            interview with Anne Johnstone, 'Happy Ending, and that's
            for Beginners', Herald, 24 June 1997.

Page 152   'like Graham Greene, my faith is sometimes about if my
            faith will return': interview with Georgie Greig, Tatler,
            10 January 2006.

Page 152   *'Caravaggio's* Supper at Emmaus *when Jesus reveals himself'*: Fraser, *An Interview with J.K. Rowling*, p. 17.

Page 153   *'Hope you have – er – a good holiday'*: PS, ch. 17.

Page 153   *'Harry Potter lives with his aunt, uncle and cousin'*: quoted on HP Lexicon, www.hp-lexicon.org/about/sources/jkr.com/jkr-com-trans-ps-synop.html.

Page 154   *the ninth richest person in the 'celebrity world'*: Independent, 15 August 2006.

Page 155   *In the dream they moved around her*: diary, 19 December 2006, official website, www.jkrowling.com.

Page 155   *'I scared Stephen King'*: www.mugglenet.com/jkr/jonyc/night2/kate.shtml.

Page 156   *According to the Pentagon, the Harry Potter books in 2006*: report in the *Scotsman*, 16 September 2006.

Chapter Five: Themes and Features

Page 158   *'I'll use the Invisibility Cloak,' said Harry*: PS, ch. 16.

Page 158   *'We're coming with you'*: DH, ch. 6.

Page 158   *Harry and Ron about what Dumbledore had said at the feast*: OP, ch. 12.

Page 158   *'A warmth was spreading through him'*: HBP, ch. 5.

Page 164   *the stories could be useful for teacher training*: see *Phi Delta Kappan: The Professional Journal for Education*, 85/4 (2003), 310–15; Margaret Zoller Booth and Grace Marie Booth, 'What American Schools Can Learn from Hogwarts School of Witchcraft and Wizardry', online article; both at www.pdkintl.org/kappan/k0312boo.htm.

Page 168   *Harry's quest takes the shape of the traditional hero's journey*: this is applied to many contemporary plots of successful moves by Christopher Vogler in *The Writer's Journey: Mythic Structure for Storytellers and Screenwriters* (2nd edn, London: Pan Books, 1999).

Page 172   *'The clock on the wall opposite him had only one hand'*: CS, ch. 3.

Page 172   *'It was a very odd watch. It had twelve hands but no numbers'*: PS, ch. 1.

Page 172   *'Death and bereavement and what death means'*: interview with Malcolm Jones, 'Why Harry's Hot', *Newsweek*, 17 July 2000.

Page 174   *walking 'palely where their living selves once trod'*: OP, ch. 38.

Page 174   *'To the well-organized mind, death'*: PS, ch. 17.

Page 174	*'It is the unknown we fear when we look upon death'*: HBP, ch. 26.
Page 175	*the 'last and greatest of his protectors had died'*: HBP, ch. 30.
Page 175	*'It's going to be all right, sir'*: HBP, ch. 26.

Chapter Six: Spiritual World View

Page 176	*J.K. Rowling's . . . themes . . . illuminate a very definite world view*: on world views, see James W. Sire, *The Universe Next Door* (4th edn, Downers Grove, Ill.: InterVarsity Press, 2004).
Page 178	*'our Hogwarts is in danger'*: OP, ch. 11.
Page 178	*[Hermione] reckons Quidditch . . . creates tensions and bad feelings*: OP, ch. 26.
Page 178	*the alchemical types of Paracelsus*: see articles on Paracelsus in *Wikipedia* and *Encyclopedia Britannica*, and see also Paracelsus, the *Liber de Nymphis, sylphis, pygmaeis et salamandris et de caeteris spiritibus*.
Page 179	*the Myers–Briggs classification*: see www.myersbriggs.org.
Page 181	*Voldemort 'cannot possess you without enduring mortal agony'*: HBP, ch. 23.
Page 181	*'In spite of the temptation you have endured, all the suffering'*: HBP, ch. 23.
Page 182	*'His mother died in the attempt to save him'*: GF, ch. 33.
Page 182	*'That's chess. . . . You've got to make some sacrifices'*: PS, ch. 16.
Page 182	*love is more powerful than Voldemort's kind of magic*: see the important exchange between Tom Riddle and Dumbledore in *HBP*, ch. 20, as Tom asks to teach at Hogwarts in the early days of Dumbledore's headmastership.
Page 183	*The room . . . 'contains a force that is at once more wonderful'*: OP, ch. 37.
Page 183	*the popular satirical online magazine the* Onion: issue 26 July 2000; see www.snopes.com/humor/iftrue/potter.htm.
Page 183	*Harry Potter books have been high on the list of banned books*: see 'Most Challenged Books of 21st Century (2000–2005)', American Library Association Website, www.ala.org.
Page 183	*'As good almost kill a man as kill a good book'*: John Milton, *Areopagitica* (1644).
Page 184	*'the values it espouses resonate at critical points with Christian morality'*: Francis Bridger, *A Charmed Life: The*

Spirituality of Potterworld (2001; New York: Doubleday, 2002).

Page 184   *'the kind of wisdom we find in the book of Proverbs'*: Bridger, *A Charmed Life*, pp. 87–8.

Page 184   *'the sheer wonder of existence, the magic of being'*: John Killinger, *God, the Devil, and Harry Potter: A Christian Minister's Defense of the Beloved Novels* (New York: St Martin's Press, 2002), p. 138.

Page 184   *'the world of Harry Potter would be inconceivable'*: Killinger, *God, the Devil, and Harry Potter*, p. 14.

Page 185   *'People tend to find in books what they look to find'*: quoted in Connie Neal, *The Gospel According to Harry Potter: Spirituality in the Stories of the World's Most Famous Seeker* (Louisville, Ky: Westminster John Knox Press, 2002), p. x.

Page 186   *read the Harry Potter stories in the context of the tradition of English Literature*: even when authors have not been confessing Christians, there is a rich pattern of reference to the Judaeo-Christian Scriptures in English Literature, as is evidenced in the magisterial *Dictionary of Biblical Tradition in English Literature*, ed. David Lyle Jeffrey (Grand Rapids, Mi.: Eerdmans, 1992). It is not possible to read classic texts of English Literature fully without some knowledge of the biblical tradition. John Granger's most recent book, *Unlocking Harry Potter: Five Keys for the Serious Reader* (Wayne, Pa.: Zossima Press, 2007), was too late for its insights to impact on this *Companion*. In it he deepens his analysis to take account of J.K. Rowling as a contemporary writer with 'edgy relevance', shaped but not controlled by her postmodernist milieu. His exploration of her 'narrative misdirection' is particularly interesting, which relates to my discussion of appearance and reality, pp. 169–71, 241–3. I look forward to his next book, which he says will be called *Harry Meets Hamlet and Scrooge: Reading the English Greats with Harry Potter*, and which will explore J.K. Rowling in the context of mainstream English literary tradition (cf. Chapter Five above, which specifically looks at the tradition of children's literature).

Page 187   *'a strong sign of the author's xian religious background'*: http://harrypottertorah.blogspot.com/2007/08/harry-potter-and-deathly-hallows-jewish.html.

Page 188   *'The consequences of our actions are always so complicated'*: *PA*, ch. 22.

Page 189   'You will find that I will only truly *have left this school*': CS,
           chs 14, 15.
Page 190   'He'll be famous . . . there will be books written about
           Harry': PS, ch. 1.
Page 190   'because Voldemort made a grave error, and acted on
           Professor Trelawney's words': HBP, ch. 24.
Page 190   'the difference between being dragged into the arena': HBP,
           ch. 24.
Page 191   [Trelawney's] prophecy about Voldemort's servant
           (Wormtail): PA, ch. 22.
Page 192   'The music was growing louder': CS, ch. 17.
Page 192   'Dumbledore's man through and through': HBP, ch. 17.
Page 192   'it was his own grief turned magically to song': HBP, ch. 29.
Page 193   The phoenix 'was resting its beautiful head against Harry's
           injured leg': GF, ch. 36.
Page 193   [Harry] sees the stag, as white as a unicorn: PA, chs 20, 21.

Chapter Seven: Images of Good and Evil

This chapter draws upon Colin Duriez, 'Voldemort, Death Eaters,
Dementors and the Dark Arts: A Contemporary Theology of Spiritual
Perversion in the Harry Potter Stories,' in Christopher Partridge and Eric
Christianson (eds), *The Lure of the Dark Side: Satan and Demonology in
Popular Culture* (London: Equinox, 2008).

Page 194   'Magic in the sense in which it happens in my books':
           interview with Evan Solomon, CBC Newsworld, *Hot Type*,
           13 July 2000.
Page 194   'Yes, I am [a Christian] . . . Which seems to offend': Max
           Wyman, 'You can Lead a Fool to a Book but you can't Make
           them Think', *Vancouver Sun* (British Columbia), 26 October
           2000.
Page 195   Jerram Barrs . . . writes of J.K. Rowling's 'very clear moral
           universe': Jerram Barrs, 'Harry Potter and his Critics', in
           *Perspectives: The Newsletter of Covenant Theological
           Seminary's Francis Schaeffer Institute* (2003), available at
           www.covenantseminary.edu/resource.
Page 195   'only "real" witchcraft elements in the books are the real
           stereotypes that have dogged witchcraft': 'Witchcraft and
           Harry Potter',
           http://paganwiccan.about.com/library/blharrypotter.htm.
Page 195   'Evil as presented in the Harry Potter books': Rabbi Noson
           Weisz, 'Harry Potter and the War between Good and Evil',

www.aish.com/societywork/arts/Harry_Potter_and_the_War
_Between_Good_and_Evil.asp.

Page 195   *J.K. Rowling's portrayal of evil [reflects] a rich tradition of
             fantasy literature*: see Chapter Four above, which discusses
             the history of fantasy and Romanticism behind Rowling's
             stories.

Pages 196–7 *The philosopher's stone is the distinctive quest of the
             alchemist*: in US editions the first book is less accurately and
             satisfactorily called *Harry Potter and the Sorcerer's Stone*.

Page 197   *goeteia or Satanic magic*: for an analysis and critique of
             Lewis's exposition, see Tom Shippey, 'New Learning and
             New Ignorance: Magia, Goeteia, and the Inklings', in
             Eduardo Segura and Thomas Honegger (eds), *Myth, Art and
             Magic* (Zollikofen: Walking Tree Publishers, 2007). Tom
             Shippey's essay explores Lewis's view of magic in relation to
             his fiction, and that of fellow Inklings, including Tolkien.
             Shippey points out that Lewis's polemical point in making
             this distinction between a mechanical and a spiritual or
             holistic view of nature, and high and black magic, is
             represented (not entirely consistently) in his fictional
             character Merlin in his *That Hideous Strength*.

Page 197   *In the sixteenth century . . . there was an 'animistic or genial
             cosmology'*: C.S. Lewis, *English Literature in the Sixteenth
             Century Excluding Drama* (London: Oxford University
             Press, 1954), p. 3.

Page 197   *'By reducing Nature to her mathematical elements'*:
             C.S. Lewis, *English Literature*, pp. 3–4.

Page 198   *'This is not merely a matter of ruling out bad 'uses' of
             essentially neutral powers'*: Benjamin Lipscomb and
             Christopher Stewart, 'Magic, Science, and the Ethics of
             Technology', in Mercedes Lackey (ed.), *Mapping the World
             of Harry Potter: Science Fiction and Fantasy Writers Explore
             the Bestselling Fantasy Series of All Time* (Dallas, Tex.:
             Benbella Books, 2005), p. 90.

Page 199   *Neither ability [to think and imagine] can be explained
             adequately by material causes*: in this they are rather like
             magic. They are also like supernatural processes, including
             miracles, as argued in the case of thought by C.S. Lewis, in
             Miracles (2nd edn, London: Collins Fontana, 1960),
             p. 154.

Page 201   *[St Augustine's] view is expounded*: in St Augustine,
             Confessions, bk 7.

Page 201   '*It was manifested unto me, that those things be good which yet are corrupted*': St Augustine, *Confessions*, bk 7.

Page 202   '*The Dark Arts . . . are many, varied, ever-changing and eternal*': HBP, ch. 9.

Page 203   '*There is no good and evil, there is only power, and those too weak to seek it*': PS, ch. 17.

Page 203   instincts for '*cruelty, secrecy and domination*': HBP, ch. 13.

Page 204   '*the most dangerous Dark Wizard of all time*': HBP, ch. 13.

Page 204   *In George MacDonald . . . a giant's strength is stored . . . apart from his body*: George MacDonald, 'The Giant's Heart', in George MacDonald, *The Gifts of the Christ Child*, ed. Glenn Edward Sadler (Oxford: A.R. Mowbray, 1973).

Page 205   '*the life or strength of a man or creature may reside in some other place or thing*': J.R.R. Tolkien, 'On Fairy Stories', in *Tree and Leaf Including the Poem* Mythopoeia (London: HarperCollins, 1992), p. 20.

Page 205   '*I shall enchant my heart, and I shall place it*': Tolkien, 'On Fairy Stories', p. 20. Tolkien quotes E.A. Wallis Budge, *Egyptian Reading Book for Beginners* (1896), p. xxi.

Chapter Eight: The Great Tradition of Children's Literature

Page 208   *necessarily . . . a sketch . . . and largely concerns literature in Britain*: these necessities of selection mean, sadly, that there is not space to discuss non-British authors writing for children such as Ursula LeGuin, Robert O'Brien and Madeleine L'Engle.

Page 208   *a discovery of childhood*: this is not to deny or minimalise the contribution of social construction to both the strengths and weakness of our modern perception of childhood. One important distortion that has been constructed is a longstanding identification of fantasy and fairy story with children's literature, an identification Tolkien and C.S. Lewis battled long and hard to refute. (See my *J.R.R. Tolkien and C.S. Lewis: The Story of a Friendship* (Stroud: Sutton Publishing, 2005), particularly pp. 95–107, 129–30.) The idea of a discovery of childhood can be paralleled with the discovery of the knowability of the contingent natural world, based on faith in its rational principles from theism, which gave rise to modern science in the seventeenth century. What has turned out, in social terms, to be the most successful and important collaboration in human history has a comparatively recent origin, tied in with a discovery of the 'world of science'.

Page 208   *He drew attention to their essential humility*: Luke 7: 32.

Page 210   *'There was a time'*: from William Wordsworth, 'Intimations
             of Immortality from Recollections of Early Childhood'.

Page 211   *'The genre was finished . . . it was impossible to keep it
             going'*: Isobel Quigly, *The Heirs of Tom Brown: The English
             School Story* (Oxford: Oxford University Press, 1984),
             p. 276.

Page 212   *'The public school turned out to be a remarkably convenient
             setting'*: Quigley, *Heirs*, p. 43.

Page 214   *'Childhood is my creed in both art and literature'*: quoted in
             John Fowles, *Wormholes: Essays and Occasional Writings*
             (London: Jonathan Cape, 1998), p. 213.

Page 215   *'magic . . . in one way is the wild imagination actualized'*:
             Colin Manlove, *From Alice to Harry Potter: Children's
             Fantasy in England* (Christchurch, NZ: Cybereditions,
             2003), p. 187.

Page 218   *'a fairly good imitation of Grimm and Dickens, mixed with
             some true Alpine feeling of my own'*: quoted in 'John
             Ruskin', in *The Oxford Companion to Children's Literature*,
             ed. Humphrey Carpenter and Mari Prichard (Oxford and
             New York: Oxford University Press, 1984).

Page 220   *what is most difficult for the writer is deciding what is* not
             possible in the world of the story: interview with BBC Radio
             Bristol, 12 November 2001.

Page 220   *'Much of the amusement of worlds-where-magic-works
             stories'*: 'Magic', in John Clute and Peter Nicholls (eds), *The
             Encyclopedia of Science Fiction* (London: Orbit, 1993).

Page 221   *'The way this influence [of magic] works is most easily seen'*:
             Diana Wynne Jones, in 'Magic', in John Clute and John
             Grant (eds), *The Encyclopedia of Fantasy* (London: Orbit,
             1997), p. 616.

Page 222   *'Any sufficiently advanced technology is indistinguishable
             from magic'*: Arthur C. Clarke quoted in Clute and Nicholls
             (eds), *The Encyclopedia of Science Fiction*, p. 765.

Page 222   *'Even fairy-stories as a whole have three faces'*: Tolkien,
             'On Fairy Stories', p. 28.

Page 223   *'caught sight of himself'*: PA, ch. 4.

Page 224   *'and what are "toves"?'*: Lewis Carroll, *Through the
             Looking-glass* (1872), ch. VI.

Page 226   *'This is a different kind of literature. It expresses a child's
             ideal world'*: Manlove, *From Alice to Harry Potter*,
             p. 192.

Chapter Nine: The Storyteller's Craft

Page 227   *magic 'can be seen as a metaphor for the special powers of childhood'*: Lurie, *Boys and Girls Forever*, p. 113.

Page 229   *[Samuel Taylor Coleridge's belief that] the human mind . . . is active in making sense of the world*: the German philosopher Immanuel Kant (1724–1804) had deeply influenced the intellectual world that Coleridge inhabited, setting the problem of how the mind was active in knowledge rather than passive in it.

Page 229   *'[Coleridge's] face . . . was turned . . . in the opposite direction to the one which natural science was taking'*: quoted in the online *Encyclopedia Barfieldiana*, www.owenbarfield.com/Encyclopedia_Barfieldiana/People/Coleridge.html, accessed 8 June 2006.

Page 229   *'This power, first put into action by the will and understanding'*: S.T. Coleridge, *Biographia Literaria* (1817), ch. XIV.

Page 230   *'The Imagination then I consider either as primary, or secondary'*: S.T. Coleridge, *Biographia Literaria*, ch. XIII.

Page 231   *'To me, George MacDonald's most extraordinary, and precious, gift'*: W.H. Auden, Afterword to George MacDonald, *The Golden Key, with Pictures by Maurice Sendak* (New York: Farrar, Straus and Giroux, 1976), p. 86.

Page 231   *[MacDonald's] enormous importance in shaping fantasy in children's literature*: see Marion Lochhead, *The Renaissance of Wonder in Children's Literature* (Edinburgh: Canongate, 1977).

Page 231   *'The imagination of man is made in the image of the imagination of God'*: George MacDonald, 'The Imagination: Its Functions and Culture', in MacDonald, *A Dish of Orts* (London: Sampson Low, 1893), ch. 1.

Page 232   *'Every new embodiment of a known truth'*: MacDonald, *A Dish of Orts*, ch. 1.

Page 232   *'One difference between God's work and man's'*: MacDonald, 'The Fantastic Imagination', in *A Dish of Orts*, ch. 14.

Page 236   *Raphael . . . Plato . . . Aristotle*: as observed by Francis Schaeffer, in *How Should We Then Live? The Rise and Decline of Western Thought and Culture* (Old Tappan, NJ: Fleming H. Revell, 1976), p. 52.

Page 237   *the secondary world is significantly developed . . . [in] fantasy*: see the helpful discussion of similarities and

differences between fantasy and fairy story in Maria
Nikolajeva's long article, 'Fantasy Literature and Fairy
Tales', in Jack Zipes (ed.), *The Oxford Companion to Fairy
Tales* (Oxford: Oxford University Press, 2000); see also Mike
Ashley's extensive article 'Fairytale' and the article largely by
Mike Ashley, 'Children's Fantasy', in John Clute and John
Grant (eds), *The Encyclopedia of Fantasy* (London: Orbit,
1997).

Page 238   *'From the moment I had the idea for the book'*: BBC radio
interview with James Naughtie, 'James Naughtie talks to J.K.
Rowling about one of her novels, *Harry Potter and the
Philosopher's Stone*', Radio 4's Book Club programme,
1 August 1999.

Page 240   *'Both were dressed as Muggles, though very inexpertly'*: GF,
ch. 7.

Page 241   *'It is our choices, Harry, that show what we truly are'*: CS,
ch. 18.

Page 241   C.S. Lewis gave the name 'undeception': C.S. Lewis, 'A Note
on Jane Austen', in C.S. Lewis, *Selected Literary Essays*
(Cambridge: Cambridge University Press, 1969).

Page 241   *'the undeception, structurally considered, is the very pivot'*:
Lewis, *Selected Literary Essays*, p. 178.

Page 244   *'The five years I spent on* Harry Potter and the Philosopher's
Stone *were spent constructing The Rules'*: interview with
J.K. Rowling, South West News Service, Bristol, 2000.

Page 244   *'The journey to King's Cross was very uneventful'*: PA, ch. 5.

Page 246   *Talking animals have a long tradition in literature*: see
Margaret Blount, *Animal Land: The Creatures of Children's
Fiction* (London: Hutchinson, 1974).

Page 248   *The shape-shifting . . . in fantasy is usually meant quite
radically*: see John Clute and David Langford,
'Metamorphosis', in Clute and Grant (eds), *The
Encyclopedia of Fantasy*.

Page 252   *'Parvati positively beamed'*: HBP, ch. 15.

Page 254   *'I went to the Yale University bookstore and bought and
read'*: Harold Bloom, 'Dumbing down American Reading',
Boston Globe, 24 September 2003.

Page 254   *'He was in a very good mood until lunchtime'*: PS, ch. 1.

Page 254   *'"Let Hedwig out," he told Ron'*: CS, ch. 3.

Page 255   *'If, as a boy, Hagrid had heard that a monster'*: CS, ch. 14.

Bibliography

Works by J.K. Rowling

Harry Potter and the Philosopher's Stone (London: Bloomsbury, 1997; published in the USA as *Harry Potter and the Sorcerer's Stone* (New York: Scholastic, 1998))

Harry Potter and the Chamber of Secrets (London: Bloomsbury, 1998; New York: Scholastic, 1999)

Harry Potter and the Prisoner of Azkaban (London: Bloomsbury, 1999; New York: Scholastic, 1999)

Harry Potter and the Goblet of Fire (London: Bloomsbury, 2000; New York: Scholastic, 2000)

Writing as Newt Scamander. *Fantastic Beasts & Where to Find Them* (London: Bloomsbury, 2001)

Writing as Kennilworthy Whisp. *Quidditch through the Ages* (London: Bloomsbury, 2001)

Harry Potter and the Order of the Phoenix (London: Bloomsbury, 2003; New York: Scholastic, 2003)

Harry Potter and the Half-Blood Prince (London: Bloomsbury, 2005; New York: Scholastic, 2005)

Harry Potter and the Deathly Hallows (London: Bloomsbury, 2007; New York: Scholastic, 2007)

Secondary Works

Ashenden, Gavin. 'Charles Williams and the Tradition of Alchemy', in Barbara Reynolds (ed.), VII: *An Anglo-American Review*, 18 (2001), 51–69

Ashley, Mike. 'Children's Fantasy', in *The Encylopedia of Fantasy* (London: Orbit, 1997)

Auden, W.H. 'Afterword', in George MacDonald, *The Golden Key, with Pictures by Maurice Sendak* (New York: Farrar, Straus and Giroux, 1967)

Baggett, David and Klein, Shawn E. *Harry Potter and Philosophy: If Aristotle Ran Hogwarts* (Chicago and LeSalle, Ill.: Open Court, 2004)

Beahm, George. *Fact, Fiction, and Folklore in Harry Potter's World: An Unofficial Guide* (Charlottesville, Va.: Hampton Roads, 2005)

Blount, Margaret. *Animal Land: The Creatures of Children's Fiction* (London: Hutchinson, 1974)

Bridger, Francis. *A Charmed Life: The Spirituality of Potterworld* (London: DLT, 2001; New York: Doubleday, 2002)

Briggs, Katharine. *A Dictionary of Fairies: Hobgoblins, Brownies, Bogies, and Other Supernatural Creatures* (Harmondsworth: Penguin, 1977)

Burkart, Gina. *A Parent's Guide to Harry Potter* (Downers Grove, Ill.: InterVarsity Press, 2005)

Campbell, Joseph. *The Hero with a Thousand Faces* (London: HarperCollins, 1993)

Carroll, Lewis [Charles Dodgson]. *Through the Looking-glass* (1872)

Clute, John and Langford, David. 'Metamorphosis', in *The Encyclopedia of Fantasy* (London: Orbit, 1997)

Clute, John and Grant, John (eds). *The Encyclopedia of Fantasy* (London: Orbit, 1997)

Clute, John and Nicholls, Peter (eds). *The Encyclopedia of Science Fiction* (London: Orbit, 1993)

Coleridge, S.T. *Biographia Literaria* (1817)

Dickerson, Matthew T. and O'Hara, David. *From Homer to Harry Potter: A Handbook on Myth and Fantasy* (Grand Rapids, Mich.: Brazos Press, 2006)

Dodgson, Charles. *See* Lewis Carroll

Down, Ellie. *The Unofficial Guide to Harry Potter* (Chichester: Summerdale, 2005)

Duriez, Colin. *J.R.R. Tolkien and C.S. Lewis: The Story of a Friendship* (Stroud: Sutton Publishing, 2005)

Duriez, Colin. 'Voldemort, Death Eaters, Dementors and the Dark Arts: A Contemporary Theology of Spiritual Perversion in the Harry Potter Stories', in Christopher Partridge and Eric Christianson (eds), *The Lure of the Dark Side: Satan and Demonology in Popular Culture* (London: Equinox, 2008)

Ellul, Jacques. *The Technological Society* (New York: Vintage Books, 1964)

Fisher, Margery. *Intent upon Reading: A Critical Appraisal of Modern Fiction for Children* (2nd edn, Leicester: Brockhampton Press, 1964)

Fowles, John. *Wormholes: Essays and Occasional Writings* (London: Jonathan Cape, 1998)

Fraser, Lindsey. *An Interview with J.K. Rowling* (London: Egmont Books, 2002)

Goudge, Elizabeth. *The Little White Horse* (Oxford: Lion, 2000)

Granger, John. *Looking for God in Harry Potter: Is there Hidden Meaning in the Bestselling Books?* (2002; rev. edn, Wheaton, Ill.: Tyndale House, 2006)

Granger, John. *Unlocking Harry Potter: Five Keys for the Serious Reader* (Wayne, Pa.: Zossima Press, 2007)

Green, Roger Lancelyn. *Tellers of Tales* (Leicester: Edmund Ward, 1946)

Haviland, Virginia. *Children and Literature: Views and Reviews* (London: Bodley Head, 1974)

Jeffrey, David Lyle (ed.). *Dictionary of Biblical Tradition in English Literature* (Grand Rapids, Mich.: Eerdmans, 1992)

Jones, Diana Wynne. *The Tough Guide to Fantasyland* (London: Cassell, 1996)

Killinger, John. *God, the Devil, and Harry Potter: A Christian Minister's Defense of the Beloved Novels* (New York: St Martin's Press, 2002)

Lackey, Mercedes (ed.). *Mapping the World of Harry Potter: Science Fiction and Fantasy Writers Explore the Bestselling Fantasy Series of All Time* (Dallas, Tex.: Benbella Books, 2005)

Lewis, C.S. 'A Note on Jane Austen', in C.S. Lewis, *Selected Literary Essays* (Cambridge: Cambridge University Press, 1969)

Lewis, C.S. *Miracles* (2nd edn, London: Collins Fontana, 1960)

Lewis, C.S. *English Literature in the Sixteenth Century Excluding Drama* (London: Oxford University Press, 1954)

Lipscomb, Benjamin and Stewart, Christopher. 'Magic, Science, and the Ethics of Technology', in Mercedes Lackey (ed.), *Mapping the World of Harry Potter: Science Fiction and Fantasy Writers Explore the Bestselling Fantasy Series of All Time* (Dallas, Tex.: Benbella Books, 2005)

Lochhead, Marion. *The Renaissance of Wonder in Children's Literature* (Edinburgh: Canongate, 1977)

Lurie, Alison. *Boys and Girls Forever: Children's Classics from Cinderella to Harry Potter* (London: Random House, 2003)

MacDonald, George. *A Dish of Orts* (London: Sampson Low, 1893)

MacDonald, George. *The Gifts of the Christ Child*, ed. Glenn Edward Sadler (Oxford: A.R. Mowbray, 1973)

MacDonald, George. *The Golden Key, with Pictures by Maurice Sendak* (New York: Farrar, Straus and Giroux, 1976)

Manlove, Colin. *Christian Fantasy: From 1200 to the Present* (Basingstoke and London: Macmillan, 1992)

Manlove, Colin. *From Alice to Harry Potter: Children's Fantasy in England* (Christchurch, NZ: Cybereditions, 2003)

Milton, John. *Areopagitica* (1644)

Nataf, André. *The Wordsworth Dictionary of the Occult* (Ware: Wordsworth, 1994)

Neal, Connie. *The Gospel According to Harry Potter: Spirituality in the Stories of the World's Most Famous Seeker* (Louisville, Ky: Westminster John Knox Press, 2002)

Neal, Connie. *Wizards, Wardrobes and Wookiees* (Downers Grove, Ill.: InterVarsity Press, 2007)

Nikolajeva, Maria. 'Fantasy Literature and Fairy Tales', in Jack Zipes (ed.), *The Oxford Companion to Fairy Tales* (Oxford: Oxford University Press, 2000)

The Oxford Companion to Children's Literature, ed. Humphrey Carpenter and Mari Prichard (Oxford and New York: Oxford University Press, 1984)

Quigly, Isobel. *The Heirs of Tom Brown: The English School Story* (Oxford: Oxford University Press, 1984)

Sadler, Glenn Edward (ed.). George MacDonald, *The Gifts of the Christ Child* (Oxford: A.R. Mowbray, 1973)

St Augustine. *Confessions* (AD 397)

Schaeffer, Francis. *How Should We Then Live? The Rise and Decline of Western Thought and Culture* (Old Tappan, NJ: Fleming H. Revell, 1976)

Schafer, Elizabeth D. *Exploring Harry Potter* (London: Ebury Press, 2000)

Segura, Eduardo and Honegger, Thomas (eds). *Myth, Art and Magic* (Zollikofen: Walking Tree Publishers, 2007)

Shippey, Tom, 'New Learning and New Ignorance: Magia, Goeteia, and The Inklings', in Eduardo Segura and Thomas Honegger (eds), *Myth, Art and Magic* (Zollikofen: Walking Tree Publishers, 2007)

Sire, James W. *The Universe Next Door* (4th edn, Downers Grove, Ill.: InterVarsity Press, 2004)

Smith, Sean. *J.K. Rowling: The Genius behind Harry Potter* (London: Arrow Books, 2002)

Tolkien, J.R.R. 'On Fairy Stories', in *Tree and Leaf Including the Poem Mythopoeia* (London: HarperCollins, 1992)

Vogler, Christopher. *The Writer's Journey: Mythic Structure for Storytellers and Screenwriters* (2nd edn, London: Pan Books, 1999)

White, T.H. *Mistress Masham's Repose* (London: Jonathan Cape, 1947)

White, T.H. *The Once and Future King* (London: Book Club Associates, 1973)

Zipes, Jack (ed.). *The Oxford Companion to Fairy Tales* (Oxford: Oxford University Press, 2000)

Index

For beings, places, things and events in the fictional world of Harry Potter *see* 'An A–Z', pages 43–137.